THE PRECIOUS PEARL

The Precious Pearl

Al-Jāmī's

Al-Durrah Al-Fakhirah

together with his

Glosses

and the

Commentary

of

'Abd al-Ghafūr al—Lārī

Translated with an Introduction,
Notes, and Glossary
by
Nicholas Heer

State University of New York Press • Albany • 1979

Published by
State University of New York Press
Albany, New York 12246

Composed by
Typography Services
Albany, New York 12211

Printed in the United States of America

Library of Congress Cataloging in Publication Data

Jāmī, 1414-1492.
al-Jāmī's al-Durrah al-fākhirah—
The precious pearl.

(Studies in Islamic philosophy and science)
"Glossary of terms":
Bibliography: p.
1. God (Islam) 2. Sufism—Early works to 1800.
I. al-Lārī, 'Abd al-Ghafūr, d. 1506.
II. Heer, Nicholas. III. Title: al-Durrah al-fākhirah.
IV. Title: The precious pearl. V. Series.
BP166.2.J3513 297'.211 78-12607

CONTENTS

ACKNOWLEDGEMENTS

I should like to acknowledge my indebtedness to the following libraries and their curators for supplying the microfilms and photographic copies of the manuscripts used in editing and translating the Arabic texts: the Princeton University Library, and especially Professor Rudolf Mach, Curator of the Robert Garrett Collection, and Alexander P. Clark, Curator of Manuscripts; the Dār al-Kutub al-Miṣrīyah, and in particular its Curator of Manuscripts, the late Fu'ād Sayyid; the Institute of Arabic Manuscripts of the Arab League, Cairo, especially the late Rashād 'Abd al-Muṭṭalib; the Staatsbibliothek Preussischer Kulturbesitz in Berlin and the head of its Tübinger Depot, Dr. Wilhelm Virneisel; the Staatsbibliothek Preussischerkulturbesitz in Marburg; the Oriental Department of the Leiden University Library; The John Rylands Library in Manchester; the India Office Library in London; The Asiatic Museum in Leningrad; the Dār al-Kutub al-Ẓāhirīyah in Damascus; and the Asiatic Society in Calcutta.

I should also like to express gratitude to my colleagues at the University of Washington, Professor Farhat J. Ziadeh and Professor Michael Loraine, for their valuable assistance and helpful suggestions, and to Professor George Makdisi of the University of Pennsylvania, who first encouraged me to undertake this work. My thanks are also due to Mrs. Jeanette Thomas for typing my entire manuscript.

Finally, I should like to thank the Executive Committee of the Society for the Study of Islamic Philosophy and Science and in particular its Secretary-Treasurer, Professor Parviz Morewedge, for making possible the publication of this volume.

INTRODUCTION

1. The Author of *al-Durrah al-Fākhirah*

Nūr al-Dīn 'Abd al-Raḥmān ibn Aḥmad al-Jāmī, the author of *al-Durrah al-Fākhirah,* was born in Kharjird, a town in the district of Jām,[1] on 23 Sha 'bān 817/1414.[2] As a youth he entered the Niẓāmīyah School in Herat, where he attended the class of Junayd al-Uṣūlī on Arabic rhetoric. Here he proved to be a superior student, for although he had expected the class to be studying the *Mukhtaṣar al-Talkhīṣ,*[3] he found upon entering that the students had already advanced to the *Sharḥ al-Miftāḥ*[4] and the *Muṭawwal.*[5] He was nevertheless able to understand these works without difficulty and to complete not only the *Muṭawwal* but its gloss as well. Among other scholars under whom he studied in Herat were 'Alī al-Samarqandī, a former student of al-Sayyid al-Sharīf al-Jurjānī, and Shihāb al-Dīn al-Jājirmī, who had studied under Sa'd al-Dīn al-Taftāzānī.

To pursue his education further al-Jāmī then moved to Samarqand, where he studied under Qāḍī-Zādah al-Rūmī,[6] the famous astronomer at the observatory of the Tīmūrid ruler, Ulugh Beg. Here again he demonstrated his brilliance and superior intelligence, first by winning a debate with his teacher and later by suggesting a number of corrections and emendations for the improvement of two of Qāḍī-Zādah's most famous works, the *Sharḥ al-Tadhkirah,*[7] and the *Sharḥ Mulakhkhaṣ al-Jaghmīnī.*[8] Qāḍī-Zādah was so impressed with his new student's intellectual powers that he claimed no one al-Jāmī's equal had ever crossed the Oxus into Samarqand since its founding. On a later occasion in Herat al-Jāmī was asked to solve some very abstruse astronomical problems by the learned astronomer 'Alī al-Qūshjī.[9] Much to al-Qūshjī's chagrin he was able to solve them without any difficulty whatsoever.

Al-Jāmī's first encounter with Ṣūfism was at the age of five, when he was taken by his father to see the great Naqshbandī saint Khwājah Muḥammad Pārsā,[10] who was then passing through Jām on his way to Mecca to perform the pilgrimage. Later al-Jāmī was himself initiated into the Naqshbandī order by Sa'd al-Dīn al-Kāshgharī,[11] whose spiritual lineage extended back to the founder of the order, Bahā' al-Dīn al-Naqshband,[12] through Niẓām al-Dīn Khāmūsh,[13] and 'Alā' al-Dīn al-'Aṭṭār.[14]

Other Ṣūfīs with whom al-Jāmī associated were Fakhr al-Dīn Lūristānī,[15] Khwājah Burhān al-Dīn Abū Naṣr Pārsā,[16] Bahā' al-Dīn 'Umar,[17] Khwājah Shams al-Dīn Muḥammad Kūsū'ī,[18] Jalāl al-Dīn Pūrānī,[19] and Shams al-Dīn Muḥammad Asad.[20]

A Ṣūfī for whom al-Jāmī had a special regard and esteem was his friend and contemporary Nāṣir al-Dīn 'Ubayd Allāh al-Aḥrār.[21] Although al-Jāmī met him in person on only four occasions, he nevertheless carried on an extensive correspondence[22] with him for many years and mentioned him by name in several of his poetical works.[23]

Al-Jāmī's later life was spent in Herat, where he enjoyed the patronage of Sulṭān Ḥusayn Bāyqarā, the Tīmūrid ruler of Khurāsān from 873 to 911 A.H. Al-Jāmī was one of a number of illustrious scholars, poets, and artists whom Sulṭān Ḥusayn had attracted to his court. Among them were the Turkī poet Mīr 'Alī-Shīr Nawā'ī, a close friend of al-Jāmī and the author of a biography of him entitled *Khamsat al-Mutaḥayyirīn,*[24] and the two painters Bihzād and Shāh Muẓaffar.[25]

In the middle of Rabī' al-Awwal 877, when he was sixty years of age, al-Jāmī set out in a caravan for Mecca with the intention of performing the pilgrimage. He arrived in Baghdad at the beginning of Jumādā al-Ākhirah and soon thereafter travelled to Karbalā' to visit the tomb of al-Ḥusayn. Shortly after his return to Baghdad he was falsely accused of having ridiculed the beliefs of the Shī'ites in a passage in the first *daftar* of his *Silsilat al-Dhahab.* The reason for this accusation was that a certain man named Fatḥī, who had travelled with the caravan from Herat, quarreled with some of the other caravan members and, wishing to take revenge on them, incited the Shī'ite population of the city against the caravan. He did this by showing to a group of Shīʿites a passage from al-Jāmī's *Silsilat al-Dhahab* from which he had removed certain verses and substituted others, thus giving to the passage an anti-Shīʿite bias.[26] Al-Jāmī, however, easily silenced his accusers by producing, at a public meeting called for the occasion, the full and correct text of the work.

Having stayed in Baghdad for four months, al-Jāmī resumed his journey to Mecca passing through al-Najaf on his way in order to visit the tomb of ʿAlī. When he had completed the pilgrimage, he returned home by way of Damascus and Aleppo, spending forty-five days in Damascus for the purpose of hearing traditions from Muḥammad al-Khayḍarī,[27] a famous traditionist and Shāfiʿite *qāḍī.*

Although he had yet to write most of his greatest poetical works, al-Jāmī's reknown had by this time spread throughout the Islamic world. When the Ottoman sultan, Muḥammad II, learned that al-Jāmī had set out on the pilgrimage, he sent a certain ʿAṭā' Allāh al-Kirmānī[28] to Damascus to invite al-Jāmī to visit Istanbul and to present him with a gift of 5000 *ashrafīs*[29] with the promise of 100,000 more should he accept the invitation. When al-Kirmānī arrived in Damascus, however, al-Jāmī had already left for Aleppo, and when al-Jāmī heard that al-Kirmānī was following him to Aleppo, he set out at once for Tabrīz, for he apparently did not want to be put in the position of refusing the sultan's invitation.

Upon his arrival in Tabrīz, he was well received by the Āq Qūyunlū ruler, Ūzūn Ḥasan, who not only presented him with many fine gifts but also invited him to remain in Tabrīz. Al-Jāmī, however, giving as his excuse the need to care for his aged mother, insisted on returning to Herat and the court of his patron Ḥusayn Mīrzā Bāyqarā.

Some years later, shortly before his death in 886 A.H., Muḥammad II again sent an envoy with precious gifts to al-Jāmī, this time with the request that al-Jāmī write a work comparing and judging the respective positions of the theologians, the philosophers, and the Ṣūfīs. Al-Jāmī acceded to this request and wrote the work identified with *al-Durrah al-Fākhirah.*[30]

Still later al-Jāmī was again invited to Istanbul by Muḥammad

II's successor, Bāyazīd II. On this occasion al-Jāmī accepted the sultan's invitation[31] and travelled as far as Hamadhān before he decided to turn back because of an epidemic of plague in the Ottoman territories.[32]

Al-Jāmī died in Herat on 18 Muḥarram 898/1492 at the age of eighty-one and was buried next to his spiritual guide, Sa'd al-Dīn al-Kāshgharī.[33]

2. Al-Jāmī's Works

Al-Jāmī was the author of a large number of Persian and Arabic works, both in prose and in verse, on a wide range of subjects.[1] His disciple, 'Abd al-Ghafūr al-Lārī, lists forty-five titles in the *Khātimah* to his *Ḥāshiyah* on al-Jāmī's *Nafaḥāt al-Uns.*[2] The same titles are given by Sām Mīrzā in his *Tuḥfah-i Sāmī,* although in a somewhat different order.[3]

Al-Jāmī's principal poetical works, all of which are in Persian, are the *Haft Awrang,* containing seven *mathnawīs: Silsilat al-Dhahab,* the first *daftar* of which was composed in 876,[4] and the second in 890, *Salāman wa-Absāl, Tuḥfat al-Aḥrār,* composed in 886, *Subḥat al-Abrār, Yūsuf wa-Zulaykhā,* composed in 888, *Laylā wa-Majnūn,* composed in 889, and *Khirad-namah-i Sikandarī*; and three *dīwāns: Fātiḥat al-Shabāb,* compiled in 884, *Wāsiṭat al-'Iqd,* compiled in 894, and *Khātimat al-Ḥayāh,* compiled in 896.[5]

In addition to *al-Durrah al-Fākhirah,* al-Jāmī wrote a number of other works dealing with the doctrines of the Ṣūfīs. These include his *Lawā'iḥ,* a Persian work in prose and poetry which has been published in facsimile and translated into English by E.H. Whinfield and Mīrzā Muḥammad Qazwīnī;[6] a commentary on Ibn 'Arabī's *Fuṣūs al-Ḥikam* completed in 896;[7] *Naqd al-Nuṣūṣ fī Sharḥ Naqsh al-Fuṣūṣ,* a commentary in Persian and Arabic on Ibn 'Arabī's own abridgement of his *Fuṣūṣ al-Ḥikam,* composed in 863;[8] and *Risālah fī al-Wujūd,* a short essay in which al-Jāmī attempts to demonstrate the external existence of existence.[9]

Other prose works of importance are his *Nafaḥāt al-Uns min Ḥaḍarāt al-Quds,* begun in 881 and completed in 883, and containing biographies in Persian of some 614 Ṣūfīs;[10] *al-Fawā'id al-Ḍiyā'īyah,* a commentary composed in 897 for his son Ḍiyā' al-Dīn Yūsuf on Ibn al-Ḥājib's famous work on Arabic syntax, *al-Kāfiyah;*[11] and finally his *Bahāristān,* a Persian work written in 892 in imitation of Sa'dī's *Gulustān.*[12]

3. *Al-Durrah al-Fakhirah*

A. *The Circumstances of its Composition.* As has been mentioned, the Ottoman sultan, Muḥammad II, requested that al-Jāmī write a treatise judging the respective positions of the theologians, the Ṣūfīs, and the philosophers. Ṭāshkubrīzādah, in his biography of al-Jāmī in *al-Shaqā'iq al-Nu'mānīyah* relates the circumstances of this request as follows:

> Al-Mawlā al-A'ẓam Sayyidī Muḥyī al-Dīn al-Fanārī related that his father, al-Mawlā 'Alī al-Fanārī, who was *qāḍī* in al-'Askar al-Manṣūr under Sulṭān Muḥammad Khān, said, "The Sulṭān said to me one day that there was need for an adjudication *(muḥākamah)*[1] between those groups investigating the sciences of reality *('ulūm al-ḥaqīqah),* namely, the theologians, the Ṣūfīs, and the philosophers." My father replied, "I said to the Sulṭān that no one was more capable of such an adjudication between these groups than al-Mawlā 'Abd al-Raḥmān al-Jāmī." He then said, "Sulṭān Muḥammad Khān accordingly sent an envoy with precious gifts to him and requested of him the aforementioned adjudication. Al-Jāmī thereupon wrote a treatise in which he adjudicated between those groups with respect to six questions,[2] including the question of existence. He sent it to Sulṭān Muḥammad Khān stating that should the treatise prove acceptable, he would supplement it with an explanation of the remaining questions. Otherwise there would be nothing to gain in his wasting his time further. The treatise, however, arrived in Constantinople after the death of Sulṭān Muḥammad Khān." Al-Mawlā Muḥyī al-Dīn al-Fanārī said furthermore that this treatise remained with his father, and I believe he said that it is still with him.[3]

There can be little doubt that the treatise referred to in this account is *al-Durrah al-Fākhirah,* for no other work of al-Jāmī can be described as an adjudication between theologians, Ṣūfīs, and philosophers. This identification is further supported by the fact that this same passage from *al-Shaqā'iq al-Nu'mānīyah* is quoted on the title pages of two of the manuscripts used in the edition of the Arabic text, Yahuda 3872 and 'Aqā'id Taymūr 393.

Not only does this account explain why al-Jāmī wrote *al-Durrah al-Fākhirah,* it also provides an explanation for the fact that both short and long versions of the work exist. The short version, which contains paragraphs 1-73 only, is apparently the original text sent to Sulṭān Muḥammad II, whereas the long version, containing the supplemental paragraphs 74-92, represents the completed work.

The account, furthermore, provides a completion date for the original version of *al-Durrah al-Fākhirah,* namely, the year 886/1481, the date of Muḥammad II's death. The work was thus written when al-Jāmī was sixty-nine years of age, after he had written *Naqd al-Nuṣūṣ,* the first *daftar* of *Silsilat al-Dhahab, Nafaḥāt al-Uns,* and the first *Dīwān,* but before he composed most of his other major works.

B. *Al-Jāmī's Method of Adjudication in al-Durrah al-Fākhirah.* In making his *muḥākamah,* or adjudication, between the theologians, philosophers, and Ṣūfīs, al-Jāmī takes up eleven questions, all of which the theologians and the philosophers had debated for centuries. These questions, listed in the order in which they are taken up, are:

1. The nature of God's existence and its relation to His essence, that is, is it superadded to His essence or identical with it?

2. God's unity and the necessity of demonstrating it.

3. The nature of God's attributes and their relation to His essence, that is, are they superadded to his essence or identical with it?

4. The nature of God's knowledge and the problem of attributing knowledge to God without compromising His unity or necessary existence.

5. God's knowledge of particulars and the problems encountered in attributing this type of knowledge to God.

6. The nature of God's will and whether His will is an attribute distinct from His knowledge.

7. The nature of God's power and the related question of

whether God is a free agent or a necessary agent.

8. The question of whether the universe is eternal or originated together with the question of whether an eternal universe can result from a free agent or not.

9. The nature of God's speech and the question of whether the Qur'an is eternal or created.

10. The voluntary acts of humans and whether they occur through the power of God or man.

11. The emanation of the universe from God and the question of whether it is possible for multiple effects to result from a single cause.[4]

In general al-Jāmī first presents the opposing positions of the theologians and the philosophers and then the Ṣūfī position. He presents the Ṣūfī position not merely as a rationally possible alternative to the theological and philosophical positions but as a clearly superior position, either because it reconciles the opposing views of the theologians and philosophers on a particular question, or because it avoids problems necessarily resulting from positions the theologians or the philosophers hold.

For example, the Ṣūfī position that God's attributes are identical with His essence externally but superadded to it in the mind represents a position midway between the theologians' position that God's attributes are superadded to His essence and that of the philosophers who assert that His attributes are identical with His essence. The Ṣūfī position that the universe is eternal even though God is a free agent reconciles the philosophers' assertion that because God is a necessary agent, the universe is eternal, with the theologians' assertion that because the universe is originated, God is a free agent.

However, on the question of whether God's existence is superadded to His essence or identical with it, the Ṣūfīs maintain an entirely different position. Instead of considering God as composed of essence and existence, they equate Him with absolute existence. They thus not only avoid the problem of determining the relation of His existence to His essence, but in addition do not have to prove God's unity, as the theologians and philosophers must do, since it is impossible to imagine multiplicity in an absolute concept.

C. *The Sources Used by al-Jāmī in al-Durrah al-Fākhirah.* In presenting the respective positions of the theologians, the philosophers, and the Ṣūfīs, al-Jāmī has relied heavily on a number of standard and well-known works. In fact much of the material presented in *al-Durrah al-Fākhirah,* and in the *Glosses* as well, consists of passages quoted or paraphrased from these works. Sometimes al-Jāmī acknowledges these passages as quotations and indicates their source, but often he simply incorporates them into his text as if he had written them himself.[5] The principal theological works from which al-Jāmī quotes are al-Jurjānī's *Sharḥ al-Mawāqif* and al-Taftāzānī's *Sharḥ al-Maqāṣid.* Extensive passages from al-Ṭūsī's *Sharḥ al-Ishārāt* and his *Risālah* written in answer to Ṣadr al-Dīn al-Qūnawī's questions are quoted in presenting some of the positions of the philosophers.

As might be expected, al-Jāmī's sources for the Ṣūfī position are both numerous and varied. Among the works he quotes extensively are al-Fanārī's *Miṣbāḥ al-Uns,* al-Qayṣarī's *Maṭla' Khuṣūṣ al-Kilam,* al-Hamadhānī's *Zubdat al-Ḥaqā'iq,* Ibn 'Arabī's *al-Futūḥāt al-Makkīyah,* and al-Qūnawī's *Kitāb al-Nuṣūṣ* as well as his *I'jāz al-Bayān.*

D. *The Various Titles by which the Work is Known.* The title given to *al-Durrah al-Fākhirah* varies from manuscript to manuscript. The two most common titles are *al-Durrah al-Fākhirah* (The Precious Pearl), and *Risālah fī Taḥqīq Madhhab al-Ṣūfīyah wa-al-Mutakallimīn wa-al-Ḥukamā'* (A Treatise Dealing with the Verification of the Doctrines of the Ṣūfīs, the Theologians and the Philosophers), or some variant of this latter title derived from the first sentence of the work's second paragraph. Al-Jāmī's disciple, 'Abd al-Ghafūr al-Lārī, in listing al-Jāmī's works, gives the title as *Risālah-i Taḥqīq-i Madhhab-i Ṣūfī wa-Mutakallim wa-Ḥakīm.*[6] Often the two titles are combined, as in the Cairo printed edition of 1328.

A few manuscripts, including Yahuda 3872 and 'Aqā'id Taymūr 393, have an additional subtitle, *Ḥuṭṭa Raḥlak,* meaning "put down your saddle bag." Jacobus Ecker, in describing the manuscripts he used in preparing his Latin translation of selected passages from the work mentions that Gotha MS. No. 87 also bears this subtitle. He further states that in the colophon of this manuscript the copyist has written that the meaning of *Ḥuṭṭa Raḥlak* is *Inzil hāhuna, fa-mā ba'd 'Abbādān qaryah,* that is, "Dismount here, for there are no towns after 'Abbādān." Ecker interprets this to mean: If you read this small treatise on God's existence and attributes, and if you learn those things contained in it, that is sufficient, for there is no other work on these matters to be read or known.[7]

Ibrāhīm al-Kūrānī in his *al-Amam li-Īqāẓ al-Himam* combines all three titles and calls the work *al-Durrah al-Fākhirah al-Mulaqqabah bi-Ḥuṭṭa Raḥlak fī Taḥqīq Madhhab al-Ṣūfīyah wa-al-Mutakallimīn wa-al-Ḥukamā' al-Mutaqaddimīn.*[8]

Houtsma 464 bears yet another title, *Risālat al-Muḥākamāt,* or *Treatise of Adjudications,* evidently in reference to the adjudication requested of al-Jāmī by Sulṭān Muḥammad II.

4. 'Abd al-Ghafūr al-Lārī, the Author of the *Commentary* on *al-Durrah al-Fākhirah*

Raḍī al-Dīn 'Abd al-Ghafūr al-Lārī, the author of the *Commentary* on *al-Durrah al-Fākhirah was* both a disciple *(murīd)* and a student *(shāgird)* of al-Jāmī. Like al-Jāmī, he was also among the group of illustrious men in Herat who enjoyed the patronage of the Tīmūrid sultan, Ḥusayn Bāyqarā. The biographical sources[1] do not mention the date of his birth, but do state that he was from Lār[2] and that he died in Herat on 5 Sha'bān 912 and was buried next to the tomb of al-Jāmī.

In addition to his *Commentary* on *al-Durrah al-Fākhirah,* al-Lārī was the author of the previously mentioned *Ḥāshiyah,* or gloss, on al-Jāmī's *Nafaḥāt al-Uns* together with the *Khātimah,* or *Takmilah,* containing the biography of al-Jāmī.[3] He also wrote a *ḥāshiyah* on al-Jāmī's *al-Fawā'id al-Ḍiyā'īyah,*[4] and a Persian commentary on *al-Uṣūl al-'Asharah* (or *Risālah fī al-Ṭuruq*) of Najm al-Dīn al-Kubrā.[5]

5. Other Commentaries on *al-Durrah al-Fakhirah*

A number of other commentaries have been written on *al-Durrah al-Fākhirah,* of which the following have proved helpful in preparing the present translation.

Al-Taḥrīrāt al-Bāhirah li-Mabāḥith al-Durrah al-Fākhirah by Ibrāhīm ibn Ḥasan al-Kūrānī[1] is a collection of glosses on the text of *al-Durrah al-Fākhirah* as well as on al-Jāmī's *Glosses.* From the first lines of the work it is apparent that these glosses were collected by one of Ibrāhīm al-Kūrānī's students. The work is not included in the list of al-Kūrānī's works given by al-Baghdādī in his *Hadīyat al-'Ārifīn,*[2] nor is it mentioned by Brockelmann. Two manuscripts of the work are in the Robert Garret Collection of the Princeton University Library. One, Yahuda 4049, consists of twenty-one folios and was copied in 1118 A.H. by a former student of al-Kūrānī named Mūsā ibn Ibrāhīm al-Baṣrī for Sibṭ Shaykh al-Islām Aḥmad Afandī. The other, consisting of folios 185b-199b of Yahuda 5373,[3] was copied by a certain Yaḥyā in 1120 A.H. Some of the individual glosses of this work are found in the margins of *al-Durrah al-Fākhirah* in 'Aqā'id Taymūr 393, Yahuda 3049, and Yahuda 3872.

Al-Risālah al-Qudsīyah al-Ṭāhirah bi-Sharḥ al-Durrah al-Fākhirah by Ibrāhīm ibn Aḥmad al-Kurdī al-Ḥusaynābādī[4] is a commentary on the long version of *al-Durrah al-Fākhirah* as well as twenty of al-Jāmī's glosses. According to a statement of the author at the end of the work, it was completed in 1106 A.H. Three manuscripts of the work are known. One, cited by Brockelmann, is in the *Maktabat al-Baladīyah* in Alexandria, and another forms part of MS No. 3337 in the *Maktabat al-Awqāf* in Baghdad.[5] A third, in Dār al-Kutub al-Ẓāhirīyah in Damascus, consists of folios 89b-124b of MS 'Āmm 9276, which also contains copies of *al-Durrah al-Fākhirah* and al-Lārī's *Commentary.*[6]

Al-Farīdah al-Nādirah fī Sharḥ al-Durrah al-Fākhirah by Abū al-'Iṣmah Muḥammad Ma'ṣūm ibn Mawlānā Bābā al-Samarqandī[7] is a lengthy commentary on the long version of *al-Durrah al-Fākhirah* and thirty-two of al-Jāmī's glosses. Apparently only one manuscript of the work is known, MS No. 1364 (Delhi 1841), in the India Office Library in London. Unfortunately this copy, consisting of 318 folios, is badly worm-eaten and water-stained and, consequently, somewhat difficult to read.[8]

Sharḥ al-Durrah al-Fākhirah by an unknown author is another lengthy commentary on the long version and a few of the glosses. The only known copy of this work is MS No. 1125 (Ar. 640), consisting of 163 folios, in the Library of the Asiatic Society in Calcutta.[9]

6. The Arabic Texts

Manuscript copies of both the short and long versions of *al-Durrah al-Fākhirah* are numerous and are to be found in almost every library of Arabic or Persian manuscripts. The text of the long version was printed in Cairo in 1328, and parts of the short version were published in Latin translation by Jacobus Ecker as part of a dissertation printed in Bonn in 1879.[1] Copies of al-Jāmī's *Glosses* and al-Lārī's *Commentary,* however, are much less numerous.

The translations of *al-Durrah al-Fākhirah,* the *Glosses,* and the *Commentary* presented here have been made on the basis of my edition of the Arabic texts which are to appear in the Wisdom of Persia Series published by the Institute of Islamic Studies, McGill University, Tehran Branch.

In preparing that edition of the texts a total of twenty-four manuscripts, in addition to the Cairo printed edition of 1328, were used. Of these twenty-five copies, fifteen contained the text of the short version and the remainder the text of the long version. Eighteen contained at least some of the *Glosses,* and six also contained al-Lārī's *Commentary.*

A description of these twenty-five copies follows:

'Āmm 9276. Dār al-Kutub al-Ẓāhirīyah, Damascus. Contains the long version with glosses (fols. 140b-149b) and al-Lārī's *Commentary* (fols. 125b-137b). At the end of the commentary the supplemental paragraphs of the long version appear again with some variant readings (fols. 137b-139b). Also contained

in this manuscript is a copy in the same hand of *al-Risālah al-Qudsīyah al-Ṭāhirah bi-Sharḥ al-Durrah al-Fākhirah* of Ibrāhīm ibn Ḥaydar ibn Aḥmad al-Kurdī al-Ḥusaynābādī (fols. 89b-124b). At the end of this work the copyist has given his name as Muḥammad ibn 'Abd al-Laṭīf al-Ḥanbalī with the date 5 Jumādā al-Ūlā 1127.

'Aqā'id Taymūr 393. Dār al-Kutub al-Miṣrīyah, Cairo (*Fihris al-Khizānah al-Taymūrīyah,* IV, 122). Contains the short version and glosses (fols. 200b-209b) and, in a different hand, al-Lārī's *Commentary* (fols. 189a-200a). The copy of the *Commentary* was completed by Aḥmad ibn Muḥammad on 23 Shawwāl 1085 in Medina. The manuscript also contains a copy of al-Jāmī's *Risālah fī al-Wujūd* (fols. 168a-180a) and on the margins of *al-Durrah al-Fākhirah,* in addition to al-Jāmī's own glosses, portions of Ibrāhīm al-Kūrānī's glosses, *al-Taḥrīrāt al-Bāhirah.* Written on fol. 200b is the passage from *al-Shaqā'iq al-Nu'mānīyah* previously quoted, giving the circumstances of the composition of *al-Durrah al-Fākhirah.*

Bukhārā 427-8. Asiatic Museum, Leningrad. Contains the long version and glosses (fols. 31b-53a), and al-Lārī's *Commentary* (fols. 53b-74b). The copyist of both works was Mullā Mīrzā 'Abd al-Rasūl al-Tājir al-Bukhārī, who completed the copy of the *Commentary* at the beginning of Rabī' al-Ākhir 1314.

Cairo 1328. Printed at the end (pp. 247-296) of *Asās al-Taqdīs fī 'Ilm al-Kalām* of Fakhr al-Dīn al-Rāzī. Cairo: Maṭba'at Kurdistān al-'Ilmīyah, 1328.

Ḥikmah 24. Maktabat al-Baladīyah, Alexandria. Contains the short version and glosses (fols. 1b-13a). Neither copyist nor date is mentioned.

Houtsma 464. Robert Garrett Collection, Princeton University Library (Ḥittī, *Descriptive Catalogue,* p. 478). Contains short version with no glosses (fols. 55a-64b). No date or copyist mentioned.

Loth 670. India Office Library, London (Loth, *Catalogue,* p. 185). Contains short version and glosses (fols. 1b-15a). No date or copyist mentioned. On folios 15b-33b is a copy of 'Abd al-Ghafūr al-Lārī's commentary on Najm al-Dīn al-Kubrā's *al-Uṣūl al-'Asharah.* Following this is a copy of al-Jāmī's *Sharḥ*

Ḥadīth Abī Dharr al-'Uqaylī.

Majāmi' Ṭal'at 217. Dār al-Kutub al-Miṣrīyah, Cairo. Contains short version with glosses (fols. 84a-96a). At the end of the short version the supplemental paragraphs of the long version have been added in a different hand (fols. 96a-98b). These have been joined to the short version by pasting a piece of paper over the original colophon and then continuing the text on it. Neither date nor copyist is mentioned.

Majāmi' Ṭal'at 274. Dār al-Kutub al-Miṣrīyah, Cairo. Contains long version but none of the glosses (pp. 187-199). No date or copyist is mentioned.

Majāmi' Taymūr 134. Dār al-Kutub al-Miṣrīyah, Cairo. Contains long version and glosses (fols. 140a-159b). No date or copyist is mentioned.

Or. Oct. 1854. Staatsbibliothek Preussischer Kulturbesitz, Marburg. Contains short version and glosses (fols. 63a-70b). Copied by Muḥammad ibn Muḥammad al-Bukhārī. Also included in the same hand is a copy of al-Jāmī's *Risālah fī al-Wujūd* (fols. 69b-70b).

Rylands 111. The John Rylands Library, Manchester (Mingana, *Catalogue,* p. 164). An incomplete copy containing paragraphs 1-23 only (fols. 1a-13a) and a few of the glosses. It is dated 1859 A.D.

Sprenger 677. Staatsbibliothek Preussischer Kulturbesitz, Berlin (Ahlwardt, *Verzeichnis,* II, 535). Contains short version without glosses (fols. 91a-107a). Copy was completed at the end of Shawwāl 1066 by Yūsuf ibn Abī al-Jalāl 'Abd Allāh al-Jāwī al-Maqāṣīrī, who also copied Yahuda 3872 nine years later in 1075.

Sprenger 1820c. Staatsbibliothek Preussischer Kulturbesitz, Berlin (Ahlwardt, *Verzeichnis,* II, 536). Contains short version and a few of the glosses (fols. 58a-68a). Copy is dated Muḥarram 1082, but the copyist is not mentioned. Also contains a copy of al-Jāmī's *Risālah fī al-Wujūd* (fols. 99b-100b).

Taṣawwuf 300. Dār al-Kutub al-Miṣrīyah, Cairo. Contains long version with glosses (pp. 1-51) and al-Lārī's *Commentary* (pp. 54-91). Both works were copied by Ibrāhīm ibn Ḥasan al-Ṭabbākh. *Al-Durrah al-Fākhirah* was completed on 10 Ramaḍān 1290 and the commentary on 15 Shawwāl of the same year. At the end of *al-Durrah al-Fākhirah,* on p. 51, the copyist has reproduced the *ijāzah* of Ibrāhīm ibn Ḥasan al-Kūrānī[2] to Aḥmad ibn al-Bannā' dated 23 Dhū al-Qa'dah 1084, which he says he found on the manuscript from which this copy was made. In the *ijāzah* Ibrāhīm al-Kūrānī states that his own authority to transmit this work goes back to al-Jāmī through his teacher, Ṣafī al-Dīn Aḥmad ibn Muḥammad [al-Qushāshī] al-Madanī,[3] Abū al-Mawāhib Aḥmad ibn 'Alī al-Shinnāwī,[4] al-Sayyid Ghaḍanfar ibn Ja'far al-Ḥusaynī al-Nahrawālī,[5] and Mullā Muḥammad Amīn, the nephew *(ibn ukht)* of al-Jāmī. This *isnād* is the same as the one given by al-Kūrānī in his *al-Amam li-Īqāẓ al-Himam.*[6]

Taṣawwuf Ṭal'at 1587. Dār al-Kutub al-Miṣrīyah, Cairo. Contains short version and no glosses (fols. 116a-132a). The manuscript is dated the end of Jumādā al-Ūlā 969, but name of copyist is not given.

Warner Or. 702(3). Leiden University Library (Voorhoeve, *Handlist,* p. 357). Contains short version and glosses (fols. 162a-165a). Although date and copyist are not mentioned, the manuscript is carefully written and includes all the original glosses.

Warner Or. 723(2). Leiden University Library (Voorhoeve, *Handlist,* p. 357). Contains short version without glosses (fols. 19b-27b). No mention made of date or copyist.

Warner Or. 997(1). Leiden University Library (Voorhoeve, *Handlist,* p. 357). Contains short version without glosses (fols. 2b-9b). Neither copyist nor date is mentioned.

Yahuda 1308. Robert Garrett Collection, Princeton University Library. Contains short version (fols. 1a-15a) with none of the glosses except No. 45, which has been incorporated into the text at the very end. Although the copyist is not mentioned, the manuscript is dated the middle of Dhū al-Qa'dah 1177. Fols. 15b-137b contain a copy of al-Jāmī's *Tafsīr.*

Yahuda 3049. Robert Garrett Collection, Princeton University Library. Contains long version and glosses (thirteen unnumbered fols.) but no date or name of copyist. Some of the glosses of Ibrāhīm al-Kūrānī known as *al-Taḥrīrāt al-Bāhirah li-Mabāḥith al-Durrah al-Fākhirah* are also found in the margins.

Yahuda 3179. Robert Garrett Collection, Princeton University Library. Contains short version and a few of the glosses (fols. 6b-11a). The manuscript is undated, and the copyist is not named.

Yahuda 3872. Robert Garrett Collection, Princeton University Library. Contains long version with all forty-five of the glosses (fols. 3a-23a) as well as al-Lārī's *Commentary* (fols. 28b-39a) and al-Jāmī's *Risālah fī al-Wujūd* (fols. 24a-27b). All three works were copied in Medina at the *ribāṭ* of al-Imām 'Alī al-Murtaḍā by Yūsuf al-Tāj ibn 'Abd Allāh ibn Abī al-Khayr al-Jāwī al-Maqāṣirī al-Qala'ī (?) al-Manjalāwī, who, as has been mentioned, was also the copyist of Sprenger 677. The three works are dated respectively 2,3, and 9 Rabī' al-Thānī 1075. On fol. 23a the copyist states that he wrote this copy on the order of his teacher and spiritual guide, al-Muḥaqqiq al-Rabbānī al-Mullā Ibrāhīm al-Kūrānī. Although there is no *ijāzah* by Ibrāhīm al-Kūrānī on the manuscript itself, it would appear from this statement that Yūsuf al-Tāj was studying these three works under him when he copied them. The *isnād* of Ibrāhīm al-Kūrānī's authority to teach these works has already been given in the description of Taṣawwuf 300. Yūsuf al-Tāj, as his *nisbah,* al-Jāwī, indicates, was originally from Indonesia. His *nisbah* al-Maqāṣirī refers to Macassar on the island of Celebes. According to P. Voorhoeve,[7] he is to be identified with the famous saint known as Shaykh Joseph, who was banished by the Dutch to the Cape of Good Hope in 1694 A.D. Shaykh Joseph was born in Macassar in 1036/1626, left for Mecca and Medina in 1054/1644, and died in Capetown in 1110/1699.[8] The passage previously quoted from *al-Shaqā'iq al-Nu'mānīyah* describing the circumstances in which al-Jāmī wrote *al-Durrah al-Fākhirah* is written on fol. 3a. Written in the margins of *al-Durrah al-Fākhirah,* in addition to al-Jāmī's glosses, and in a different hand, are some of the glosses of Ibrahīm al-Kūrānī known collectively as *al-Taḥrīrāt al-Bāhirah li-Mabāḥith al-Durrah al-Fākhirah.*

Yahuda 5373. Robert Garrett Collection, Princeton University Library. A large collection of works and chapters from works all of which are copied in the same hand and deal with various aspects of *waḥdat al-wujūd* Ṣūfism. Included are the long version of *al-Durrah al-Fākhirah* with the glosses (fols. 8b-32b), the *Commentary* of al-Lārī (fols. 33b-47b), al-Jāmī's *Risālah fī al-Wujūd* (fols. 1b-4a), and al-Kūrānī's *al-Taḥrīrāt al-Bāhirah* (fols. 185b-199a). The copy of *al-Durrah al-Fākhirah* is dated 6 Rabī' al-Awwal and that of the *Commentary* 19 Rabī' al-Awwal 1104. At the end of the copy of *al-Taḥrīrāt al-Bāhirah,* which is dated 19 Jumādā al-Ākhirah 1120, the copyist has given his name simply as Yaḥyā.

Yahuda 5930. Robert Garrett Collection, Princeton University Library. Contains short version of *al-Durrah al-Fākhirah* with a few of the glosses (fols. 326a-334b). Al-Jāmī's *Risālah fī al-Wujūd* is found on fols. 334b-336b. No date or copyist is mentioned.

7. The Establishment of the Texts.

In establishing the Arabic texts of all three works an attempt was made to divide the manuscripts into groups on the basis of their variant readings. From each group one or two representative manuscripts were then selected, and these manuscripts were then collated and their variant readings cited in the notes to the Arabic edition.

The selection of these representative manuscripts was based on a number of considerations. These included the care with which a manuscript had been copied, as evidenced by the lack of obvious mistakes, the fact that a manuscript had been collated by the copyist with other copies, as indicated by marginal notations, the fact that the version of the text copied had been transmitted by an authorized teacher, and the reputation of the copyist as a scholar in the subject of the work in question. On the basis of these considerations Yahuda 3872 must be regarded as the best and most authoritative of all the manuscripts, so its readings were usually adopted in cases where no one reading was supported by a majority of the selected manuscripts.

A. *The Text of al-Durrah al-Fākhirah.* The text of *al-Durrah al-Fākhirah* exists in both short and long versions. The short version ends with paragraph 73, and, as previously stated, probably represents the original text of the work which al-Jāmī sent to Sulṭān Muḥammad II.[1] The long version contains the additional paragraphs 74-92, which were apparently written later in order to complete the work. Only ten of the twenty-five copies used in establishing the Arabic text contain the long version. In one, Majāmī' Ṭal'at 217, the additional paragraphs of the long version have been added in a different hand to the end of a copy of the short version. In another, 'Āmm 9276, the additional paragraphs appear twice, once in their proper place and once again at the end of al-Lārī's *Commentary.* Because these additional paragraphs have at times been copied separately from the rest of the text, they were considered to constitute a distinct work in themselves with respect to the collation of the manuscripts and their distribution into groups. Consequently in what follows the short version has generally been referred to as the original text, whereas the additional paragraphs of the long version have been called the supplement.

Of the twenty-five copies of the original text consulted, eight can be classified according to variant readings as forming one definite group and five more as forming another group. The first of these groups can be further divided into two subgroups, one of which comprises Cairo 1328, Majāmī' Ṭal'at 274, Taṣawwuf 300, and Yahuda 3872, the other 'Aqā'id Taymūr 393, Majāmī' Ṭal'at 217, Sprenger 677, and Taṣawwuf Ṭal'at 1587. The second group consists of Ḥikmah 24, Or. Oct. 1854, Warner Or. 702(3), Yahuda 3049, and Yahuda 5373. The remaining twelve manuscripts do not seem to fall into any definite groups. Of the total of twenty-five, seven representative manuscripts, Majāmī' Ṭal'at 217, Taṣawwuf 300, and Yahuda 3872, from the first group, Or. Oct. 1854 and Yahuda 5373 from the second group, and Loth 670 and Warner Or. 997(1) from the remaining manuscripts were chosen for the final collation, and their variant readings were cited in the notes to the Arabic edition.

The eleven copies of the supplement fall into four groups. The first of these contains Cairo 1328, Majāmī' Ṭal'at 274, Taṣawwuf 300, and Yahuda 3872. The second group includes Bukhārā 427-8, Yahuda 3049, and Yahuda 5373, and the third

'Āmm 9276 (both copies) and Majāmī' Ṭal'at 217. Majāmī' Taymūr 134 evidently forms a group of its own. Of these eleven copies, four, one from each group, were chosen for collation. These are Yahuda 3872, Yahuda 5373, Majāmī' Ṭal'at 217, and Majāmī' Taymūr 134.

B. *The Glosses.* Al-Jāmī's *Glosses* are generally found written in the margins of the manuscripts opposite the statement or passage in the text to which they refer. Occasionally, as in Yahuda 5930 and Yahuda 1308, a gloss has been incorporated into the text, and sometimes, as in Warner Or. 702(3) and Bukhārā 427-8, the glosses have been written on separate slips of paper which have then been inserted between the folios of the manuscript. At the end of each gloss the word *minhu* (by him) is usually written to indicate that the gloss is by the author himself and to distinguish it from the many other glosses and notes which fill the margins of many of the manuscripts.

Only eighteen of the twenty-five copies of *al-Durrah al-Fākhirah* were found to contain any of the glosses at all, and only one, Yahuda 3872, contained all of the forty-five glosses included in the present translation. In the table of glosses the particular glosses contained in each of these manuscripts are indicated. It should be noted that twelve of the glosses, Nos. 5, 13, 15, 18, 20, 23-25, and 40-43 occur in appreciably fewer manuscripts than do the other glosses, and with the obvious exception of 'Aqā'id Taymūr 393,[2] are usually in manuscripts containing the long versions of the text.[3] This can be clearly seen by comparing the glosses contained in the two manuscripts of the long version with the most glosses, namely Yahuda 3872 and Yahuda 5373, with the two manuscripts of the short version containing the most glosses, namely Warner Or. 723(2) and Or. Oct. 1854. It therefore seems possible that these twelve glosses were added by al-Jāmī to the original thirty-three at some later time, perhaps at the time the supplement was added, although it should be noted that none of the forty-five glosses refer to passages or statements in the supplement.[4]

The table also indicates which of the glosses are dealt with in al-Lārī's *Commentary* as well as in the other commentaries

TABLE OF GLOSSES

NUMBER OF GLOSS	1	2	3	4	5	6	7	8	9	10	11	12	13	14	15	16	17	18	19	20	21	22	23	24	25	26	27	28	29	30	31	32	33	34	35	36	37	38	39	40	41	42	43	44	45	
Āmm 9276			X	X		X	X		X			X	X	X					X							X	X	X							X		X							X		15
Taṣawwuf 300			X	X	X	X		X		X	X	X	X				X	X		X													X		X			X	X				X			17
Yahuda 3049	X	X	X			X		X	X		X	X		X	X	X	X		X			X									X						X	X	X							18
Bukhārā 427-8	X	X		X	X		X	X	X	X		X	X				X		X			X				X	X	X	X	X	X	X	X	X	X	X	X	X	X							27
Majāmīʿ Ṭalʿat 217	X	X		X	X	X	X		X	X	X	X	X	X		X	X		X	X		X				X	X	X	X	X	X		X	X	X	X	X	X	X			X				31
Majāmīʿ Taymūr 134	X	X	X	X	X	X	X				X	X		X		X	X		X		X	X		X		X	X	X	X	X	X	X	X	X	X	X	X	X	X					X	X	32
Yahuda 5373	X	X		X	X	X	X	X	X	X	X	X	X	X	X	X	X	X	X	X	X	X				X	X	X	X	X	X	X	X	X	X	X	X	X	X	X	X	X		X	X	40
Yahuda 3872	X	X	X	X	X	X	X	X	X	X	X	X	X	X	X	X	X	X	X	X	X	X	X	X	X	X	X	X	X	X	X	X	X	X	X	X	X	X	X	X	X	X	X	X	X	45
Warner Or. 702(3)	X	X	X	X		X	X	X	X	X	X	X		X		X	X		X		X	X	X		X	X	X	X	X	X	X	X	X	X	X	X	X	X	X					X	X	35
Or. Oct. 1854	X	X	X	X		X	X	X	X	X	X	X				X	X		X		X	X				X	X	X	X	X	X	X	X	X	X	X	X	X	X					X	X	32
Ḥikmah 24	X	X	X	X		X	X	X	X	X	X	X		X		X	X		X		X	X				X		X	X	X	X	X					X									24
Loth 670				X		X	X	X	X	X		X		X		X			X		X	X						X		X	X				X	X	X	X	X		X			X	X	23
ʿAqāʾid Taymūr 393				X	X	X		X		X	X	X	X	X			X	X	X	X			X	X									X				X	X	X	X			X			21
Sprenger 1820 c	X															X	X		X			X				X					X			X	X		X									10
Rylands 111	X			X			X		X	X						X																														6
Yahuda 3179	X								X																																		X		X	4
Yahuda 5930	X							X							X																															3
Yahuda 1308																																													X	1
No. of MSS Containing Gloss	13	9	8	13	7	12	11	11	12	11	10	13	7	10	4	11	12	4	13	5	7	11	3	3	2	10	8	10	8	9	11	7	9	8	11	8	13	11	11	3	3	3	4	7	8	
Muḥammad Maʿṣūm	X	X		X		X	X	X	X	X	X	X	X	X		X	X		X		X			X		X	X	X	X	X	X	X		X	X	X	X	X					X	X		32
al-Husaynābādī	X					X	X	X	X	X						X					X	X				X	X	X	X	X	X			X	X		X		X						X	20
al-Lārī		X			X					X		X				X	X					X			X						X						X	X	X			X	X	X		15
al-Kūrānī	X	X										X				X	X																				X									6
Anonymous												X										X					X		X	X							X									6
No. of commentaries containing Gloss	3	3	0	1	1	2	2	2	2	3	1	4	1	1	0	4	3	0	1	0	2	3	0	1	1	2	3	2	3	3	3	1	0	2	2	1	5	2	3	0	0	1	2	2	1	

consulted.[5] It was not possible to use these commentaries in establishing the Arabic text of the *Glosses,* since, with the exception of the commentary of Muḥammad Ma'ṣūm, the glosses are rarely quoted in their entirety. Unfortunately the poor condition of the manuscript of Muḥammad Ma'ṣūm's commentary prevented its use for this purpose.

Several of the manuscripts, particularly Majāmī' Taymūr 134, contain glosses which are attributed to al-Jāmī by means of the word *minhu,* but which are not contained in any of the other manuscripts, or at most in only one other. Are these glosses to be considered authentic or not? None of them occur in either Yahuda 3872 or Taṣawwuf 300, both of which must be considered authoritative manuscripts because of their transmission through Ibrāhīm al-Kūrānī, nor are any of them mentioned in al-Lārī's *Commentary* or any of the other commentaries which have been consulted. Although it is possible that as yet unexamined manuscripts of *al-Durrah al-Fākhirah* may also contain additional glosses attributed to al-Jāmī, and that some or all of these glosses may ultimately be shown to be authentic, the Arabic edition and translation of the *Glosses* was nevertheless limited to the forty-five glosses contained in Yahuda 3872. It should be noted that each of these forty-five glosses appears in at least two other manuscripts with the exception of gloss No. 25, which appears in only one other manuscript. However, since this gloss is quoted by al-Lārī in his *Commentary,* there can be no doubt as to its authenticity.

A comparison of variant readings in the original thirty-three glosses reveals that nine of the eighteen manuscripts containing these glosses fall into two distinct groups. The first of those includes 'Āmm 9276, 'Aqā'id Taymūr 393, Bukhārā 427-8, Taṣawwuf 300, and Yahuda 3872. The other contains Ḥikmah 24, Or. Oct. 1854, Warner Or. 702(3), and Yahuda 5373. Four of the remaining manuscripts, Loth 670, Majāmī' Ṭal'at 217, Majāmī' Taymūr 134, and Yahuda 3049 cannot be placed in either of these groups, nor do they seem to constitute any additional group or groups in themselves. The other five manuscripts contain too few glosses for a comparison of variant readings to be made.

Since of these eighteen manuscripts only Yahuda 3872 and Warner Or. 702(3) contain all thirty-three original glosses, it was not possible to use the same manuscripts in establishing the texts of all thirty-three. As a general rule, four manuscripts were collated for each gloss. These were Yahuda 3872 and Warner Or. 702(3), representing each of the two groups, and one other manuscript from each group selected from among those manuscripts which happen to contain the gloss in question.

Of the additional glosses, Nos. 5 and 13 are each contained in seven manuscripts. Six manuscripts, 'Aqā'id Taymūr 393, Bukhārā 427-8, Majāmī' Ṭal'at 217, Taṣawwuf 300, Yahuda 3872 and Yahuda 5373, contain both of these glosses, Majāmī' Taymūr 134 contains gloss No. 5 and 'Āmm 9276 contains gloss No. 13. Variant readings in these two glosses indicate that four of these eight manuscripts, 'Aqā'id Taymūr 393, Taṣawwuf 300, Yahuda 3872, and Yahuda 5373, form one group, and that the remaining four constitute a second group. For these two glosses two manuscripts from the first group, Yahuda 3872 and 'Aqā'id Taymūr 393, and two from the second group were collated and their variant readings cited in the notes to the Arabic edition.

The other additional glosses, Nos. 15, 18, 20, 23-25, and 40-43, are contained in too few manuscripts for any definite groups to be determined from a comparison of variant readings. In most cases, therefore, all the manuscripts containing these glosses were collated and their variant readings cited in the notes to the Arabic text.

C. *Al-Lārī's Commentary.* Al-Lārī's *Commentary* is found in only six of the manuscripts which contain *al-Durrah al-Fākhirah.* These are 'Āmm 9276, 'Aqā'id Taymūr 393, Bukhārā 427-8, Taṣawwuf 300, Yahuda 3872, and Yahuda 5373. All of those manuscripts except 'Aqā'id Taymūr 393 contain the long version of *al-Durrah al-Fākhirah.* On the other hand, no copies of the *Commentary* were found in any manuscript which did not contain *al-Durrah al-Fākhirah* with at least some of the glosses.

On the basis of a comparison of variant readings these six manuscripts fall into two groups. The first of these includes

Bukhāra 427-8, Yahuda 3872, and Yahuda 5373, and the second 'Āmm 9276, 'Aqā'id Taymūr 393, and Taṣawwuf 300. Two manuscripts from each group were used in the collation, Yahuda 3872 and Yahuda 5373 from the first group and 'Aqā'id Taymūr 393 and Taṣawwuf 300 from the second.

8. Notes on the Signs and Symbols Used

A. In *al-Durrah al-Fākhirah.*

1. Numerals within square brackets, [ ], refer to al-Jāmī's *Glosses* and are placed at the point in the text where the gloss is to be read.
2. A" v" indicates that the word or phrase which follows is dealt with in al-Lārī's *Commentary.*

B. In al-Lārī's *Commentary.*

1. Italics are used to indicate words and phrases quoted from *al-Durrah al-Fākhirah* or the *Glosses.*
2. Numerals at the head of sections refer to the corresponding paragraph numbers of *al-Durrah al-Fākhirah.*
3. Numerals within square brackets at the head of sections refer to the numbers of the corresponding glosses.

NOTES TO THE INTRODUCTION

Section 1

1. The district of Jām is located in the northeast corner of the province of Qūhistān near the Herat River. See Guy Le Strange, *The Lands of the Eastern Caliphate,* pp. 356-58.

2. The principal sources for al-Jāmī's life are: 1) the biographical account given by his disciple 'Abd al-Ghafūr al-Lārī in the *Khātimah,* or *Takmilah,* appended to his *Ḥāshiyah* on al-Jāmī's *Nafaḥāt al-Uns* (See Charles Ambrose Storey, *Persian Literature,* I, pp. 956-958); 2) al-Kāshifī's *Rashaḥāt-i 'Ayn al-Ḥayāt,* completed in 909 (Storey, *Persian Literature,* I, p. 964); 3) Mīr 'Alī-Shīr Nawā'ī's *Khamsat al-Mutaḥayyirīn,* written in Turkī in memory of al-Jāmī (Storey, *Persian Literature,* I, pp. 789-790); and 4) Ṭāshkubrīzādah's *al-Shaqā'iq al-Nu'mānīyah,* I, pp. 389-392.

Other sources include: al-Shawkānī, *al-Badr al-Ṭāli',* I, pp. 327-328; al-Laknawī, *al-Fawā'id al-Bahīyah,* pp. 86-88; al-Sanhūtī, *al-Anwār al-Qudsīyah,* pp. 152-153; al-Nabhānī, *Jāmi' Karāmāt al-Awliyā',* II, p. 154; Dārā Shikūh, *Safīnat al-Awliyā',* pp. 82-84.

Modern accounts of his life are given by Edward Granville Browne in his *Literary History of Persia,* III, pp. 507-548; Arthur John Arberry in his *Classical Persian Literature,* pp. 425-450; by William Nassau Lees in the English preface to his edition of al-Jāmī's *Nafaḥāt al-Uns*; and by 'Alī-Aṣghar Ḥikmat in his book, *Jāmī,* published in Tehran in 1320/1942.

Except where other sources are cited, the brief account of al-Jāmī's life given here is based on al-Kāshifī's *Rashaḥāt,* pp. 133-163; and al-Lārī's *Khātimah,* especially fols. 156b-158b, 170a-170b, and 172b-173b.

3. The shorter commentary by Sa'd al-Dīn al-Taftāzānī on *Talkhīṣ al-Miftāḥ,* an abridgement of the third part of al-Sakkākī's *Miftāḥ al-'Ulum* by Jamāl al-Dīn al-Qazwīnī. See Carl Brockelmann, *Geschichte der arabischen Litteratur I,* pp. 352-354.

4. Any one of several commentaries on the third part of al-Sakkākī's *Miftāḥ al-Ulūm.* See Brockelmann, *Geschichte,* I, pp. 352-354.

5. The longer commentary of al-Taftāzānī on al-Qazwīnī's *Talkhīṣ al-Miftāḥ.* See Brockelmann, *Geschichte,* I, pp. 352-354.

6. His full name was Shihāb al-Dīn Mūsā ibn Muḥammad ibn Maḥmūd al-Rūmī. See Khayr al-Dīn al-Ziriklī, *al-A'lām,* VIII, p. 282; Brockelmann, *Geschichte,* II, 275; Ṭāshkubrīzādah, *al-Shaqā'iq al-Nu'mānīyah,* I, pp. 77-81

(under the biography of his grandfather, Maḥmūd). The year 815 given as the date of his death by Brockelmann is clearly an error. Al-Ziriklī places his death at about 840. Since he worked on the famous *zīj* of Ulugh Beg after Ghiyāth al-Dīn Jamshīd's death in 832 (or 833 according to some sources), but died himself before the *zīj* was completed in 841, his death could only have occurred within this period. See Aydın Sayılı, *The Observatory in Islam,* pp. 259-289; Edward Stewart Kennedy, *The Planetary Equatorium,* pp. 3-7, and Brockelmann, *Geschichte,* II, pp. 275-276. If Qāḍī-Zādah died as late as 841, al-Jāmī would at that time have been only twenty-four.

7. A commentary on *al-Tadkhirah al-Nāṣirīyah* by Naṣīr al-Dīn al-Ṭūsī. See Brockelmann, *Geschichte,* II, pp. 674-675.

8. A commentary on *al-Mulakhkhaṣ fī al-Hay'ah* by Maḥmūd ibn Muḥammad ibn 'Umar al-Jaghmīnī. See Brockelmann, *Geschichte,* I, p. 624, Supplement, I, p. 865.

9. 'Alā' al-Dīn 'Alī ibn Muḥammad al-Qūshjī, a former student of Qāḍī-Zādah, completed Ulugh Beg's *zīj* after his teacher's death. See Brockelmann, *Geschichte,* II, p. 305, Supplement, II, p. 329.

10. His full name was Muḥammad ibn Muḥammad ibn Maḥmūd al-Ḥāfiẓ al-Bukhārī. A disciple of Bahā' al-Dīn al-Naqshband, the founder of the Naqshbandī order, he died unexpectedly in 822 in Medina after completing the pilgrimage. See al-Jāmī, *Nafaḥāt al-Uns,* pp. 392-396; al-Sanhūtī, *al-Anwār al-Qudsīyah,* pp. 142-145; Dārā Shikūh, *Safīnat al-Awliyā',* p. 79; al-Kāshifī, *Rashaḥāt,* pp. 57-63.

11. He died in 860. See al-Jāmī, *Nafaḥāt al-Uns,* pp. 403-405; al-Kāshifī, *Rashaḥāt,* pp. 117-133; al-Sanhūtī, *al-Anwār al-Qudsīyah,* pp. 151-152; Dārā Shikūh, *Safīnat al-Awliyā',* pp. 81-82 (under the name Niẓām Khāmūsh).

12. He died in 791. See al-Jāmī, *Nafaḥāt al-Uns,* pp. 384-389; al-Kāshifī, *Rashaḥāt,* pp. 53-57; Dāra Shikūh, *Safīnat al-Awliyā',* pp. 78-79; and al-Sanhūtī, *al-Anwār al-Qudsīyah,* pp. 126-142.

13. See al-Jāmī, *Nafaḥāt al-Uns,* pp. 400-402; al-Kāshifī, *Rashaḥāt,* pp. 108-117; and al-Sanhūtī, *al-Anwār al-Qudsīyah,* pp. 150-151.

14. See al-Jāmī, *Nafaḥāt al-Uns,* pp. 389-392; al-Kāshifī, *Rashaḥāt,* pp. 79-90; Dārā Shikūh, *Safīnat al-Awliyā',* p. 80; and al-Sanhūtī, *al-Anwār al-Qudsīyah,* pp. 145-148.

15. See al-Jāmī, *Nafaḥāt al-Uns,* pp. 452-453.

16. He was the son of Khwājah Muḥammad Pārsā, mentioned earlier. See al-Jāmī, *Nafaḥat al-Uns,* pp. 396-397; al-Kāshifi, *Rashaḥāt,* pp. 63-64; Dārā Shikūh, *Safīnat al-Awliyā',* pp. 79-80; and al-Sanhūtī, *al-Anwār al-Qudsīyah,* p. 144.

17. See al-Jāmī, *Nafaḥāt al-Uns,* pp. 455-456.

18. See *ibid.,* pp. 496-498.

19. See *ibid.,* pp. 501-503.

20. See *ibid.,* pp. 456-457.

21. He was born in 806 and died in 895. See al-Jāmī, *Nafaḥāt al-Uns,* pp. 406-413; al-Sanhūtī, *al-Anwār al-Qudsīyah,* pp. 157-175; Ṭāhkubrīzādah,

al-Shaqā'iq al-Nu'mānīyah, I, pp. 381-389; Dārā Shikūh, *Safīnat al-Awliyā',* pp. 80-81; and especially al-Kāshifī, *Rashaḥāt,* pp. 207-242.

22. Al-jāmī's letters to 'Ubayd Allāh al-Aḥrār are preserved in his *Risālah-i Munsha'āt.* See Ḥikmat, *Jāmī,* p. 205.

23. As, for example, in the first *daftar* of his *Silsilat al-Dhahab* (al-Jāmī, *Haft Awrang,* p. 158), in his *Tuḥfat al-Aḥrār* (al-Jāmī, *Haft Awrang,* p. 384), and in his third *dīwān (Khātimat al-Ḥayāt).* See Ḥikmat, *Jāmī,* pp. 72-76.

24. See Storey, *Persian Literature,* I, pp. 789-795.

25. See Bābur, *Bābur-nāma,* pp. 283-292.

26. The passage in question is entitled "Dar bayān-i ānkih akthar-i khalq-i 'ālam rūy-i parastish dar mawhūm wa-mukhayyal dārand," which may be translated "In explanation of the fact that most of the people of the world have the object of [their] worship in their own imagination and fancy." See al-Jāmī, *Haft Awrang,* p. 52.

27. See al-Ziriklī, *al-A'lām,* VII, p. 280, and autograph No. 1240 opposite p. 273; and Brockelmann, *Geschichte,* II, p. 120, Supplement, II, p. 116.

28. He is perhaps to be identified with a certain 'Aṭā' Allāh al-'Ajamī, whose biography is given in Ṭāshkubrīzādah's *al-Shaqā'iq al-Nu'mānīyah,* I, p. 334.

29. The *ashrafī* was a gold coin first issued by the Mamlūk sultan, al-Ashraf Barsbāy, and weighing about 3.41 grams or .11 of a troy ounce. See Jere Bacharach, "The Dinar Versus the Ducat," *International Journal of Middle East Studies* 4, pp. 77-96. Five thousand *ashrafīs* would therefore weigh about 17,050 grams or 550 ounces.

30. See Ṭāshkubrīzādah, *al-Shaqā'iq al-Nu'mānīyah,* I, pp. 390-391.

31. Two letters of Bāyazīd II to al-Jāmī with al-Jāmī's answers are preserved in Farīdūn Beg's *Munsha'āt al-Salāṭīn,* I, pp. 361-364. See Ḥikmat, *Jāmī,* pp. 44-47.

32. See Ṭāshkubrīzādah, *al-Shaqā'iq al-Nu'mānīyah,* I, pp. 389-390.

33. For the description of his tomb, see Ḥikmat, *Jāmī,* pp. 214-228.

Section 2

1. No complete or exhaustive list of al-Jāmī's works has yet been compiled. One of the problems facing the compiler of such a list is that al-Jāmī seems to have given definite titles only to his major works. Consequently, the titles of his minor works often differ from copy to copy, each title being based on a different key word or expression to be found in the initial paragraphs of the text. Accurate identification of a copy of a particular work must, therefore, be based on the beginning lines of the work at least, if not on the entire text.

The most thorough lists compiled to date are the following:

1. The description of MS No. 894, containing thirty-seven of al-Jāmī's works, given by Edward Sachau and Hermann Ethé in their *Catalogue of the Persian, Turkish, Hindustani and Pushtu Manuscripts in the Bodleian Library,*

pp. 608-615.

2. The description of MS No. 1357, containing twenty-two of al-Jāmī's prose works, given by Hermann Ethé in his *Catalogue of the Persian Manuscripts in the Library of the India Office,* II, pp. 762-765.

3. The list compiled by A.T. Tagirdzhanov on pp. 311-318 of his *Opisanie Tadzhikskikh i Persidskikh Rukopisei Vostochnogo Otdela Biblioteki LGU.*

4. 'Alī Aṣghar Ḥikmat's description of twenty of al-Jāmī's works on pp. 166-213 of his book, *Jāmī.*

5. The list of printed editions and translations of al-Jāmī's works on pp. 26-35 of Edward Edwards's *A Catalogue of the Persian Printed Books in the British Museum.*

2. See fol. 172b of British Museum MS Or. 218.

3. See pp. 86-87.

4. This is the date given in the colophon of the first *daftar* on p. 183 of Aqā Murtaḍā's edition of the *Haft Awrang.* Although al-Jāmī often mentioned the date for the completion of a work, usually in its last lines, he did not do so in the case of this work. However since the first *daftar* is dedicated to Sulṭān Ḥusayn Bāyqarā, it must have been written between the year 873, the year of his accession, and 877, the year al-Jāmī was unjustly accused of having ridiculed Shī'ite beliefs because of what he was alleged to have written in this work.

5. For a detailed description of the *Haft Awrang* and the three *dīwāns,* see Browne, *Literary History,* III, pp. 516-548; and Ḥikmāt, *Jāmī,* pp. 183-203 and 207-212.

6. Vol. XVI, New Series, Oriental Translation Fund. Reprinted with Additions and Corrections. London 1928.

7. Printed in the margin of 'Abd al-Ghanī al-Nābulusī's *Jawāhir al-Nuṣūṣ fī Ḥall Kalimāt al-Fuṣuṣ* (Cairo, 1304-1323).

8. Lithographed in Bombay in 1307.

9. See my edition and translation of this work, "Al-Jāmī's *Treatise on Existence,*" in *Islamic Philosophical Theology,* ed. Parviz Morewedge.

10. See Storey, *Persian Literature* I, pp. 954-959.

11. See Brockelmann, *Geschichte,* I, p. 369, Supplement, I, p. 533; and Browne, *Literary History,* III, p. 514.

12. See Browne, *Literary History,* III, p. 515.

Section 3

1. The *muḥākamah* was a genre of writing in which the author compared two opposing points of view or positions and then attempted an adjudication or possibly a reconciliation between them. Probably the most famous work of this type was Quṭb al-Dīn al-Rāzī's *al-Muḥākamāt,* in which he attempted to reconcile the opposing views of Fakhr al-Dīn al-Rāzī and Naṣīr

al-Dīn al-Ṭūsī as expressed in their respective commentaries on Ibn Sīnā's *Ishārāt.*

2. The six questions referred to here are apparently those pertaining to God's existence, His unity, His knowledge, His will, His power, and His speech, all of which are dealt with in the original or short version. The long version includes two additional questions dealing with the impotence of contingent being and the emanation of multiplicity from unity.

3. Ṭāshkubrīzādah, *al-Shaqā'iq al-Nu'mānīyah,* I, pp. 390-391.

4. The first nine of these questions are treated in the original version whereas the last two are dealt with in the supplemental paragraphs of the long version. The nine questions treated in the original version can be reduced to the six questions mentioned in *al-Shaqā'iq al-Nu'mānīyah* by combining the two questions dealing with God's knowledge, considering the question of the dependence of an eternal effect on a free agent as part of the question of God's power, and considering the question of God's attributes in general as a preface to the following questions dealing with the attributes in detail.

5. Insofar as has been possible the sources of all quotations and paraphrases, whether acknowledged by al-Jāmī or not, have been indicated in the notes to the translation of *al-Durrah al-Fākhirāh* and the *Glosses.*

6. See his *Khātimah,* British Museum MS Or. 218, fol. 172b.

7. Jacobus Ecker, *Gâmii de Dei Existentia et Attributis Libellus,* p. 26.

8. Al-Kūrānī, *al-Amam li-Īqāẓ al-Himam,* p. 107.

Section 4

1. The principal source for al-Lārī's life is al-Kāshifī's *Rashaḥāt,* pp. 163-173. Other sources include Bābur's *Bābur-nāma,* pp. 284-285; Dārā Shikūh, *Safīnat al-Awliyā',* p. 84; al-Sanhūtī, *al-Anwār al-Qudsīyah,* p. 153; and al-Lāhawrī, *Khazīnat al-Aṣfiyā',* I, p. 598.

2. The name of a city and district in the province of Fārs. See G. LeStrange, *Lands of the Eastern Caliphate,* p. 291.

3. See Storey, *Persian Literature,* I, pp. 956-958.

4. See Brockelmann, *Geschichte,* I, p. 369, Supplement, I, p. 533.

5. See Brockelmann, *Geschichte,* I, p. 787. A copy of this work is to be found on folios 15b-33b of MS Loth 670 in the India Office Library. See the description of this manuscript in Section 6 of the Introduction, p. 12.

Section 5

1. For the author, see Brockelmann, *Geschichte,* II, p. 505, Supplement, II, p. 520; and al-Ziriklī, *al-A'lām,* I, p. 28.

2. See Vol. I, p. 35.

3. See the description of this manuscript in Section 6 of the Introduction, p. 15.

4. For the author, see Brockelmann, *Geschichte,* Supplement, II, p. 619. For the work itself, see *Ibid.,* II, p. 266, Supplement, III, p. 1271; and al-Baghdādī, *Īḍāḥ al-Maknūn,* I, p. 567.

5. See Muḥammad As'ad Ṭalas, *al-Kashshāf 'an Makhṭūṭāt Khazā'in Kutub al-Awqāf,* p. 277.

6. See the description of this manuscript in Section 6 of the Introduction, p. 11.

7. He is also the author of a gloss on al-Taftāzānī's commentary on *al-'Aqā'id* of al-Nasafī (See Brockelmann, *Geschichte,* Supplement, I, p. 759), of a Persian *tafsīr* on *sūrah* 108 of the Qur'ān, and of another work, in Arabic, entitled *Risālat Abḥāth* (see Wladimir Ivanow, *Descriptive Catalogue of the Persian Manuscripts in the Collection of the Asiatic Society of Bengal,* p. 471).

8. See *Catalogue of the Arabic Manuscripts in the Library of the India Office,* II, 168.

9. See Wladimir Ivanow and M. Hidayat Hosain, *Catalogue of the Arabic Manuscripts in the Collection of the Royal Asiatic Society of Bengal,* I, pp. 583-584.

Section 6

1. *Gâmii de Dei Existentia et Attributis Libellus "Stratum Solve!" sive "Unio Pretiosus."* Pars Prior. Prolegomena una cum capitibus selectis in Latinum sermonem translatis. Dissertatio quam ad summos in philosophia honores auctoritate amplissimi philosophorum ordinis in alma litterarum Universitate Fridericia Guilelmia Rhenana rite impetrandos scripsit et una cum sententiis controversis die X mensis Martii a. MDCCCLXXIX hora XII publice defendit Jacobus Ecker. Bonnae.

The translation, which includes only paragraphs 1-3, 27-29, and 60-71 was based on five manuscripts: Warner 702(3), Warner 997(1), Warner 723(2), Gotha 87(7) [See Pertsch, *Die arabischen Handscriften,* p. 156], and Loth 670. With the exception of the Gotha manuscript, all of these were used in the preparation of the edition on which the present translation in based.

2. See Brockelmann, *Geschichte,* II, p. 505, Supplement, II, p. 520; and al-Ziriklī, *al-A'lām,* I, p. 28.

3. See Brockelmann, *Geschichte,* II, p. 514, Supplement, II, p. 535.

4. *Ibid.,* II, p. 514, Supplement, II, p. 534.

5. See 'Abd al-Ḥayy al-Ḥasanī, *Nuzhat al-Khawāṭir,* V, p. 301.

6. Al-Kūrānī, *al-Amam,* pp. 107-108.

7. See his *Handlist of Arabic Manuscripts,* pp. 41, 52, 341, 354, 539.

8. See Brockelmann, *Geschichte,* II, p. 556; and G.W.J. Drewes, "Sech Joesoep Makasar" *Djawa,* 1926, No. 2, pp. 83-88.

Section 7

1. See Section 3 of the Introduction, p. 5.

2. This exception might be explained as a case of the glosses from a manuscript of the long version being added later to the margins of a copy of the short version. Since none of the glosses refer to the supplemental paragraphs of the long version, a copyist interested only in adding the glosses to his own copy might not notice the additional paragraphs at the end of the manuscript from which he was copying.

3. The exceptions are Gloss 15, which appears in Yahuda 5930, Glosses 23 and 25, which appear in Warner Or. 702(3), Gloss 41, which appears in Loth 670, and Gloss 43, which appears in Yahuda 3179.

4. Other explanations for the reduced occurrence of these twelve glosses are, of course, possible. Glosses may be left out by a copyist because they are too long to fit into the space available in the margin. On the other hand, a copyist may overlook glosses consisting of only a few words. It might also be argued that these twelve glosses are not authentic, and that is why they occur in so few of the manuscripts. This argument can be countered, however, by the fact that all twelve occur in Yahuda 3872, the most authoritative of the manuscripts.

5. These are the commentaries described in Section 5 of the Introduction.

The
Translation
of
al-Jāmī's
AL-DURRAH AL-FĀKHIRAH

In the name of God, the Merciful, the Compassionate.

1. [v]Praise be to God, Who became manifest *(tajallā)* through His essence *(bi-dhātihi)* to His essence *(li-dhātihi),* so that the manifestations *(majālī)* of His essence and of His attributes [v]became individuated *(ta'ayyana)* in His inner knowledge, [v]the effects *(āthār)* of these manifestations being then reflected [v]upon His outward aspect *(ẓāhir)* from within *(al-bāṭin),* [v]such that unity *(al-waḥdah)* became multiplicity *(kathrah),* [v]as you see and behold. May God's blessing and peace be upon him through whom [v]this multiplicity reverted to its original unity, and upon his family and companions, [v]who have inherited of this virtue a large portion.

2. *To Proceed,* this is a treatise dealing with the verification of the doctrines of the Ṣūfīs, the theologians, and the early philosophers, and with the establishment of their beliefs concerning the existence of the Necessary Existent in Himself *(al-Wājib li-Dhātihi),* the realities *(ḥaqā'iq)*[1] of His names and attributes, the manner in which multiplicity emanates from His unity without any impairment *(naqṣ)* to the perfection of His sanctity and glory, and other subsequent inquiries *(mabāḥith)* prompted by thought *(al-fikr)* and reason *(al-naẓar).* It is hoped that God will permit every unbiased seeker to benefit from this treatise and that He will protect it from every unthinking bigot, for He is sufficient for me and an excellent guardian.

3. *Preface.* Know [v]that there is in existence a necessary existent *(wājib),* [v]for otherwise that which exists *(al-mawjūd)* would be restricted to contingent being *(al-mumkin),* [v]and consequently nothing would exist at all. [v]This is because contingent being, even though multiple *(muta'addid),* is not self-sufficient *(lā yastaqill)* with respect to its existence, as is obvious, nor with respect to bringing another into existence, since the stage of bringing-into-existence *(martabat al-ījād)* is consequent to that of existence.[1] Thus, if there is neither existence nor

bringing-into-existence, there can be nothing that exists, either through itself or through another. Thus the existence of the Necessary Existent *(al-Wājib)* is proven.

4. The apparent position *(madhhab)* of both al-Shaykh Abū al-Ḥasan al-Ash'arī[1] and al-Shaykh Abū al-Ḥusayn al-Baṣrī[2] of the Mu'tazilites is that the existence of the Necessary Existent *(al-Wājib)* indeed the existence of everything, is identical with its essence *(dhāt)* [V]both in the mind *(dhihnan)* and externally *(khārijan).* [V]This implies that existence is common *(ishtirāk)* to proper existences *(al-wujūdāt al-khāṣṣah)*[3] in name only *(lafẓan)* rather than in meaning *(ma'nan),* and this is obviously false, because, as has been explained elsewhere in works dealing with this subject, [V]belief concerning [the existence of] something in an absolute sense endures even though belief as to its particular characteristic *(khuṣūṣīyah)* ceases, [V]and because [existence] is subject to division in meaning *(al-taqsīm al-ma'nawī).*[4] Some people, therefore, did not interpret their position literally, but claimed that [V]what they meant by identity *(al-'aynīyah)* was indistinguishability in the external world, that is, that there is not in the external world something which is the quiddity *(al-māhīyah)* and something else subsisting in it *(qā'im bihā)* externally which is existence, as one who follows their proofs understands.

5. The majority of the theologians *(jumhūr al-mutakallimīn)* took the position that existence is a single concept *(mafhūm wāḥid)* common to all existences, and that this single concept becomes multiple and is divided into portions *(ḥiṣṣah)* through its attribution to things *(al-ashyā'),* as, for example, the whiteness of this snow [as distinguished from the whiteness of] that snow. [V]The existences of things are these portions, and these portions along with that concept *(al-mafhūm)* intrinsic to them *(al-dākhil fīhā)* are external *(khārijah)* to the essences of things and only mentally superadded to them *(zā'idah 'alayhā)* in the view of their verifiers *(muḥaqqiqīhim),*[1] and both mentally and externally in the view of others.[[1]]

6. The gist *(ḥāṣil)* of the position of the philosophers[1] is that existence is a single concept common to all [proper] existences. These [proper] existences, however, are dissimilar

realities which are multiple in themselves not merely through the accident of attribution *('āriḍ al-iḍāfah),* for in that case they would be similar to each other *(mutamāthilah)* and agree in reality, nor through specific differences *(al-fuṣūl),* for in that case absolute existence *(al-wujūd al-muṭlaq)* would be their genus *(jins).* On the contrary, existence is an accident concomitant with them *('āriḍ lāzim lahā)* like the light of the sun and the light of a lamp. Although both sun and lamp differ in reality *(al-ḥaqīqah)* and in concomitants *(al-lawāzim),* they, nevertheless, have in common the accident of light. [v]Similar to this are the whiteness of snow and the whiteness of ivory, or quantity and quality, which have in common accidentality *(al-'araḍīyah),* or even substance and accident, which have contingency *(al-imkān)* and existence in common. However, since each [proper] existence does not have its own name, as is the case with the divisions of contingent being *(aqsām al-mumkin)* or the divisions of accident *(aqsām al-'araḍ),* it was imagined that the multiplicity *(takaththur)* of existences and their division into portions was due entirely to their attribution to the quiddities which are their substrata, like the whiteness of this snow and [the whiteness] of that, or the light of this lamp and [the light] of that. Such, however, is not the case. On the contrary, they are different and dissimilar realities subsumed under this concept which inheres [in them] but is external to them. When one considers that this concept becomes multiple and is divided into portions through its attribution to quiddities, then [one realizes] that these portions also are external to those existences with dissimilar realities *(al-wujūdāt al-mukhtalifat al-ḥaqā'iq).*[2]

7. Three things are thus [involved]: the concept of existence *(mafhūm al-wujūd),* its portions individuated through its attribution to quiddities, and the proper existences with dissimilar realities *(al-wujūdāt al-khāṣṣah al-mukhtalifat al-ḥaqā'iq).* The concept of existence is essential *(dhātī)* and intrinsic to *(dākhil fī)* its portions, but both[3] are external to *(khārij 'an)* proper existences. Proper existence is [v]identical with the essence in the case of the Necessary Existent *(al-Wājib),* but superadded *(zā'id)* and external *(khārij)* in the case of everything else.

8. [V]*Ramification.* If you have understood this, we say further:[1] Just as it is possible for this general concept *(al-mafhūm al-'āmm)* to be superadded to Necessary Existence *(al-Wujūd al-Wājibī)* and to contingent proper existences, on the assumption that the latter are dissimilar realities, it is also possible for it to be superadded to a single absolute and existent reality *(ḥaqīqah wāḥidah muṭlaqah mawjūdah)* which is the reality of Necessary Existence *(ḥaqīqat al-Wūjud al-Wājib)*[[4]] as is the position taken by the Ṣūfīs who hold the doctrine of the unity of existence *(waḥdat al-wujūd).* This superadded concept would then be a mental entity *(amr i'tibārī)*[2] existing only in the intellect *(al-'aql),* and its substratum *(ma'rūḍ)* would be an external and real existent *(mawjūd ḥaqīqī khārijī)* which is the reality of existence.[[5]]

9. Furthermore,[1] [V]that existence is predicated by analogy *(al-tashkīk al-wāqi' fīhi)* does not indicate that it is an accident with respect to its singulars *(afrād),*[[6]] for no proof has been adduced to show that it is impossible for quiddities and essential attributes *(al-dhātīyāt)* to differ by analogousness *(bi-al-tashkīk).*[2] The strongest argument they have mentioned is that if a quiddity or an essential attribute differs in its particulars *(al-juz'īyāt),* then neither the quiddity nor the essential attribute is one. [V]This [argument], however, is refuted *(manqūḍ)*[3] by the case of the accident.[[7]] [V]Also, a difference in completeness or incompleteness in the same quiddity, such as a cubit or two cubits of measure does not imply a difference in the quiddity itself.[[8]]

10. Al-Shaykh Ṣadr al-Dīn al-Qūnawī said in his *al-Risālah al-Hādiyah:*[1] If a reality differs "by being more powerful *(aqwā),* prior *(aqdam),* stronger *(ashadd),* or superior *(awlā)* in something, all of that is due, in the opinion of the verifier *(al-muḥaqqiq),* to its manifestation *(al-ẓuhūr)* rather than to any multiplicity *(ta'addud)* occurring in the reality [itself] which is becoming manifest. [This is so] regardless of whether that reality is one of knowledge, of [real] existence, or of something else. There is, thus, a recipient *(qābil)* predisposed for the manifestation *(ẓuhūr)* of the reality such that the reality is more complete in its manifestation in one recipient than it is in its

manifestation in another, even though the reality [itself] is one in all [recipients]. The inequality *(al-mufāḍalah)* and dissimilarity *(al-tafāwut)*[9] occurs between its manifestations in accordance with the command causing its manifestation *(al-amr al-muẓhir)* and requiring an individuation *(ta'ayyun)* of that reality which is different from its individuation[2] in some other matter. There is, thus, no multiplicity *(ta'addud)* in the reality as such, nor is there any division *(tajzi'ah)* or partition *(tab'īḍ)*. What has been said to the effect that if light and knowledge necessitated [respectively] the cessation of night-blindness *(al-'ashā)* and the existence of something known, then every light and knowledge would do the same, is true, [v]as long as one does not mean by this that there is any difference in the reality."

11. Moreover, the basis *(mustanad)* of the position taken by the Ṣūfīs is mystical revelation and insight *(al-kashf wa-al-'iyān)* rather than reason and demonstration *(al-naẓar wa-al-burhān)*.[10] For indeed, since they have turned towards God in complete spiritual nudity *(al-ta'riyah al-kāmilah)* by wholly emptying their hearts [v]of all worldly attachments *(al-ta'alluqāt al-kawnīyah)* [v]and the rules of rational thought *(al-qawānīn al-'ilmīyah)*, and by unifying the will *(tawaḥḥud al-'azīmah)*, persisting in concentration *(dawām al-jam'īyah)*, and persevering along this path without slackening, interruption of thought *(taqsīm khāṭir)* or dissolution of will *(tashattut al-'azīmah)*, God has granted to them [v]a revealing light *(nūr kāshif)* to show them things as they really are.[1] This light appears within [v]at the appearance of a level beyond the level of the intellect *(ṭawr warā' ṭawr al-'aql)*. Do not think the existence of that improbable, for beyond the intellect are many levels whose number is hardly known except by God.[11]

12. The relation of the intellect to this light is the same as the relation of the estimation *(al-wahm)* to the intellect. And just as it is possible for the intellect to judge something to be true which cannot be apprehended by the estimation, such as the existence of a being *(mawjūd)*, for example, which is neither within the world nor outside it,[1] so also can that revealing light judge to be true certain things which cannot be apprehended by the intellect, [12,13] such as the existence of an all-encompassing

and absolute reality *(ḥaqīqah muṭlaqah muḥīṭah)* unlimited by any determination *(taqayyud)* and unrestricted by any individuation *(ta'ayyun),* although the existence of such a reality is not [a proposition] of this sort, [V]for many of the philosophers and theologians have taken the position that natural universals *(al-kullī al-ṭabī'ī)*[2] exist in the external world. Moreover, all those who have undertaken to prove the impossibility [of this proposition] have used premisses which are not free from suspicion of being defective. The intention here, however, is merely to eliminate from this proposition *(al-mas'alah)* any logical impossibility along with the usual reasons for thinking it improbable, not to establish it with proofs and demonstrations. Indeed, those who have studied this proposition, either to verify or support it or to invalidate or impair it, have been able to produce only insufficient proofs and demonstrations of it or to point out uncertainties *(shukūk)* and raise weak and unfounded objections *(shubah)* against it.

13. One of the proofs for the impossibility of the [external] existence of natural universals is that given by al-Muḥaqqiq al-Ṭūsī in his *Risālah* written in answer to the questions asked him by al-Shaykh Ṣadr al-Dīn al-Qūnawī.[1] He argues that "a concrete thing *(al-shay' al-'aynī)* does not subsist in *(lā yaqa' 'alā)* numerous things, because if it were in each one of those things, it would not be one concrete thing *(shay' bi-'aynih)* but rather [many] things. Alternatively, if it were in the whole [of them] insofar as [they are] a whole *(min ḥayth huwa kull),* the whole constituting in this respect a single thing, then it would not subsist in [numerous] things. If, on the other hand, it were in the whole in the sense of being divided among its units *(āḥād),* then there would be in each unit only a part of that thing. Thus if it is neither in the units nor in the whole, it does not subsist in them."

14. Al-Mawlā al-'Allāmah Shams al-Dīn al-Fanārī answered him in his commentary on *Miftāḥ al-Ghayb.*[1] Choosing the first alternative *(al-shiqq al-awwal)*[2] [for refutation] he said: "The meaning of the realization *(taḥaqquq)* of a universal reality *(al-ḥaqīqah al-kullīyah)* in its singulars *(afrād)* is its realization at one time qualified by this individuation *(al-ta'ayyun)* and at

another by that individuation. This does not necessitate its being many things, just as the transformation *(taḥawwul)* of a single individual into different *(mukhtalifah)* or even completely distinct *(mutabāyinah)*[3] states does not necessitate its being [many] individuals." He then said: "Should you say: How can what is one in essence *(al-wāḥid bi-al-dhāt)* be described by contrary qualities *(al-awṣāf al-mutaḍāddah)* like easternness and westernness, or knowledge or ignorance, and so forth? I should answer: You think this improbable because you make universals analogous to particulars and the invisible world *(al-ghā'ib)* analogous to the visible world *(al-shāhid)*. There is no proof for the impossibility of this with respect to universals."

15. Another [proof] is that of al-Mawlā Quṭb al-Dīn al-Rāzī,[1] which states that numerous realities such as genus, difference, and species, are all realized in one singular *(fard)*. If they existed [externally], however, predication between them would be impossible because of the impossibility of predication between multiple [external] existents *(mawjūdāt muta'addidah)*.

16. Al-'Allāmah al-Fanārī[1] answered him saying that "it is possible for numerous related realities *(ḥaqā'iq mutanāsibah)* to exist through a single existence which includes them as such, just as fatherhood subsists in the sum total of the parts of the father as a whole." The lack of multiple existences *('adam al-wujūdāt al-muta'addidah)* does not imply the lack of existence absolutely. Indeed they explicitly state that the creation *(ja'l)* of the genus, the difference, and the species is one.[2]

17. As for the proofs for the existence of natural universals in general,[[14]] they are not such as to be useful [in proving] this thesis *(al-maṭlūb)* to the point of certainty but only to the point of probability, although they are mentioned in the well-known works [dealing with this subject] together with the objections raised against them. We have, therefore, avoided taking up these proofs and shall concern ourselves only with what serves to prove this thesis itself.

18. We say, therefore, that there is no doubt that the Source of Existents *(Mabda' al-Mawjūdāt)* exists,[[15]] and that this source can be either the reality of existence *(ḥaqīqat al-wujūd)* or something else. It cannot, however, be something else, since

everything except existence is in need of another, namely existence, in order to exist, and to be in need is inconsistent with necessary existence *(al-wujūb).* Therefore, this source must be the reality of existence. [V]Moreover, if it is absolute *(muṭlaq),* then the thesis *(al-maṭlūb)* is proven. If, on the other hand, it is individuated *(muta'ayyin),* then it is impossible for its individuation to be intrinsic to it *(dākhil fīhi),* for otherwise the Necessary Existent *(al-wājib)* would be compound. Its individuation must, therefore, be extrinsic *(khārij)* [to it]. It follows that the Necessary Existent is a simple entity *(maḥḍummā),* which is existence, and that its individuation is an attribute inhering [in it].

19. Should you ask: Why is it not possible for its individuation to be identical with it? I should answer: If by individuation you mean that through which it is individuated, then it is possible for it to be identical with it. However, this does not harm our position, because if that through which it is individuated is its essence, [V]then it cannot in itself be individuated, otherwise an endless chain would result. On the other hand, if what is meant is the individuation *(al-tashakhkhuṣ)* itself, then this cannot be identical with its essence, because it is one of the second intelligibles *(al-ma'qūlāt al-thāniyah)*[1], to which nothing corresponds in the external world.[16]

20. It is evident to anyone familiar with the doctrines promulgated in their books that what is related of their revelations *(mukāshafāt)* and visions *(mushāhadāt)* attests only to the affirmation of the existence of an absolute essence *(dhāt muṭlaqah)* encompassing the intellectual and concrete planes *(al-marātib al-'aqlīyah wa-al-'aynīyah)* and expanding over both mental and external existents, but having no individuation which prevents it from appearing in other individuations whether divine or created. Thus, it is not impossible to affirm of it an individuation which is consistent with *(yujāmi')* all individuations and is not inconsistent with *(lā yunāfī)* any of them, which is identical with its essence and not superadded to it either in the mind or externally, [V]and which the intellect, should it conceive of it in a certain individuation, would be unable to imagine as being common *(mushtarak)* to many in the same way that universals

are common to their particulars, but would be able to conceive of as being transformed into or as appearing in numerous forms *(al-ṣuwar al-kathīrah)* and infinite manifestations *(al-maẓāhir al-ghayr al-mutanāhiyah),* both cognitively and concretely *('ilman wa-'aynan)* and in the invisible world as well as the visible *(ghayban wa-shahādatan),* in accordance with various relations *(al-nisab al-mukhtalifah)* and different aspects *(al-i'tibārāt al-mutaghāyirah).*[1] [17]

21. [V]Consider this by analogy with the rational soul *(al-nafs al-nāṭiqah),* which pervades the parts of the body and their external senses and internal faculties *(quwāhā al-bāṭinah);* [V]or even better *(bal)* by analogy with the perfectional rational soul *(al-nafs al-nāṭiqah al-kamālīyah),* which, if realized *(taḥaqqaqat)* as a manifestation of the comprehensive name *(maẓharīyat al-ism al-jāmi'),*[1] is spiritualized *(kān al-tarawḥun)*[2] of some of its concomitant realities *(ḥaqā'iqihā al-lāzimah)* and appears in numerous forms without determination *(taqayyud)* or limitation *(inḥiṣār),* all of which can be predicated of it and of each other because of the unity of its individual essence *('ayn)* just as it becomes many because of the variation of its forms.

22. For this reason it was said [18] of Idrīs that he was Ilyās sent to Baalbek,[1] not in the sense that his individual essence *(al-'ayn)* shed the Idrīsid form *(al-ṣūrah al-idrīsīyah)* and put on the Ilyāsid form, since this would be a profession of metempsychosis *(al-tanāsukh),* but rather in the sense that the ipseity *(huwīyah)*[2] of Idrīs, while subsisting in his individual existence *(annīyah)*[3] and form *(ṣūrah)* in the fourth heaven, nevertheless appeared and became individuated *(ta'ayyanat)* in the individual existence of Ilyās, who remains to this time. Thus the ipseity of Idrīs with respect to his individual essence *(al-'ayn)* and reality *(al-ḥaqīqah)* is one, but with respect to formal individuation *(al-ta'ayyun al-ṣūrī)* is two. In like manner Jibrīl, Mīkā'īl, and 'Izrā'īl appear at one and the same time in 100,000 places in different forms, all of which subsist in them.

23. [V]Similar to this are the spirits of the perfect *(arwāḥ al-kummal).* For example, it is related of Qaḍīb al-Bān al-Mawṣilī[1] that he was seen at one and the same time in numerous gatherings, in each of which he was occupied with a different matter.

And since the estimations *(awhām)* of those immersed in time and place could not understand this account, they received it with opposition and resistance and judged it false and erroneous. Those, on the other hand, who had been granted success in escaping from this predicament *(al-maḍīq),* [V]seeing him exalted above time and place, realized that the relation of all times and places to him was one and the same; and they thus believed it possible [V]for him to appear in every time and every place, for any matter he wished, [V]and in any form he desired.

24. [V]*Analogy.* If a single particular form *(ṣūrah wāḥidah juz'īyah)* is impressed *(inṭaba'at)* in many mirrors which differ with respect to being large or small, long or short, flat, convex or concave, and so forth, then there can be no doubt that this form multiplies *(yatakaththar)* in accordance with the multiplicity of the mirrors, and that its impressions differ in accordance with the differences in the mirros. Furthermore, this multiplicity [of impressions] does not impair the unity of the [original] form, nor does the appearance [of the form] in any one of these mirrors preclude it from appearing in the others. The True One *(al-Wāḥid al-Ḥaqq),* "and God's is the loftiest likeness,"[1] is thus analogous to the one form, whereas quiddities *(al-māhīyāt)* are analogous to the many mirrors with their differing predispositions *(isti'dādāt).* God appears in each and every individual essence *('ayn)* in accordance with that essence, without any multiplicity *(takaththur)* or change *(taghayyur)* occuring in His holy essence. Moreover, His appearing in accordance with the characteristics *(aḥkām)* of any one of these individual essences does not prevent Him from appearing also in accordance with the characteristics of the others, as you have learned from the foregoing analogy.

25. *On His Unity (waḥdah).* Inasmuch as the Necessary Existent *(al-Wājib),* in the opinion of the majority of theologians, is a reality *(ḥaqīqah)* existing through a proper existence *(wujūd khāṣṣ),* [V]and, in the opinion of their two leaders *(shaykhayhim)* and the philosophers, is [itself] a proper existence, they all found it necessary, in order to prove His unicity *(waḥdānīyah)* and deny a partner to Him, to make use of proofs and demonstrations, which they have provided in their works. The Ṣūfīs

who profess the unity of existence *(waḥdat al-wujūd),* however, since it was evident to them that the reality of the Necessary Existent *(ḥaqīqat al-Wājib)* is absolute existence *(al-wujūd al-muṭlaq),* did not find it necessary to put forward a proof for the assertion of His unity [V]and the denial of a partner to Him. [V]In fact, it is impossible to imagine in Him any duality *(ithnaynīyah)* and multiplicity *(ta'addud)* without considering individuation *(ta'ayyun)* and determination *(taqayyud)* to be in Him also. For everything multiple, whether seen, imagined or apprehended, [V]is either an existent *(al-mawjūd)* or attributive existence *(al-wujūd al-iḍāfī)*[1] not absolute [existence] *(al-muṭlaq),* since its opposite is nonexistence *(al-'adam),* [V]which is nothing.[2]

26. Furthermore, the True Existence *(al-Wujūd al-Ḥaqq)* possesses a unity *(waḥdah)* which is not superadded to His essence, [V]but is rather His being considered as He is in Himself *(min ḥayth huwa huwa),* for when considered in this way *(bi-hādhā al-i'tibār)* His unity is not an attribute *(na't)* of the One *(al-Wāḥid),* but is rather identical with Him. This is what the verifiers *(al-muḥaqqiqīn)* mean by essential oneness *(al-aḥadīyah al-dhātīyah),* [V]from which are derived the unity *(al-waḥdah)* and the multiplicity *(al-kathrah)* which are familiar to all *(al-jumhūr),* namely numerical unity and multiplicity. [V]Moreover, if it is considered as being devoid of all aspects *(al-i'tibārāt),* [V]it is called oneness *(aḥadīyah),* but if considered as being qualified by them, it is called singleness *(wāḥidīyah).*[1]

27. *On His Attributes in General.* The Ash'arites took the position[1] that God has eternal and existent attributes superadded to His essence. He is, thus, knowing through knowledge, powerful through power, willing through will, and so forth.[19] The philosophers, on the other hand, took the position that His attributes are identical with His essence, not in the sense that there is an essence which has an attribute and that the two are in reality united, but rather in the sense that what results from *(yatarattab 'alā)* His essence is what [in other cases] results from an essence and attribute together. For example, your own essence is not sufficient to reveal things to you but requires for this the attribute of knowledge which subsists in

you. God's essence is altogether different, for, in order that things be revealed and made apparent to Him, God does not need an attribute subsisting in Him. Indeed, all concepts *(al-mafhūmāt)* are revealed to Him through His essence, so that, in this respect, His essence is the reality of knowledge. It is the same in the case of His power, for His essence is effective *(mu'aththirah)* in itself rather than through an attribute superadded to it, as in the case of our own essences. Thus, in this respect, His essence is power, and consequently His essence and attributes are in reality united, although they differ from each other with respect to aspect *(al-i'tibār)* and concept *(al-mafhūm).*

28. [v]As for the Ṣūfīs, they took the position that God's attributes were identical with His essence with respect to existence *(bi-ḥasab al-wujūd)* but other than it with respect to intellection *(al-ta'aqqul)*.[[20]] Al-Shaykh [Muḥyī al-Dīn Ibn 'Arabī] said: "Some [v]denied His attributes, although the intuition *(dhawq)* of the prophets and saints testifies to the contrary; others affirmed them and judged them to be [v]completely different from His essence. This is complete unbelief and pure polytheism.

29. Someone,[[21]] may God sanctify his soul, said:[1] "Whoever affirms [God's] essence but does not affirm [His] attributes is an ignorant innovator *(mubtadi'),* and whoever affirms attributes which are entirely different from [His] essence is an unbelieving dualist *(thanawī kāfir)* as well as ignorant." [v]He also said: "Our essences are imperfect *(nāqiṣah)* and are only perfected by attributes. God's essence, however, is perfect *(kāmilah)* and [v]in no way is in need [v]of anything, for everything which is in need of something in any way is imperfect, and imperfection does not befit the Necessary Existent. His essence is [v]sufficient for everything and [v]with respect to everything. It is, thus, knowledge with respect to objects of knowledge *(al-ma'lūmat),* power with respect to objects of power *(al-maqdūrāt),* and will with respect to objects of will *(al-murādāt).* It is one and [v]has no duality *(ithnaynīyah)* in it whatsoever."[[22]]

30. *On His Knowledge.* [v]All are in agreement in affirming His knowledge except a small and insignificant group of early philosophers. Since the theologians affirmed attributes super-

added to His essence, [v]they found no difficulty with respect to the connection *(ta'alluq)* of His knowledge with things outside His essence by means of forms *(ṣuwar)* corresponding to those things and superadded to Him.

31. Since the philosophers, on the other hand, did not affirm the attributes, their doctrine was confused on this question. The gist *(ḥāṣil)* of what al-Shaykh [Ibn Sīnā] said in *al-Ishārāt*[1] was: "Since the First *(al-Awwal)* [v]apprehends *('aqala)* His essence by means of His essence and because His essence is the cause *('illah)* of multiplicity *(al-kathrah),* [v]it follows that He apprehends multiplicity because of His apprehension of His essence by means of His essence. Thus, his apprehension of multiplicity is a concomitant *(lāzim)* effected by Him *(ma'lūl lahu),* and the forms of multiplicity, which are the objects of His apprehension *(ma'qūlāt),* are also His effects *(ma'lūlāt)* and His concomitants ranked in the order of effects and therefore posterior to *(muta'akhkhirah 'an)* the reality of His essence as an effect is posterior to its cause. His essence is not constituted *(mutaqawwimah)* by them or by anything else. It is one, and the multiplicity of concomitants *(al-lawāzim)* and effects *(al-ma'lūlāt)* is not inconsistent with the unity of their cause *('illah),* of which they are the concomitants, regardless of whether these concomitants are established *(mutaqarrirah)* in the cause itself or distinct *(mubāyinah)* from it. Therefore, the establishment *(taqarrur)* of caused multiplicity *(al-kathrah al-ma'lūlah)* in the essence of the Self-Subsistent One, who is prior to them with respect to causality *(al-'illīyah)* and existence, does not necessitate His being multiple. The gist of this is that the Necessary Existent is one, and His unity does not cease on account of the multiplicity of the forms established in Him."

32. To this the learned commentator [Naṣīr al-Dīn al-Ṭūsī][1] objected: "There is no doubt that to acknowledge the establishment of concomitants of the First in His essence is to acknowledge that a single thing can be [v]both an agent *(fā'il)* and a recipient *(qābil)* at the same time, that the First is qualified [v]by attributes that are neither relative *(iḍāfīyah)* nor negative *(salbīyah),* that He is [v]a substratum *(maḥall)* for His multiple

and contingent effects, may He be high exalted above that, [v]that His first effect[23] is not distinct *(mubāyin)* from His essence, [v]and that He does not bring into existence *(lā yūjid)* anything which is distinct from Him through His own essence directly but rather through the mediacy *(tawassuṭ)* of entities subsisting in Him, as well as other [propositions] which contradict the apparent [v]positions *(madhāhib)* of the philosophers. In fact, the early philosophers who denied God's knowledge, as well as [v]Plato, who affirmed the self-subsistence of intelligible forms *(al-ṣuwar al-ma'qūlah),* and the Peripatetics, who affirmed the union of knower *(al-'āqil)* and known *(al-ma'qūl),* took these absurd positions only in order to avoid committing themselves to such ideas as these."

33. [v]He then indicated[24] what he himself believed the truth to be, saying:[1] "Just as an apprehender in perceiving his own essence through his essence does not require a form [v]other than the form of his own essence through which he is what he is, so also in perceiving that which emanates from his essence he does not need any form other than the form of the emanation through which the emanation is what it is. Consider your own case when you apprehend something [v]by means of a form which you have imagined or brought to mind. This form does not emanate absolutely from you alone, but rather with a certain participation of something else. Nevertheless, you do not apprehend this form through another form, but rather, just as you apprehend that thing through the form, so also do you apprehend the form itself through that same form without there being any doubling of forms within you. [v]Indeed, the only things that double are your [mental] considerations *(i'tibārāt)* connected with your essence and that form [v]only,[25] [v]or by way of superimposition *(al-tarakkub).*[26] [v]If such is your situation *(ḥāl)* with respect to what emanates from you with the participation of something besides yourself, what, then, do you think of the situation of an apprehender *(al-'āqil)* with respect to what emanates solely from his own essence without the intervention *(mudākhalah)* of anything else?"

34. "Do not think that a condition for your apprehending this form is your being a substratum *(maḥall)* for it,[27] for you

apprehend your own essence, although you are not a substratum for it. Your being a substratum for that form is merely a condition for the occurrence *(ḥuṣūl)* of that form to you, and the occurrence is, in turn, a condition for your apprehending the form. Therefore, if the form occurs to you in any way other than by inhering *(al-ḥulūl)* in you, then the apprehension *(al-ta'aqqul)* also occurs without inhering in you. It is well known that the occurrence [of the form] of a thing to its agent *(fā'il),* insofar as it occurs to something other than itself, [V]is not inferior to its occurrence to its recipient *qābil).*[28] [V]Therefore, the essential effects *(al-ma'lūlāt al-dhātīyah)* [V]of the Apprehender and Agent through His essence*(al-'āqil al-fā'il li-dhātihi)* [V]occur to Him without inhering in Him, and He apprehends them without their being inherent in Him."

35. "Having presented the foregoing I proceed as follows: You have leaned that the First apprehends His essence without there being any difference *(taghāyur),* with respect to existence *(fī al-wujūd),* between His essence and His apprehension of His essence, except as conceived in the minds of those considering [this] *(fī i'tībār al-mu'tabirīn).* Moreover, you have concluded *(ḥakamta)* that His apprehension of His essence is the cause *('illah)* of His apprehension of the first effect *(al-ma'lūl al-awwal).* Therefore, if you have concluded that the two causes, namely, His essence and His apprehension of His essence, are one thing with respect to existence without there being any difference between them, you can conclude that the two effects also, namely, the first effect and the First's apprehension of it, are, with respect to existence, one thing without there being any difference between them which would require one of them to be distinct *(mubāyin)* from the First and the other to be established *(muqarrar)* in Him. Therefore, just as you concluded that the difference between the two causes was purely mental *(i'tibārī),* you can conclude that the difference between the two effects is also mental.[29] [V]The existence of the first effect is thus identical with the First's apprehension of it without there being any need for a newly effused form *(ṣūrah mustafāḍah musta'nafah)* to subsist in the essence of the First, may He be exalted above that."[30]

36. "Furthermore, since the intellectual substances *(al-jawāhir al-'aqlīyah)* apprehend those things which are not effects of theirs through the occurrence of the forms of those things in them, and since they also apprehend the Necessarily Existent First *(al-Awwal al-Wājib),* and because nothing exists which is not an effect of the Necessarily Existent First, all the forms of both universal and particular beings, exactly as they are in existence *('alā mā 'alayhi al-wujūd),* occur in them. The Necessarily Existent First apprehends these [intellectual] substances, together with these forms, not through other forms but rather through those identical substances and forms. In this way [He apprehends] existence exactly as it is *(al-wujūd 'alā mā huwa 'alayhi).* Thus, 'not an atom's weight escapes Him'[1] nor must any of the aforementioned impossibilities be resorted to." End of quotation from al-Ṭūsī.[31]

37. One of the commentators on the *Fuṣūs al-Ḥikam*[1] raised against him the objection that [v]because those intellectual substances are contingent *(mumkinah),* they are therefore originated *(ḥādithah)* and preceded by essential nonexistence *(al-'adam al-dhātī),* as well as known to the Truth *(al-Ḥaqq)* before their existence. How, then, can the First's knowledge *('ilm)* of them be identical with their existence? Furthermore, [such a position] nullifies divine providence *(al-'ināyah),* which is explained by the philosophers [v]as [God's] active and eternal knowledge *(al-'ilm al-azalī al-fi'lī)* connected with universals in a universal manner *(kullīyan)* [v]and with particulars in a universal manner also [v]and which is prior to the existence of things. Moreover, it also implies that His essence, [v]with respect to the most noble of His attributes, is in need of that which is other than He and emanates from Him.[32] The truth is that one who is fair-minded will realize that He who created *(abda'a)* things and brought them out of nonexistence into existence, whether that nonexistence was temporal *(zamānī)* or not, knew both the realities of those things and their concomitant mental and external forms *(ṣuwaruha al-lāzimah lahā al-dhihnīyah wa-al-khārijīyah)* before He brought them into existence. [v]Otherwise, it would have been impossible to give them existence. Thus, knowledge of them is not the same as

their existence. Moreover, the doctrine that it is impossible for His essence and His knowledge, which is identical with His essence, to be a substratum *(maḥall)* for multiple entities [v]is valid only if they are distinct from Him, as in the opinion of those veiled from the truth *(al-maḥjūbīn 'an al-ḥaqq)*. [v]If, on the other hand, they are identical with Him with respect to existence *(al-wujūd)* and reality *(al-ḥaqīqah)*, but different from Him with respect to determination *(al-taqayyud)* and individuation *(al-ta'ayyun)*, then it is not impossible [for Him to be a substratum]. [v]In reality, however, He is neither subsistent *(ḥāll)* nor is He a substratum *(maḥall)*, but is, rather, a single thing appearing sometimes with the quality of being a substratum *(al-maḥallīyah)* and at other times with the quality of being subsistent *(al-ḥāllīyah)*.

38. *Further Substantiation.* If the First knows His essence through His essence, He is, considering that He knows and is known, both a knower *('ālim)* and something known *(ma'lūm)*, and, insofar as He knows His essence through His essence and not through a form superadded to Him, He is knowledge *('ilm)*. Three things are thus involved which are indistinguishable from each other except as considered in the mind *(bi-ḥasab al-i'tibār)*. If His essence is considered *(u'tubira)* as being a cause *(sabab)* for His appearing to Himself, then luminosity *(al-nūrīyah)* attaches to Him. If He is considered as being a giver of existence *(wājid)* to the object of His knowledge *(ma'lūm)* and not a depriver of it *(ghayr fāqid lahu)*, as being present with it *(shāhid iyyāhu)* and not being absent from it *(ghayr ghā'ib 'anhu)*, then the relation *(nisbah)* of existence *(al-wujūd)*, of presence *(al-shuhūd)*, of giving existence *(al-wājidīyah)*, of receiving existence *(al-mawjūdīyah)*, of being present *(al-shāhidīyah)*, and of being the object of presence *(al-mashhūdīyah)* is determined.[1]

39. There is no doubt that His knowledge of His essence and of these considerations *(al-i'tibārat)*, which are His attributes, does not require a form superadded to Him. Neither does His knowledge of the quiddities *(māhīyāt)* of things or their ipseities *(huwīyāt)*, for their quiddities and ipseities are nothing but His transcendent essence *(al-dhāt al-muta'āliyah)* clothed in

these aforementioned considerations whose intellections are derived one from another *(al-muntashi'at al-ta'aqqul ba'ḍuhā 'an ba'ḍ),* collectively and individually *(jam'an wa-furādā)* in either a universal or a particular manner *('alā wajh kullī aw juz'ī).*[33] Thus, in knowing them He does not need a superadded form *(ṣūrah zā'idah),* and consequently there is neither act *(fi'l)* nor receptivity *(qabūl),* nor subsistent *(ḥāll)* nor substratum *(maḥall).* Moreover, He has no need, with respect to any of His perfections, for what is other than He and emanates from Him. High may He be exalted above what the evildoers say!

40. *That His Knowledge of His Essence is the Source (mansha') of His Knowledge of All Other Things.* The philosophers said: the First knows things by reason of His knowledge of His essence. This is because He knows His essence, which is the origin *(mabda')* of the particulars of things *(tafāṣīl al-ashyā').* He thus possesses a simple entity *(amr basīṭ),* which is the origin of His knowledge of the particulars of things, and this is His knowledge of His essence. This is because knowledge of the cause entails knowledge of its effects regardless of whether these effects occur through an intermediary *(wāsiṭah)* or not. Thus, His knowledge of His essence, which is the essential cause *('illah dhātīyah)* of the first effect *(al-ma'lūl al-awwal),* includes knowledge of the first effect. Then the combination [of the two] is a proximate cause *('illah qarībah)* of the second effect *(al-ma'lūl al-thānī),* so that knowledge of it is entailed also, and so on to the last effect. Thus, His knowledge of His essence includes the knowledge of all existents as a whole *(ijmālan).* Moreover, if what is in His knowledge is particularized *(fuṣṣila),* these existents then become differentiated from each other and particularized *(mufaṣṣalah).* His knowledge is thus like a simple entity *(amr basīṭ)* which is the origin *(mabda')* of the particulars of numerous things *(tafāṣīl umūr muta'addidah),* and just as His essence is the origin of the characteristics *(khuṣūṣīyāt)* of things and their particulars *(tafāṣīl),* so is His knowledge of His essence the origin of His cognitions *(al-'ulūm)*[34] of things and their particulars. [V]This is analogous to what has been said to the effect that knowledge of a quiddity

includes the knowledge of its parts *(ajzā')* as a whole *(ijmālan),* and that such knowledge is the origin of its particulars.

41. Do not let it escape you that this doctrine implies His knowledge of particulars *(al-juz'īyāt)* as particulars, for particulars are caused by Him just as are universals, and He must, therefore, know them also. Although the philosophers are known for having claimed that He has no knowledge of particulars as particulars, since this would imply change *(al-taghayyur)* in His real attributes *(ṣifātihā al-ḥaqīqīyah),* one of the more recent philosophers *(ba'ḍ al-muta'akhkhirīn)*[35] has disclaimed this, saying:[1] "The denial that His knowledge is connected with particulars is something that has been ascribed to the philosophers by those who do not understand their doctrine. [V]How can they deny that His knowledge is connected with particulars when these emanate from Him, and when, in their opinion, He apprehends His essence, and when their position is that knowledge of the cause necessitates knowledge of the effect? Indeed, having denied His being in space, they made the relation of all places to Him a single identical relation *(nisbah wāḥidah mutasāwiyah),* and having denied His being in time, [V]they also made the relation to Him of all times, past, future, and present, a single relation. They maintained that just as one who knows places, although he is not himself spatial *(makānī),* knows, nevertheless, Zayd's position with respect to 'Amr's, how each of them can be pointed out with respect to the other, and what the distance between them is, and so forth with respect to all substances of the universe *(dhawāt al-'ālam)* and just as he does not relate any of these things to himself because he is not spatial *(makānī),* so also does one who knows times, if he is not himself temporal *(zamānī)* know at what time Zayd is born and at what time 'Amr, how much time separates them, and so forth with respect to all events tied to [particular] times. He does not relate any of them to a [particular] time which is [then] present to him, and, therefore, does not say: This has passed, this has not yet happened, and this exists now. Rather, all things which are in time are present to him and equally related to him, although he knows their relationship to each other as well as the priority of some of

them to the others.[36]"

42. "Although this [doctrine] was established among them, and they determined upon it, nevertheless the estimations *(aw-hām)* of those immersed in space and time were unable to understand it, and some of them consequently judged God to be spatial, and they point to a place proper to Him. Others judged Him to be temporal and say that this has passed Him and that that has not yet happened to Him. They therefore attribute to those who deny this of Him the doctrine that He does not have knowledge of temporal particulars *(al-juz'īyāt al-zamānīyah),* although such is not the case."

43. The Ṣūfīs, may God sanctify their souls, say that inasmuch as the Truth *(al-Ḥaqq)* necessitated *(iqtaḍā)* everything either through His essence or through one or more conditions *(shurūṭ),* everything is therefore one of His concomitants or a concomitant of one of His concomitants, and so forth. Consequently, the Creator *(al-Ṣāni'),* who is not distracted from anything by anything, the Kindly One and the Well-Informed *(al-Laṭīf al-Khabīr),* who lacks no perfection, inevitably knows His essence as well as the concomitant of His essence and the concomitant of His concomitant, both collectively and individually *(jam'an wa-furādā),* as a whole and in particular *(ijmālan wa-tafṣīlan)* to an infinite degree. They also say[1] that the Truth, because of His essential absoluteness *(iṭlāqihi al-dhātī)* possesses essential coextension *(al-ma'īyah al-dhātīyah)*[2] with every existent thing, and that his being present *(ḥuḍūr)* with things is His knowledge of them, so that not an atom's weight escapes His knowledge on earth or in the heavens.

44. [v]The gist of this is that He knows things in two ways. One of these is through the chain of succession [of causes and effects] *(silsilat al-tartīb)* in a manner close to that of the philosophers.[37] The other is through his oneness *(aḥadīyah),* which encompasses all things. It is obvious, of course, that His knowledge of things by the second way is preceded by His knowledge of them by the first way, for the first is [v]absentational knowledge *('ilm ghaybī)* of them prior to their existence, and the second is presentational knowledge *('ilm shuhūdī)* of them during their existence. In reality, however, there are

not two knowledges, but rather there attaches to the first knowledge through *(bi-wāsiṭah)* the existence of its connection *(muta'alliq),* that is, the thing known *(al-ma'lūm),* a relation *(nisbah)* in consideration of which we call that knowledge presence *(shuhūd)* and attendance *(ḥuḍūr).* It is not that another knowledge has originated. Should you say that this implies that His knowledge by the second way is limited to presently existing things *(al-mawjūdāt al-ḥālīyah),* [V]I should answer yes, but all existents [V]in relation to Him are present, since [all] times are the same in relation to Him as well as present *(ḥāḍirah)* with Him, as has just been mentioned in the quotation from one of the verifiers *(ba'ḍ al-muḥaqqiqīn).*[1]

45. *On His Will (al-irādah).* Both the theologians and the philosophers agreed in asserting the doctrine that He is willing *(murīd),* although there was great difference as to what was meant by His will. In the view of the theologians from among the people of the approved way *(ahl al-sunnah)* His will is an eternal attribute *(ṣifah qadīmah)* superadded *(zā'idah)* to His essence, as is the case with the rest of His real attributes *(al-ṣifāt al-ḥaqīqīyah).* In the opinion of the philosophers, however, it is His knowledge of the most perfect order *(al-niẓām al-akmal),* which they call providence *('ināyah).* Ibn Sīnā said: "Providence is the First's all-encompassing knowledge of everything and of how everything should be, so as to be in the best order *(aḥsan al-niẓām).* Thus, the First's knowledge of the correct manner *(kayfīyat al-ṣawāb)* for the arrangement of the existence of the whole *(tartīb wujūd al-kull)* is the fountainhead *(manba')* for the effusion *(fayaḍān)* of good *(al-khayr)* over the whole, without there arising any intention *(qaṣd)* or desire *(ṭalab)* on the part of the True First *(al-Awwal al-Ḥaqq).*"[1]

46. In clarification of the two positions we can say that it is obvious that [V]our mere knowledge of what can possibly emanate from us is not sufficient for its occurrence. On the contrary, we experience within ourselves a certain psychical state *(ḥālah nafsānīyah)* following upon our knowledge of what it would contain of benefit *(al-maṣlaḥah).* We then need to move the members [of the body] by means of the force *(al-qūwah)* distributed in our muscles. It is our essence *(dhāt),*

then, that is the agent *(al-fā'il),* and our muscular force that is the power *(al-qudrah).* Moreover, the conceiving *(taṣawwur)* of that thing [which is to emanate] is [our] awareness *(al-shu'ūr)* of the object of that power *(al-maqdūr),* and the knowledge of the benefit [to be derived] is [our] knowledge of the goal *(al-ghāyah).* The psychical state called inclination *(al-mayalān)* [V]is what follows upon [our] desire *(al-shawq)* which, in turn, stems from [our] knowledge of the goal. These are all entities distinct from each other, and each one has a role *(madkhal)* in the emanation of that thing.

47. Those theologians who deny that His acts are motivated by purposes *(aghrāḍ)* affirm of Him an essence and a power *(qudrah)* superadded to His essence, as well as knowledge of the object of that power *(al-maqdūr)* and of the benefit [to be found] in it, also superadded to His essence, and will *(irādah).* They ascribe a role in bringing-into-existence *(al-ījād)* to all of these with the exception of the knowledge of the benefit, [V]for it is a purpose and goal not a final cause *('illah ghā'īyah).*

48. The philosophers, on the other hand, affirmed of Him an essence and a knowledge of things which is identical with His essence. They make His essence and His knowledge together sufficient for bringing-into-existence *(al-ījād),* because His knowledge is identical with both His power and His will and is consequently sufficient for emanation *(al-ṣudūr).* [V]He does not possess a state similar to the psychical inclination *(al-mayalān al-nafsānī)* which humans possess. What in our case emanates from the essence together with its attributes [V]emanates from Him through the essence alone. This is the meaning of the union *(ittiḥād)* of attributes with essence. The emanation of an act from Him is not like its emanation from us, nor is it like its emanation from such things as fire and the sun which have no awareness of what emanates from them.

49. As for the verifying Ṣūfīs *(al-ṣūfīyah al-muḥaqqiqūn),* they affirm of Him a will superadded to His essence, [V]but with respect to intellection *(bi-ḥasab al-ta'aqqul)* rather than externally *(bi-ḥasab al-khārij),* just like the rest of the attributes. They thus differ from the theologians, who affirm a will superadded to His essence externally, and from the philosophers,

who deny His will altogether.

50. *On His Power (al-qudrah).* [v]All of the religionists *(al-millīyūn)*[1] took the position that He is powerful *(qādir),* that is, that both the bringing-into-existence *(ījād)* of the world and abstaining *(tark)* [from it] are proper for Him,[38] and that neither of these is a concomitant *(lāzim)* of His essence, such that its separation from it is impossible. As for the philosophers, they said that His bringing-into-existence of the world according to its actual order *('alā al-niẓām al-wāqi')* is one of the concomitants of His essence and cannot be divorced from it. Thus they denied power to Him in the aforementioned sense because of their belief that it was an imperfection *(nuqṣān),* but affirmed of Him necessitation *(al-ījāb)*[2] maintaining it to be complete perfection *(al-kamāl al-tāmm).* As for His being powerful in the sense that if He wills He acts, and if He does not will He does not act, this is agreed upon by both parties,[39] [v]except that the philosophers took the position that His will to act *(mashī'at al-fi'l),* which is [the same as] His effusion *(al-fayḍ)* and liberality *(al-jūd),* is concomitant *(lāzimah)* with His essence, just as His other attributes of perfection *(al-ṣifāt al-kamālīyah)* are concomitant with it, and that, therefore, the separation *(infikāk)* of the two is impossible. Thus the antecedent of the first hypothetical proposition *(muqaddam al-sharṭīyah al-ūlā)* is necessarily true, and the antecedent of the second cannot possibly be true. Both hypothetical propositions are therefore true with respect to the Creator *(al-Bārī).*[3]

51. As for the Ṣūfis, may God sanctify their souls, they not only affirm of Him a will *(irādah)* superadded to His essence, but also knowledge of the most perfect order *(al-niẓām al-akmal),* [v]and free choice *(ikhtiyār)* in bringing the world into existence, although not in the same sense as intended by human free choice *(ikhtiyār al-khalq),* which is a wavering *(taraddud)* between two things the occurrence of each of which is possible for a person until one of the two preponderates for him because of a greater profit or benefit which he desires. This type [of choice] is objectionable with respect to God, because He is one in essence *(aḥadī al-dhāt),* single in attributes *(wāḥidī al-ṣifāt).* [v]His command *(amr)* is one. His knowledge both of

Himself and of things is one knowledge. [V]Thus, wavering *(taraddud)* and the possibility of two different decisions *(ḥukmayn mukhtalifayn)* are inapplicable to Him. In fact, nothing other than what is known and willed within Him is possible. Divine choice *(al-ikhtiyār al-ilāhī)* thus [stands] between [V]compulsion *(al-jabr)* and free choice as these are understood by humans. The objects of His knowledge, whether their existence has been decreed or not, are inscribed in the expanse of His knowledge *(murtasimah fī 'arṣat 'ilmihi)* eternally and everlastingly *(azalan wa-abadan)* and are arranged in the most perfect order in the thing itself *(fī nafs al-amr),*[1] although this is hidden from most people. [Choice as to] which of two things is superior *(al-awlawīyah bayn amrayn)* is only to be attributed to one who imagines each of them to be possible and is wavering [between them]. In the thing itself *(fī nafs al-amr),* however, [V]what actually occurs *(al-wāqi')* is necessary, and nothing else can possibly exist.

52. You may object that al-Farghānī, may God have mercy on him, in his commentary on *al-Qaṣīdah al-Tā'īyah*[1] proved, by [citing] God's statement: "Hast thou not seen how thy Lord hath spread the shade," that is, the shade of creation *(al-takwīn)* over created things *(al-mukawwanāt),* [V]"and if He willed He would have made it still,"[2] and would not have spread it, that if the Truth *(al-Ḥaqq)* had not willed to bring the world into existence it would not have appeared, [V]and that it was possible for Him that He not will, so that it would not appear. To this I should answer that their doctrine that if He did not will, it would not occur, is true, for there occurs in tradition the statement: "What He does not will, is not."[3] However, for a hypothetical proposition to be true, as we said before, it is not necessary that its antecedent be true or even possible. Thus, the rule of necessity *(qā'idat al-ījāb)* [in bringing the world into existence] is not inconsistent with this [tradition], [V]nor is decisive choice *(al-ikhtiyār al-jāzim),* as mentioned above. Therefore, their statement concerning the general bringing-into-existence *(al-ījād al-kullī)* of the world, "that it was possible for Him that He not will, so that it would not appear," [V][serves] either to deny the compulsion imagined by weak intellects, [V]or

[to show] that God, in consideration of His unitary essence *(dhātihi al-aḥadīyah)* is independent *(ghanī)* of the worlds. *(al-'ālamīn).*

53. The Ṣūfīs, then, agree with the philosophers that it is impossible for the antecedent of the second hypothetical proposition[1] to be true. They differ from them, however, [v]in affirming a will *(irādah)* superadded to His knowledge of the most perfect order *(al-niẓām al-akmal)* but concomitant *(lāzimah)* with it, such that it is impossible for it to be separated from His knowledge, just as it is impossible for His knowledge to be separated from His essence.

54. *On the Question of Whether an Eternal Effect (al-athar al-qadīm) Can Depend on a Free Agent (al-mukhtār) or Not.* It should be noted that the theologians and, indeed, the philosophers as well, agreed that what is eternal *(al-qadīm)* does not depend on a free agent *(al-fā'il al-mukhtār),* because the act of the free agent is preceded by the intention *(al-qaṣd)* to bring something into existence and is of necessity contemporaneous *(muqārin)* with the nonexistence of that thing whose bringing-into-existence is intended. The theologians affirmed the free choice of the agent and denied [the existence of] an eternal effect, whereas the philosophers affirmed [the existence of] an eternal effect and denied the free choice [of the agent]

55. As for the Ṣūfīs, may God sanctify their souls, [v]they allowed the dependence of an eternal effect on a free agent and combined affirmation of [the agent's] free choice with belief in the existence of an eternal effect. They said:[1] Clear mystical revelation *(al-kashf al-ṣarīḥ)* has shown that if a thing *(al-shay')* necessitates an entity *(amr)* through its essence rather than through a condition superadded to its essence, which is what is called "other" *(ghayr),* or if that thing includes one or more conditions which are identical with its essence, such as relations and attributions *(al-nisab wa-al-iḍāfāt),* then it continues [necessitating] that entity and endures with it as long as its essence endures, as, for example, the Most Exalted Pen *(al-Qalam al-A'lā)*, for it was the first thing created, there being no intermediary *(wāsiṭah)* between it and its Creator, and it endures as long as [its Creator] endures. It is as if they had

adhered to what al-Āmidī[2] said to the effect that the priority of bringing-into-existence by intention *(qaṣdan)* to the existence of the effect *(al-ma'lūl)* is just like the priority of bringing-into-existence by necessity *(ījāban)*. Just as the priority of necessary bringing-into-existence *(al-ījād al-ījābī)* is an essential rather than a temporal priority *(sabq bi-al-dhāt lā bi-al-zamān)*, so also is it possible here for intentional bringing-into-existence *(al-ījād al-qaṣdī)* to be contemporaneous with the thing intended *(al-maqṣūd)* but to be prior to it in essence. In this way it is possible for a certain existent to be necessarily existent from eternity through the Necessary Existent in Himself *(al-Wājib li-Dhātihi)*, [v]even though He is a free agent *(mukhtār)*. Thus, the two are contemporaneous, although they differ with respect to essential priority and posteriority, just as the movement of the hand is essentially prior to the movement of the ring even though it is contemporaneous with it *(ma'ahā fī al-zamān)*.

56. It may be objected that when we consult our inner sense *(wijdān)* and properly observe the meaning of intention, we learn of necessity that it is impossible to intend to bring into existence something [already] existing, because intention must be contemporaneous *(muqārin)* with the nonexistence of the effect. Thus, the effect of the free agent must definitely be originated *(ḥādith)*. To this we should answer that the priority of intention to bringing-into-existence is like the priority of the bringing-into-existence to existence in that they are both essential priorities. Thus, their contemporaneous existence is possible because what is impossible is the intention of bringing-into-existence [v]something existing through a prior existence. In summary, if intention is a sufficient [cause] for the existence of the thing intended *(al-maqṣūd)*, then it is contemporaneous with it. If it is not sufficient, it may precede it temporally, as is the case when we intend our acts.

57. It may further be objected that when we consult our inner sense and observe the meaning of intention, we conclude that the intention to bring something into existence *(tahṣīl al-shay')* and to effect it *(al-ta'thīr fīhi)* is inconceivable except when that thing is not yet in existence, whereas to necessitate it *(ījāb)* is inconceivable except when it is in existence, even

though its [cause] is prior to it in essence *(bi-al-dhāt)*. This interpretation is self-evident and depends only upon the proper conception of the meaning of intention and will. To this we should answer that one who consults his inner sense perceives only his own imperfect, originated will and intention, not [God's] perfect, eternal will, and there is no doubt that the two differ qualitatively *(ḥukman)*. The former is not sufficient to bring the thing willed *(al-murād)* into existence, and the thing willed, therefore, lags greatly behind it. The latter, however, is sufficient, and consequently the thing willed cannot lag behind it.[40] How, then, can one of these wills be compared to the other?

58. It should be known that the attributes of perfection *(al-ṣifāt al-kamālīyah)*, such as knowledge *(al-'ilm)*, will *(al-irādah)* and power *(al-qudrah)*, can be considered in two ways *(lahā i'tibārān)*. One of them is to consider their relationship to the Truth, bearing in mind His Absolute unity *(waḥdatihi al-ṣirfah)* and the plane of His independence from the worlds. Considered in this way the attributes are eternal *(azalīyah)* and everlasting *(abadīyah)*, perfect with no trace of imperfection in them. The other is [to consider] the relationship of the uncreated quiddities *(al-māhīyāt al-ghayr al-maj'ūlah)*[1] to His existential light *(nūrihi al-wujūdī)* as analogous to the relationship of mirrors to what is impressed in them. It is the nature *(sha'n)* of the Manifest *(al-Mutajallī)* in His attributes of perfection to appear in accordance with the place of manifestation *(al-majlā)*, [v]rather than in accordance with Himself. Thus when He manifests Himself in a certain thing, His attributes of perfection appear in it in accordance with that thing rather than in accordance with the Manifest. [v]Imperfection, then, attaches to the attributes because of the imperfection of the place [of manifestation] *(al-maḥall)*.

59. Therefore, when a mystic perceives these attributes through his inner sense *(wijdān)*, he attributes the imperfection to the lack of receptivity in the place [of manifestation] *('adam qābilīyat al-maḥall)* and ascribes them to God as complete and sanctified above any trace of imperfection. Should he ascribe them to God as imperfect, he would do so only in

consideration of God's appearing in His places of manifestation *(majālī),* rather than in accordance with His absolute unity *(ṣirāfat waḥdatihī).* One who is not a mystic, on the other hand, [V]either ascribes these attributes to God as imperfect without differentiation of the planes [of existence] *(al-marātib)* from each other, [V]or else denies them of Him completely. [V]May God be high exalted above what the evil doers say.

60. *On His Speech (kalām).* The proof that He is a speaker *(mutakallim)*[1] is the concensus *(ijmā')* of the prophets concerning that. It is related about them by *tawātur*[2] that they used to affirm speech of Him and to say that God commanded such and such, prohibited such and such and narrated such and such, [V]and that all that is among the divisions of speech.[41]

61. It should be known that two incompatible syllogisms are involved here. The first is that God's speech is one of His attributes, that all of His attributes are eternal *(qadīm),* and that consequently God's speech is eternal. The second is that His speech is composed *(mu'allaf)* of parts consecutively ordered in existence, that everything which is like that is originated *(ḥādith),* and that therefore God's speech is originated. The Muslims thus divided into four groups. Two of these groups accepted the validity of the first syllogism, [V]one of them rejecting the minor premiss of the second syllogism, [V]and the other rejecting the major premiss. The other two groups accepted the validity of the second syllogism [V]each group rejecting one of the two premisses of the first syllogism [V]in the manner mentioned above.

62. As for the people of truth *(ahl al-ḥaqq),* some of them accepted the validity of the first syllogism and rejected the minor premiss of the second syllogism saying that[1] His speech is not of the genus of sounds *(al-aṣwāt)* and letters *(al-ḥurūf)* but, on the contrary, is an eternal attribute *(ṣifah azalīyah),* subsisting in God's essence, by which He commands, prohibits, and narrates, and so forth,[42] and which is indicated by [verbal] expression *(al-'ibārah),* writing *(al-kitābah),* or sign *(al-ishārah).* Thus if this attribute is expressed in Arabic, it is the *Qur'ān,* if in Syriac the *Injīl,* and if in Hebrew the *Tawrāh.* The difference lies in the expressions [V]rather than in the thing named

(al-musammā).

63. By way of elaboration at this point [it may be said] that if God narrates something, commands it, or prohibits it, and so forth, and if the prophets relay this to their nations by means of expressions signifying it *(bi-'ibārāt dāllah 'alayhi),* then without doubt three things are involved: meanings *(ma'ānī)* known [to God], expressions signifying them, also known [to God], and an attribute *(ṣifah)* by which God is able to make those meanings manifest through these expressions for the purpose of instructing *(ifhām)* those persons addressed *(al-mukhāṭabīn).*[43] There is no doubt as to the eternity *(qidam)* of this attribute with respect to God, nor as to the eternity of the form through which these meanings and expressions are known *(ṣūrat ma'lūmīyat tilka al-ma'ānī wa-al-'ibārāt)* to God. If, therefore, His speech is equivalent to this attribute, then there is no doubt as to its eternity. If it is equivalent to those meanings and expressions, however, then there is no doubt that they too, [v]with respect to their being known to God, are eternal. However, this eternity is not restricted to them alone but applies not only to them but also to [v]all the other expressions and significations *(madlūlāt)* of created beings *(al-makhlūqāt),* for all of these are known to God eternally and everlastingly. On the other hand, if [His speech] is equivalent to something beyond these three things, then there is no proof to establish this [v]which rests on a leg *(sāq).*

64. As for the speech of the mind *(al-kalām al-nafsī)* affirmed by the theologians, [v]if it is equivalent to this attribute, then its nature *(ḥukm)* is obvious. If, however, it is equivalent to those meanings and expressions known [to God], [v]then there is no doubt that their subsisting in God is only in consideration of the form through which they are known *(ṣūrat ma'lūmīyatihā),* and that therefore it is not an attribute in itself *(ṣifah bi-ra'sihā)* but rather one of the particulars of [His] knowledge. [v]As for the object of [His] knowledge *(al-ma'lūm),* whether it be the expressions or their significations *(madlūlāt),* it does not subsist in Him. The expressions in their basic existence *(bi-wujūdihā al-aṣīl)*[1] come under the category of successive accidents *(al-a'rāḍ al-ghayr al-qārrah).*[2] [v]As for their significations, some

of them are of the class of substances *(al-dhawāt)* and others of the class of successive accidents; [V]so how can they subsist in Him!

65. At this point let us mention [V]what the Ṣūfīs have to say, so that, God willing, the truth may become evident.[44] Al-Imām Ḥujjat al-Islām [al-Ghazālī] said:[1] "Speech is of two sorts, one of which is attributed to the Creator and the other to human beings. As for the speech which is attributed to the Creator, it is one of His attributes of lordship *(ṣifāt al-rubūbīyah).* There is, however, no similarity between the attributes of the Creator and the attributes of human beings, for the attributes of human beings are superadded to their essences, so that, through these attributes, their unity becomes multiple, their individual existence *(annīyah)* is constituted, and their definitions *(ḥudūd)* and descriptions *(rusūm)* are determined. . . . [V]God's attributes, however, do not define His essence nor do they describe Him, [V]and consequently they are not things superadded to [His] knowledge, which is the reality of His ipseity *(ḥaqīqat huwīyatihi).*"

66. "Whoever wishes to enumerate the attributes of the Creator is in error. . . . It is incumbent upon the rational person to reflect and to realize that the attributes of the Creator are not multiple, nor can they be separated one from the other except with respect to the levels of expression *(marātib al-'ibārāt)* and the sources of allusion *(mawārid al-ishārāt).* Thus, if His knowledge is related to listening to the prayer of those in need, He is said to be a hearer *(samī').* If it is related to seeing into the hearts of created beings *(ru'yat ḍamīr al-khalq),* He is said to be a seer *(baṣīr).* . . . If from the mysteries *(maknūnāt)* of His knowledge He pours forth upon someone's heart the divine secrets and the subtleties of the power of His lordship *(daqā'iq jabarūt rubūbīyatihi),* then He is said to be a speaker *(mutakallim).* It is not [true], then, that some part of Him is the instrument of hearing, and another part the instrument of sight, and yet another the instrument of speech. . . . [V]Thus, the Creator's speech is none other than His relating *(ifādah)* the mysteries of His knowledge to whomever He wishes to honor. As God said: 'And when Moses came to Our appointed

tryst and His lord had spoken unto him,"[1] God honored him with His nearness, and drew him near with His holiness, and seated him on the carpet of His intimacy, and addressed him with the most majestic of His attributes and spoke to him with the knowledge of His essence. As He wished He spoke, and as He willed He heard."

67. In *al-Futūḥāt al-Makkīyah,* may God sanctify the soul of its author, it is stated[1] that with respect to the Qur'ān's being letters "two things can be understood. The first is what is called discourse *(qawl),* speech *(kalām),* or utterance *(lafẓ),* and the second is what is called writing *(kitābah),* script *(raqm)* or calligraphy *(khaṭṭ).* Since the Qur'ān is written, it consists of written letters *(ḥurūf al-raqm),* and since it is also pronounced, it consists of spoken letters *(ḥurūf al-lafẓ).* From what, then, does its being spoken letters derive? Is it from the speech of God, which is one of His attributes, or is it from what is interpreted from it *(al-mutarjam 'anhu)?*[2] It should be known that God has informed us through His prophet that He will manifest Himself in various forms at the resurrection, and that He will be both recognized and denied. Anyone whose reality can accept this manifestation [of God] will not think it improbable that speech in [the form of] spoken letters and called the speech of God should be attributed to one of these forms [of manifestation] in a manner befitting His majesty. Just as we say that He has manifested Himself in a form befitting His majesty, so also we say that He spoke with letters and sounds as befits His majesty." Then, after a lengthy discussion, he stated: "If you examine what we have asserted, [v]you will see clearly that the speech of God is that which is recited, heard, and pronounced and is called *Qur'ān, Tawrāh, Zabūr,* and *Injīl.*"

68. Al-Shaykh Ṣadr al-Dīn al-Qūnawī, may God sanctify his soul, said in exegesis of the *Fātiḥah:*[1] "Among the sum of things that God granted to His servant," by which he meant himself, "was that He revealed to him some of the secrets of His Noble Book, which contains every important science, and showed him that it emerged from an otherwordly conflict *(muqāra'ah ghaybīyah)* occurring between the two attributes of power and

will, dyed with the nature *(ḥukm)* of that which [God's] knowledge encompassed at the plane linking the invisible and visible worlds *(al-martabah al-jāmi'ah bayn al-ghayb wa-al-shahādah)* but in accordance with the requirements of place *(al-mawṭin)* and station *(al-maqām).* He assigned to him the nature *(ḥukm)* of a person addressed [by God] *(al-mukhāṭab)* as well as such a person's condition and time as a necessary consequence *(bi-al-tab'īyah wa-al-istilzām).*

69. What is apparent from the statements of these eminent [Ṣūfīs] is [v]that the speech which is an attribute of God is none other than His relating *(ifādah)* and pouring forth *(ifāḍah)* the mysteries of His knowledge *(maknūnāt 'ilmihi)* upon whomever He wishes to honor. [V]Moreover, the books sent down composed of letters and words, such as the Qur'ān and similar books, are also His speech, although they are only some of the forms *(ṣuwar)* of that relating and pouring forth which have appeared through the mediacy of [God's] knowledge, will and power in the intermediate world linking the invisible and visible worlds *(al-barzakh al-jāmi' bayn al-ghayb wa-al-shahādah),* that is, the world of similitude *('ālam al-mithāl),* from some of His formal and similative places of manifestation *(majālīhi al-ṣūrīyah wa-al-mithālīyah)* in a manner befitting Him.

70. Thus the two syllogisms mentioned at the beginning of this discussion are not in reality incompatible, since what is meant by speech in the first syllogism is the attribute subsisting in God's essence, whereas in the second it is what has appeared in the intermediate world *(al-barzakh)* from some of the divine places of manifestation *(al-majālī al-ilāhīyah).* The disagreement occurring between the various groups of Muslims is due to the failure to distinguish between these two [kinds of] speech. God, may He be glorified, knows best.

71. Concerning God's statement: "And when thy Lord said unto the angels: Lo! I am about to place a viceroy in the earth,"[1] a certain person said:[2] "Know that this discourse *(al-muqāwalah)* varies in accordance with the different worlds in which the conversation *(al-taqāwul)* occurs. If it occurs in the similative world *(al-'ālam al-mithālī),* it is similar to sensible speech *(al-mukāmalah al-ḥissīyah)* in that the Truth *(al-Ḥaqq)* mani-

fests Himself to the angels similatively *(tajalliyan mithālīyan),* just as He manifests Himself in various forms to the people of the Hereafter *(ahl al-ākhirah)* as stated in the tradition of the transformation *(ḥadīth al-taḥawwul).*[3] If the conversation occurs in the world of spirits *('ālam al-arwāḥ),* in view of their immateriality, then it is like the speech of the mind *(al-kalām al-nafsī),* and God's speaking to the angels is His injecting *(ilqā')* the intended meaning into their hearts." From this the intelligent person becomes aware of what God's speech is as well as its various levels. Thus, at one level it is identical with the Speaker, and at another it is a meaning subsisting in Him like the speech of the mind. Finally, [V]in both the world of similitude and that of sense *('ālamay al-mithāl wa-al-ḥiss),* and in accordance with them, it is composed of letters and expressed by them.

72. *That Contingent Being Has no Power.* Al-Shaykh Abū al-Ḥasan al-Ash'arī took the position that[1] the voluntary acts of men *(af'āl al-'ibād al-ikhtiyārīyah)* occur through the power *(qudrah)* of God alone, and that their power has no effect *(ta'thīr)* on these acts. On the contrary [V]God's custom *('ādah)* is to bring power and choice into existence in a man, and then, if there is no obstacle *(māni'),* to bring into existence in him the act for which he has been empowered *(fi'lahu al-maqdūr)* contemporaneously *(muqārin)* with that power and choice. A man's act is thus created *(makhlūq)* by God, both in the sense of *ibdā'* and *iḥdāth,*[2] and is then acquired *(maksūb)* by that man. What is meant by his acquiring it is its being contemporaneous *(muqāranatuhu)* with his own power and will without, however, his having any effect *(ta'thīr)* or influence *(madhhal)* on its existence other than being a substratum *(maḥall)* for it.[45]

73. The philosophers said that such acts occur by way of necessity, and without any possibility of lagging behind *(al-takhalluf),* by means of a power which God creates in a man if such [power] is contemporaneous with the existence of the [necessary] conditions *(ḥuṣūl al-sharā'iṭ)* and the absence of obstacles *(irtifā' al-mawāni').*[1]

74. The position of the Ṣūfīs who assert the unity of existence *(waḥdat al-wujūd)* is that when the True Existence *(al-Wujūd*

al-Ḥaqq) descended *(tanazzala)* from the plane of His unity *(waḥdah)* and absoluteness *(iṭlāq)* to the planes of multiplicity and determination *(al-taqayyud),* He did so only in the oneness of the aggregate of all His attributes and names *(aḥadīyat jam' jamī' ṣifātihi wa-asmā'ihi).* For just as His essence became determined in this descent in accordance with the predispositions *(isti'dādāt)* of the recipients *(al-qawābil),* so His attributes and names became determined in accordance with them also. Thus, man's knowledge, will and power are all attributes of the Truth which have descended from the plane of their absoluteness to the planes of determination in accordance with the predispositions of men. The voluntary acts of men occur through the power of God alone, but only after that power has descended to their planes and has become manifest within them and become determined in accordance with their predispositions. Men possess no power beyond this. The meaning of such acts' being acquired *(maksūbah)* by men is that the characteristics *(khuṣūṣīyāt)* of their predispositions have a role *(madkhal)* in the determination of that power which is connected with their acts and which effects them, not that they themselves have any effect on their acts.

75. *On the Emanation of Multiplicity (al-kathrah) From Unity (al-waḥdah).* The Ash'arites affirmed the possibility of the dependence *(istinād)* of numerous effects *(āthār muta'addidah)* on a simple single cause *(mu'aththir wāḥid basīṭ).* It is not surprising that they did so, since they maintain that all of the innumerable contingent beings *(mumkināt)* are immediately dependent *(mustanidah)* on God, even though He is exalted above composition *(tarkīb).*

76. The philosophers, on the other hand, denied the possibility of the dependence of numerous effects on a simple single cause except through the multiplicity of that cause's instruments, as is the case with the rational soul, for many effects emanate from it in accordance with the multiplicity of its instruments, namely, the members of the body and the faculties inhering in them, or through the multiplicity of conditions and recipients, as is the case with the active intellect *(al-'aql al-fa''āl)* in their view, for events in the world of elements *('ālam*

al-'anāṣir) depend on it in accordance with multiple conditions and recipients.

77. However, as for what is really simple and one in every respect, such that it contains no multiplicity either with respect to its essence or its real *(ḥaqīqī)* or mental *(i'tibārī)* attributes, or with respect to instruments, conditions, or recipients, like the First Principle *(al-Mabda' al-Awwal),* it is impossible that more than one effect depend on it. On this [axiom] the philosophers based [their explanation of] the manner in which contingent beings *(al-mumkināt)* emanate from the Necessary Existent according to their doctrine, as will be shown below, God willing. Keep clearly in mind, however, that since the Ash'arites affirmed real attributes *(ṣifāt ḥaqīqīyah)* of God, He is not, in their opinion, really simple and one in all respects, and thus does not fall under this axiom *(al-qā'idah).*

78. Both of these groups have proofs for the positions they have taken and refutations *(qawādiḥ)* of the positions of their opponents. [V]It is apparent that the true position is that of the philosophers, namely, that it is impossible for multiplicity to emanate from what is really one *(al-wāḥid al-ḥaqīqī).* For this reason the verifying Ṣūfīs *(al-ṣūfīyah al-muḥaqqiqūn)* agreed with the philosophers on this [point]. They differed from them, however, with respect to the First Principle's being really one, for, as has been said, they affirm of Him attributes *(ṣifāt)* and relations *(nisab)* which differ from Him in the mind *('aqlan)* but not in the external world *(khārijan).* Thus, in view of His being the origin *(mabda')* of the world, they believe it possible for multiplicity to emanate from Him with respect to the multiplicity of His attributes and relations *(i'tibārāt).* However, with respect to His essential unity *(waḥdatihi al-dhātīyah)* there can emanate from Him only a single one of these attributes and relations. Then, through the mediacy of this one, there attaches to Him all the other relations and, through the mediacy of the multiplicity of these relations there attaches to Him a real existential multiplicity *(kathrah wujūdīyah ḥaqīqīyah).*

79. Thus, the Ṣūfīs agree with the philosophers on the impossibility of the emanation of multiplicity from what is really one *(al-wāḥid al-ḥaqīqī),* but differ from them in believing it

possible for existential multiplicity *(al-kathrah al-wujūdīyah)* to emanate from the First Principle. On the other hand, they agree with the theologians that it is possible for existential multiplicity to emanate from the First Principle but differ from them insofar as the latter believe it possible for multiplicity to emanate from what is really one.

80. Since the theologians believe it possible for multiple effects *(al-āthār al-kathīrah)* to depend on what is really one, they do not, as do the Ṣūfīs and philosophers, need to determine precisely how such multiplicity emanates from it. The philosophers,[1] for their part, believe it possible for many things to emanate from one thing by means of different aspects *(i'tibārāt)* only. For example, the number one possesses the attribute of halfness in relation to the number two and thirdness in relation to three, but possesses only indivisibility in relation to its oneness.

81. Since in their opinion the First Principle is one in all respects, the knowledge of the way in which multiplicity emanates from it requires being endowed with a certain genius *(luṭf qarīḥah)* [for such things], and we shall therefore present what is possible in this matter. Let A be the One First [Being] *(al-Wāḥid al-Awwal)* and B that which emanates from it and which is therefore at the second level *(al-martabah al-thāniyah).* Then A through the mediacy *(bi-tawassuṭ)* of B has an effect, and let that be C, and B by itself has an effect, namely, D, and these two are at the third level. Then A with C has an effect, E, and AB with C has an effect, G. A with D has an effect, H, and AB with D has an effect, I. Then B with E has an effect, J, and B with D has an effect, K. C by itself has an effect, L, G by itself has an effect, M, and CD together have an effect, N. Then from ACD there is an effect, O, from BCD and effect, P, and from ABCD an effect, Q.[1]

82. The first level is A. The second level is B from A. The third level is C from AB and D from B. The fourth level is E from AC, G from ABC, H from AD, I from ABD, J from BC, K from BD, L from C, M from D, N from CD, O from ACD, P from BCD, and Q from ABCD. These amount to twelve and are in the fourth level.

83. Furthermore, if we consider the lower [levels] with respect to the higher, for example, B with respect to A, and C with respect to A, to B, and to both of them, or, similarly, D with respect to A, to B, and to both of them, and so on in the [levels] below them, then the effects *(al-āthār)* and relations *(al-i'tibārāt)* become even more numerous. [V]Moreover, if we go beyond these levels to the fifth and sixth and what follows, the effects and relations become infinite. Thus, the First can act and have an effect in relation to each one of them, and there thus emanates from Him, because of these relations, an infinite number of existents *(mawjūdāt)* unconnected with each other.

84. The philosophers said that the first intellect *(al-'aql al-awwal),* after its emanation from the One Principle *(al-Mabda' al-Wāḥid),* contains four aspects. The first is its existence *(wujūd),* which it has from the First, [the second is] its quiddity *(māhīyah),* which it has from its essence *(dhāt),* [the third is] its knowledge of the First, which it has with respect to the First, and [the fourth is] its knowledge of its own essence, which it has with respect to itself. Thus, there emanates from it by means of these aspects *(i'tibārāt)* the form of a sphere *(ṣūrat falak)* along with its matter *(māddah),* [V]its intellect *('aql),* and its soul *(nafs).* [V]They presented this by means of analogy *(mithāl)* in order that one might understand how, as a result of many relations, numerous effects could emanate without any inconsistency with the doctrine that from what is one *(al-wāḥid)* there can emanate from one aspect *(bi-i'tibār wāḥid)* only one.

85. They did not claim that they were acquainted with the manner in which all the other numerous existents emanated, but concerned themselves only with the nine spheres *(al-aflāk al-tis'ah).* They affirmed ten intellects, only because it is impossible for there to be less than that in view of the nine universal spheres. As for there being more [than ten], they mentioned that the spheres were many, their movements varied, and that each one must have an intellect and a soul. They also did not concern themselves with the planets or the fixed stars, but maintained that it was possible for the existence of all of these

existents to emanate from the First Principle, some through the mediacy of others, and from one aspect *(i'tibār)* or another. [v]These aspects are not hypothetical *(mafrūḍah),* nor are they a complete cause of anything. They are merely aspects which have been attributed to one principle, so that its effects are multiplied. These aspects need not be concrete, existential entities *(umūr wujūdīyah 'aynīyah);* it is sufficient for them to be intellectual *('aqlīyah),* since a single agent performs multiple acts by reason of a variety of existential or privative intellectual entities *(umūr 'aqlīyah wujūdīyah aw 'adamīyah).*

86. As for the verifying Ṣūfīs, they affirmed the possibility in the One Principle of a multiplicity of aspects *(kathrat al-i'tibārāt),* each arising from the other and originating from a single aspect namely, the first emanation *(al-ṣādir al-awwal).* From it arise other aspects, and through the mediacy of these aspects emanate concrete existential entities *(umūr wujūdīyah 'aynīyah)* in a single plane.

87. These existential entities are divided first of all into two parts. One part has no contingency in it except in one respect, namely, its being in its reality contingent and created. The contingency in it is intelligible *(ma'qūl)* in this respect, and thus its receiving existence from its creator *(mūjid)* and its being qualified by it does not depend on any condition other than the Truth *(al-Ḥaqq).* This part has existential priority *(al-awwalīyah al-wujūdīyah)* in the stage of bringing-into-existence *(martabat al-ījād).* Proper to this plane are the Most Exalted Pen *(al-Qalam al-A'lā)* and the ecstatic angels *(al-malā'ikah al-muhayyamah),*[1] as well as the perfect ones *(al-kummal)* and the peerless ones *(al-afrād)* in one respect, namely, in respect to their abstracted spirits *(arwāḥuhum al-mujarradah)* rather than in respect to the connection of their spirits with their elemental bodies *(abdānihim al-'unṣurīyah).*[2] As for the other part, although it is also contingent in its essence, its existence is dependent on an existential entity *(amr wujūdī)* other than the pure True Existence *(maḥḍ al-Wujūd al-Ḥaqq).* This existential entity is either one, like the Pen *(al-Qalam)* with the Tablet *(al-Lawḥ),*[3] or more than one as in the other existents.

88. From this account it is apparent that according to the

position of the philosophers the first emanation is a concrete existent *(mawjūd 'aynī)* with no other existent in its plane. This is the first intellect. According to the position of the Ṣūfīs, however, the first emanation is a mental, intellectual relation *(nisbah 'aqlīyah i'tibārīyah)* which precedes all the other aspects *(al-i'tibārāt),* rather than the first intellect, since, as has been mentioned above, the Ṣūfīs affirm other existents in its plane.[1]

89. Al-Shaykh Ṣadr al-Dīn al-Qūnawī said:[1] "And that single entity which emanates first *(al-wāḥid al-ṣādir awwalan)* is, in our opinion, general existence *(al-wujūd al-'āmm)* which is poured forth upon the individual essences of contingents *(a'yān al-mumkināt),* that is, upon their fixed essences *(al-a'yān al-thābitah lahā).*[2] This existence is common both to the Most Exalted Pen, which is the first existent according to the philosophers and is also called the first intellect, as well as to all the other existents. This single emanation is not, however, the first intellect as mentioned by the rationalist philosophers." He then said after that: "This general existence is, in reality, not different from the inner True Existence *(al-Wujūd al-Ḥaqq al-bāṭin),* which is unconnected *(al-mujarrad)* with individual essences *(al-a'yān)* and manifestations *(al-maẓāhir)* except through relations and aspects *(nisab wa-i'tibārāt)* such as manifestation *(al-ẓuhūr),* individuation *(al-ta'ayyun),* and multiplicity *(al-ta'addud),* which occur to it through attachment *(al-iqtirān)* and through reception of the quality of being common *(qabūl ḥukm al-ishtirāk).*[3]

90. It is evident to the intelligent person *(al-faṭin)* that if general existence is not, in reality, different from the True Existence, then the [first] emanation is not general existence with respect to its reality but rather with respect to the relation of generality and expansion *(nisbat al-'umūm wa-al-inbisāṭ).* Thus, in their view, the first emanation is, in reality, the relation of generality and expansion, for if existence did not first expand and assume the forms of the essences fixed in knowledge *(al-a'yān al-thābitah fī al-'ilm),* no recipient *(qābil)* would ever be realized. Moreover, after the recipients have been realized, if it did not then expand over them, no concrete existent *(mawjūd 'aynī)* would exist at all.[1]

91. Through this relation of expansion *(al-nisbah al-inbisāṭīyah)* are realized the nominal relations *(al-nisab al-asmā'īyah)* of the Divine Essence *(al-Dhāt al-Ilāhīyah)* as well as the mundane realities *(al-ḥaqā'iq al-kawnīyah)* in the plane of the divine knowledge. This relation is prior to all the other aspects *(al-i'tibārāt)* and is not in need of any other aspect. Indeed, all the aspects result from it. The expansion of existence through its appearance in the forms of the recipients *(ṣuwar al-qawābil)* does not occur all at once, for, in accordance with the principle that it is impossible for multiplicity to emanate from what is really one, it must appear [first] in the form of one of the recipients. Then from this form is derived its appearance in the forms of the other recipients, one form being derived from another.

92. As for its expansion over the recipients in order to bring them into concrete existence *(li-ījādihā fī al-'ayn),* it is not necessary that it occur in a corresponding way *('alā tilka al-nisbah),* since it is possible for that which first emanates with concrete existence *(al-wujūd al-'aynī)* to be more than one, as is the position taken by the unitarian Ṣūfīs *(al-Ṣūfīyah al-muwaḥḥidah).*[1]

NOTES
to the Translation of al-Jāmī's
AL-DURRAH AL-FĀKHIRAH

Par. 2

1. *Ḥaqīqah* is the term used for a quiddity *(māhīyah)* which has external existence. See al-Jurjānī, *al-Ta'rīfāt,* under *al-māhīyah;* al-Aḥmadnagarī, *Dustūr al-'Ulamā',* III, p. 192, under *al-māhīyah,* and III, p. 283, under *al-ma'nā.*

Par. 3

1. For this premiss, see, for example, al-Jurjānī, *Sharḥ al-Mawāqif,* II, pp. 140-141. Al-Jāmī's argument here appears to be taken from *Sharḥ al-Mawāqif,* VIII, p. 12.

Par. 4

1. See Fuat Sezgin, *Geschichte des arabischen Schriftums,* I, p. 602.
2. See Sezgin, *Geschichte,* I, p. 627
3. *Al-wujūdāt al-khāṣṣah* are the existences of particular individual things. See Amélie Marie Goichon, *Lexique de la langue philosophique d'Ibn Sīnā,* p. 419; and Ibn Sīnā, *al-Shifā', al-Ilāhīyāt,* p. 31.
4. That is, it can be divided, for example, into necessary and contingent existence and the latter can be further divided into substantial and accidental existence. See al-Aḥmadnagarī, *Dustūr al-'Ulamā,* I, p. 333, under *al-taqsīm.* For this and other arguments that existence is common in meaning to proper existences, see al-Taftāzānī, *Sharḥ al-Maqāṣid,* I, p. 46; and al-Jurjānī, *Sharḥ al-Mawāqif,* II, pp. 112-127.

Par. 5

1. The *muḥaqqiq* is the scholar who establishes a thesis by using proofs *(dalā'il).* See al-Jurjānī, *al-Ta'rīfāt,* under *al-taḥqīq;* al-Aḥmadnagarī, *Dustūr al-'Ulamā',* III, p. 228, under *al-muḥaqqiq;* al-Tahānawī, *Kashshāf,* p. 336, under *al-taḥqīq.*

Par. 6

1. This paragraph is derived almost entirely from al-Taftāzānī, *Sharḥ al-Maqāṣid,* I, pp. 53-54.

Par. 8

1. This paragraph is identical with par. 10 of al-Jāmī's *Risālah fī al-Wujūd.* See "Al-Jāmī's Treatise on Existence" in *Islamic Philosophical Theology* by Parviz Morewedge.

2. That is, an entity that exists only in the mind of the person considering it and during the time he is considering it. See al-Jurjānī, *al-Ta'rīfāt,* under *al-amr al-i'tibārī;* al-Aḥmadnagarī, *Dustūr al-'Ulamā',* I, p. 187, under *al-amr al-i'tibārī,* and III, p. 193, under *al-māhīyah;* al-Tahānawī, *Kashshāf,* p. 72, under *al-umūr al-i'tibārīyah.* Izutzu and Mohaghegh in their edition of Hādī Sabzawārī's *Sharḥ Ghurar al-Farā'id* translate *i'tibārī* as mentally posited. See pp. 65-66, 71 of Izutsu's English introduction, "The Fundamental Structure of Sabzawari's Metaphysics."

Par. 9

1. This paragraph is apparently derived from al-Qūshjī, *Sharḥ al-Tajrīd,* p. 10; and al-Jurjānī, *Ḥāshiyat Sharḥ al-Tajrīd,* fols. 17a-17b.

2. Concepts which differ in their particulars with respect to superiority *(awlawīyah)* or lack of it, priority *(taqaddum)* or posteriority *(ta'ahkhur),* or strength *(shiddah)* or weakness *(ḍu'f)* were said to be predicated analogically *(bi-al-tashkīk)* of their particulars rather than univocally. See Quṭb al-Dīn al-Rāzī, *Taḥrīr al-Qawā'id al-Manṭiqīyah,* I, pp. 210-213; and al-Jurjānī, *al-Ta'rīfāt,* under *al-tashkīk.* It was commonly argued that since essential concepts did not differ in their particulars, only accidental concepts could be predicated analogically. See Naṣīr al-Dīn al-Ṭūsī, *Sharḥ al-Ishārāt,* p. 203; and Quṭb al-Dīn al-Rāzī, *al-Muḥākamāt,* p. 281.

3. According to works on the art of disputation *(ādāb al-baḥth)* such as al-Ījī's *Ādāb al-Baḥth,* Ṭāshkubrīzādah's *Ādāb al-Baḥth wa-al-Munāẓarah,* and Sāchaqlīzādah's *al-Risālah al-Waladīyah,* objection to a thesis may take one of the following three forms:

1. *Man',* or denial (also called *naqḍ tafṣīlī,* or particular refutation), in which the objector denies one of the premisses in the defender's proof of

his thesis.

2. *Mu'āraḍah,* or opposition, in which the objector offers a proof for a proposition incompatible with the defender's thesis.

3. *Naqḍ,* or refutation (also known as *naqḍ ijmālī,* or general refutation), in which the objector finds fault with the proof as a whole. He does this by showing either 1) that its conclusion leads to an impossibility, such as a circle or an endless chain, or 2) that the same proof can be used to demonstrate a proposition known to be false.

The present case is an example of this second type of *naqḍ.* The defender has argued as follows:

> All quiddities (essential attributes) are one.
>
> No things which differ in their particulars are one.
>
> Therefore, no things which differ in their particulars are quiddities (essential attributes).

The objector can apply this same proof to accidents and argue as follows:

> All accidents are one.
>
> No things which differ in their particulars are one.
>
> Therefore, no things which differ in their particulars are accidents.

This conclusion contradicts what is known about accidents, namely, that they do, in fact, differ in their particulars. Consequently one of the premisses of the proof must be false. Since the truth of the major premiss is admitted by both defender and objector, the minor premiss, namely, that no things which differ in their particulars are one, must be false. Since the defender's proof also contains this premiss, his proof is thereby shown to be defective.

In his *al-Risālah al-Waladīyah,* pp. 125-127, Sāchaqlīzādah gives a similar example of this type of *naqḍ.* The defender, a philosopher, gives the following proof for the eternity of the world:

> All things that are effects of an eternal being are eternal.
>
> The world is an effect of an eternal being.
>
> Therefore, the world is eternal.

The objector, applying the same proof to daily events, then argues:

> All things that are effects of an eternal being are eternal.
>
> Daily events are effects of an eternal being.
>
> Therefore, daily events are eternal.

This conclusion is obviously false, and, since the truth of the minor premiss is not in dispute, the major premiss, which is the same in both proofs, must be false.

Par. 10

1. See MS Wetzstein II 1806, fol. 57b; MS Vat. Arab. 1453, fol. 38a-38b. *Al-Risālah al-Hādiyah* as written in answer to the *Risālah* of Naṣīr al-Dīn al-Ṭūsī which in turn was written in answer to questions put to al-Ṭūsī by al-Qūnawī in his *al-Risālah al-Mufṣiḥah.* The passage quoted here is in answer to al-Ṭūsī's argument that since existence is predicated analogically rather than univocally it cannot be a single reality but is, on the contrary, many different realities. Concepts which are also predicated analogically, according to al-Ṭūsī, are light and knowledge. If light were a single reality, all types of light would be equally brilliant and would cause the cessation of night blindness. In fact, however, only sunlight is brilliant enough to do this. Likewise if knowledge were a single reality, human and divine knowledge would be the same, and human knowledge would cause the existence of the thing known just as God's knowledge does. See Naṣīr al-Dīn al-Ṭūsī, *Risālah,* MS Wetzstein II 1806, fol. 36a-36b; MS Warner Or. 1133, fols. 26a-27a; MS Vat. Arab. 1453, fol. 17a-17b.

2. All the manuscripts of *al-Durrah al-Fākhirah* as well as the two manuscripts available of *al-Risālah al-Hādiyah* read *ta'ayyunuhu,* whereas *ta'ayyunuhā,* with *hā* referring to the feminine *ḥaqīqah,* would be expected.

Par. 11

1. The preceding part of this paragraph has been summarized from pages 21 and 34 of al-Qūnawī's *I'jāz al-Bayān.* The remaining sentences of the paragraph are quoted from 'Ayn al-Quḍāh al-Hamadhānī, *Zubdat al-Ḥaqā'iq,* pp. 26-27.

Par. 12

1. On the false judgments of the estimation, see Ibn Sīnā, *al-Shifā', al-Manṭiq, al-Burhān,* pp. 64-65; also al-Jurjānī, *Sharḥ al-Mawāqif,* II, pp. 41-42; al-Kātibī, *al-Risālah al-Shamsīyah,* p. 28 of Arabic text, p. 35 of translation; and Quṭb al-Dīn al-Rāzī, *Taḥrīr al-Qawā'id al-Manṭiqīyah,* II, pp. 248-249.

Judgments of the estimation *(al-wahmīyāt)* made, however, with respect to sensibles *(al-maḥsūsāt)* were considered to be true and were sometimes included among the premisses on which demonstration was based. See al-Jurjānī, *Sharḥ al-Mawāqif,* II, pp. 41-42; and al-Taftāzānī, *Sharḥ al-Risālah al-Shamsīyah,* p. 185.

2. The natural universal *(al-kullī al-ṭabī'ī)* was usually defined as the nature *(al-ṭabī'ah)* or quiddity *(al-māhīyah)* as it is in itself *(min ḥayth hiya hiya),* absolute and unconditioned by anything *(lā bi-sharṭ shay'),* whether universality, particularity, existence, nonexistence, or anything else. It was distinguished from two other universals, the mental universal *(al-kullī al-'aqlī),* which is the nature insofar as it is a universal, that is, the nature conditioned by

universality *(bi-sharṭ lā-shay')*, and the logical universal *(al-kullī al-manṭiqī)*, which is the concept of universality itself. See Ibn Sīnā, *al-Shifā', al-Manṭiq, al-Madkhal,* pp. 65-72; al-Kātibī, *al-Risālah al-Shamsīyah,* p. 6 of the Arabic text, p. 11 of the English translation; Quṭb al-Dīn al-Rāzī, *Taḥrīr al-Qawā'id al-Manṭiqīyah,* I, pp. 289-292; and *Lawāmi' al-Asrār,* pp. 53-54.

In general the position of the philosophers was that natural universals existed externally, whereas that of the theologians was that they existed only in the mind. For the position of the philosophers, see Ibn Sīnā, *al-Shifā', al-Ilāhīyāt,* pp. 202-212; al-Ṭūsī, *Sharḥ al-Ishārāt,* pp. 192-193; al-Kātibī, *al-Risālah al-Shamsīyah,* p. 6 of the Arabic text, p. 11 of the English translation; al-Urmawī, *Maṭāli' al-Anwār,* p. 53. For that of the theologians, see Quṭb al-Dīn al-Rāzī, *Risālat Taḥqīq al-Kullīyāt;* and *Lawāmi' al-Asrār,* pp. 53-56; al-Taftāzānī, *Sharḥ al-Rīsālah al-Shamsīyah,* pp. 46-47; and al-Jurjānī, *Ḥāshiyah 'alā Sharḥ al-Maṭāli',* pp. 134-138. A summary of the objections which can be raised against the position of the philosophers on this question is given in Kāshif al-Ghiṭā', *Naqd al-Ārā' al-Manṭiqīyah,* pp. 195-207.

Par. 13

1. This is the *Risālah* written in answer to the questions contained in al-Qūnawī's *al-Risālah al-Mufṣiḥah.* See MS Wetzstein II 1806, fol. 39a-39b; MS Warner Or. 1133, fols. 30b-31a; and MS Vat. Arab. 1453, fol. 20a.

Par. 14

1. See al-Fanārī, *Misbāḥ al-Uns,* p. 35.

2. That is, if the universal subsisted in each one of a number of things, it would not be one concrete thing but many things.

3. Two universals are said to be *mutabāyin* if neither of them is true of what the other is true of. For example, no horse is a human and no human is a horse. They are said to be *mutasāwī* (coextensive) if each is true of what the other is true of. For example, every human is rational and every rational being is human. Finally one universal can be more general *(a'amm)* or more specific *(akhaṣṣ)* than the other. For example, all humans are animals but not all animals are humans. See al-Kātibī, *al-Risālah al-Shamsīyah,* p. 6 of the Arabic text, p. 11 of the English translation; Quṭb al-Dīn al-Rāzī, *Taḥrīr al-Qawā'id al-Manṭiqīyah,* I, pp. 294-298; al-Aḥmadnagarī, *Dustūr al-'Ulamā',* I, p. 270, under *al-tabāyun,* I, p. 291, under *al-tasāwī.*

Par. 15

1. Al-Jāmī is still quoting here from al-Fanārī's *Miṣbāḥ al-Uns,* p. 35. For al-Rāzī's arguments against the existence of natural universals, see his *Lawāmi' al-Asrār,* pp. 54-56; and his *Risālat Taḥqīq al-Kullīyāt,* MS Warner Or. 958 (21), especially fols. 68b-69a.

Par. 16

1. See his *Miṣbāḥ al-Uns,* p. 35.

2. That is, that the genus and the difference are created through the creation of the individual of the species and not through separate creations. All three therefore exist through the one existence of the individual. In commenting on this sentence Muḥammad Ma'ṣūm refers to Naṣīr al-Dīn al-Ṭūsī's *Tajrīd al-'Aqā'id* and the commentaries on it. See *al-Farīdah al-Nādirah,* fol. 66b; as well as al-Ḥillī, *Kashf al-Murād,* p. 45; and al-Qūshjī, *Sharḥ al-Tajrīd,* p. 108.

Par. 19

1. Second intelligibles or second intentions are universals which can only be predicated of other universals as they exist in the mind. First intelligibles, on the other hand, are universals which can be predicated of individuals existing outside the mind. For example, the universal concept human is a first intelligible which can be predicated of each individual human existing in the external world. The universal concept species, however, can only be predicated of other universal concepts, such as human, as they exist in the mind. It is therefore a second intelligible with no individuals existing outside the mind. See al-Aḥmadnagarī, *Dustūr al-'Ulama',* III, p. 290, under *al-ma'qūlāt al-thāniyah;* and al-Taftāzānī, *Sharḥ al-Maqāṣid,* I, p. 56.

Par. 20

1. According to al-Jāmī, God's names and attributes are relations *(nisab),* aspects *(i'tibārāt),* or attributions *(iḍāfāt)* connecting His essence with the objects of His knowledge, will, power, etc. See pars. 28, 29 (and 39) and glosses 22 (and 33) as well as al-Larī's commentary on par. 28.

Par. 21

1. *Al-ism al-jāmi',* also known as *al-ism al-a'ẓam,* is a term for the name *Allāh,* since this name is said to comprehend all of God's names and attributes. See *Sharḥ al-Durrah al-Fākhirah,* fol. 105a; al-Husaynābādī, *al-Risālah al-Qudsīyah,* fol. 102b; al-Kāshānī, *Iṣṭilāḥāt,* p. 89, under *al-ism al-a'ẓam;* and al-Jurjānī, *al-Ta'rīfāt,* under *al-ism al-a'ẓam.*

2. *Al-tarawḥun* is apparently derived from *rūḥānī.* In *Sharḥ al-Durrah al-Fākhirah al-tarawḥun* is defined as sanctification and shedding or casting off [of bodily attributes] *(al-taqaddus wa-al-insilākh).* See fol. 105a. See also Dozy, *Supplément,* I, p. 568, under *rawḥana.* Al-Jāmī also uses this term in his commentary on the 22nd *faṣṣ* of Ibn 'Arabī's *Fuṣūṣ al-Ḥikam.* See his *Sharḥ Fuṣūṣ al-Ḥikam,* II, 266.

Par. 22

1. Idrīs and Ilyās are each mentioned twice in the Qur'ān, without, however, being identified with each other. See Qur'ān XIX, 56 and XXI, 85 for Idrīs and VI, 85 and XXXVII, 123-130 for Ilyās. For their identity with each other and other pertinent information, see A.J. Wensinck, "Idrīs" and "Ilyās" in Gibb, *Shorter Encyclopedia of Islam,* pp. 158-159, 164-165; as well as al-Ṭabarī, *Jāmi' al-Bayān,* VII, p. 172; XVI, 72; XVII, p. 58, XXIII, p. 60; and Ibn 'Arabī, *Fuṣūṣ al-Ḥikam,* I, p. 181; II, p. 257.

2. *Huwīyah,* which has been translated here as ipseity, is commonly defined as the particular reality *(al-ḥaqīqah al-juz'īyah)* or particular quiddity *(al-māhīyah al-juz'īyah),* that is, the individuated quiddity as opposed to the universal quiddity. The word is sometimes used, however, to mean existence. See al-Jurjānī, *al-Ta'rīfāt,* under *al-māhīyah;* al-Aḥmadnagarī, *Dustūr al-'Ulamā',* III, p. 283, under *al-ma'nā,* and III, p. 478, under *al-huwīyah.* For the origin of the word, see al-Fārābī, *Kitāb al-Ḥurūf,* pp. 112-113.

3. *Annīyah (innīyah, ānīyah)* is translated here as individual existence in accordance with the definition given by al-Kāshānī in his *Iṣṭilāḥāt al-Ṣūfīyah,* p. 91. Almost identical definitions are given by al-Jurjānī, *al-Ta'rīfāt,* under *al-ānīyah,* and al-Aḥmadnagarī, *Dustūr al-'Ulamā',* I, p. 197. Much has been written on the origin and meaning of this term. See, for example, Simon van den Bergh, "Annīyah" in *The Encyclopedia of Islam,* New Edition, I, pp. 513-514; al-Fārābī, *Kitāb al-Ḥurūf,* p. 61, *Kitāb al-Alfāẓ,* p. 45; Soheil M. Afnan, *Philosophical Lexicon,* p. 12-13; Goichon, *Lexique,* pp. 9-12; Richard M. Frank, "The Origin of the Arabic Philosophical Term *Annīyah,*" in *Cahiers de Byrsa* 6 (1956): 181-201; and Marie-Thérèse d'Alverny, "Anniyya-Anitas," in *Mélanges offerts à Étienne Gilson* (Paris-Toronto 1959), pp. 59-91.

Par. 23

1. An associate of 'Abd al-Qādir al-Jīlānī, he died in 570 A.H. See al-Jāmī, *Nafaḥāt al-Uns,* pp. 524-525 of Tehran edition; al-Tādhifī, *Qalā'id al-Jawāhir,* pp. 118-120; al-Munāwī, *al-Kawākib al-Durrīyah,* fol. 207a-207b; and particularly al-Nabhānī, *Jāmi' Karāmāt al-Awliyā',* II, pp. 23-31, which reproduces the *fatwā* of al-Suyūṭī entitled *al-Munjalī fī Taṭawwur al-Walī* (Brockelmann, *Geschichte,* II, p. 201, Supplement, II, pp. 188, 195) on the question of whether a *walī* can be in two places at once.

Par. 24

1. Qur'ān, XVI, 60. The translation of this as well as the other Qur'ānic citations appearing in the texts is based on that of Mohammed Marmaduke Pickthall in *The Meaning of the Glorious Koran,* New York: New American Library, 1953.

Par. 25

1. That is, existence attributed to quiddities. According to al-Fanārī, *al-*

wujūd al-iḍāfī is another way of expressing the concept of *al-mawjūdīyah,* or being existent. See his *Miṣbāḥ al-Uns,* p. 53.

2. This last sentence is quoted from al-Fanārī, *Miṣbāḥ al-Uns,* p. 121.

Par. 26

1. For further clarification of the distinction between *aḥadīyah* and *wāḥidīyah,* see al-Tahānawī, *Kashshāf,* p. 1463, under *al-aḥadīyah,* and p. 1467, under *al-wāḥidīyah;* Reynold A. Nicholson, *Studies in Islamic Mysticism,* pp. 94-97; al-Jāmī, *Lawā'iḥ,* Flash XVII, p. 16 of English translation, fols. 11a-11b of Persian text; al-Qayṣārī, *Maṭla' Khuṣūṣ al-Kilam,* p. 11.

Par. 27

1. For the source of this paragraph, see al-Jurjānī, *Sharḥ al-Mawāqif,* VIII, pp. 44-45, 47.

Par. 29

1. 'Ayn al-Quḍāh al-Hamadhānī in his *Zubdat al-Ḥaqā'iq,* pp. 40, 42.

Par. 31

1. The quotation, which extends through par. 36, is actually from Naṣīr al-Dīn al-Ṭūsī, *Sharḥ al-Ishārāt, namaṭ* 7, pp. 329-331.

Par. 32

1. See al-Ṭūsī, *Sharḥ al-Ishārāt,* p. 329.

Par. 33

1. See al-Ṭūsī, *Sharḥ al-Ishārāt,* pp. 330-331.

Par. 36

1. Qur'ān, XXXIV, 3.

Par. 37

1. Dāwūd ibn Maḥmūd al-Qayṣarī. See his *Maṭla' Khuṣūṣ al-Kilam,* pp. 16-17, quotations from which constitute most of this paragraph.

Par. 38

1. The meaning of the last half of this paragraph is not clear to me, and I

have consequently resorted to a completely literal translation of it. Muḥammad Maʻṣūm in his commentary on *al-Durrah al-Fākhirah* entitled *al-Farīdah al-Nādirah,* fol. 142 a, interprets *al-nūrīyah* (luminosity) to mean *ʻilm* (knowledge) and *al-shāhidīyah* and *al-mashhūdīyah* to mean *al-ʻālimīyah* (being a knower) and *al-maʻlūmīyah* (being an object of knowledge) respectively. If such is the case the last half of this paragraph can be interpreted as follows:

If God's essence is the cause of His self-knowledge, that is, if He knows His essence through His essence directly rather than through a superadded form, then He can be said to be knowledge or luminosity *(al-nūrīyah).* If he is further considered as being the cause of His own existence, that is, as being a giver of existence to His essence which is also the object of His knowledge, and as being present to His essence, that is, being a knower of His essence, then He can be said to have six aspects: existence *(wujūd),* being a giver of existence *(wājidīyah),* being a recipient of existence *(mawjūdīyah),* knowledge *(shuhūd),* being a knower *(shāhidīyah),* and being an object of knowledge *(mashhūdīyah).*

Par. 41

1. Naṣīr al-Dīn al-Ṭūsī in his *Risālah* to Ṣadr al-Dīn al-Qūnawī, MS Warner Or. 1133, fol. 33a-33b; Wetzstein II 1806, fol. 41a-41b; MS Vat. Arab. 1453, fols. 21b-22a. The quotation extends to the end of par. 42.

Par. 43

1. This last sentence is quoted from al-Fanārī, *Miṣbāḥ al-Uns,* p. 60. See also, Qur'ān, X, 61, and XXXIV, 3.
2. The literal meaning of *maʻīyah* is "withness." According to al-Ḥusaynābādī in his commentary, *al-Risālah al-Qudsīyah,* fol. 112b, God's coextension is not like the coextension of substances and accidents but, on the contrary, like that of the soul with the body.

Par. 44

1. That is, the quotation from al-Ṭūsī found in paragraphs 41 and 42.

Par. 45

1. Al-Jāmī's source for the first part of this paragraph is al-Taftāzānī, *Sharḥ al-Maqāṣid,* II, p. 69. The rest of the paragraph including the quotation from Ibn Sīnā is derived from al-Jurjānī, *Sharḥ al-Mawāqif,* VIII, p. 81. The original source of the quotation from Ibn Sīnā is his *al-Ishārāt wa-al-Tanbīhāt,* Part 3, *namaṭ* 7, pp. 729-730.

Par. 50

1. Al-Jāmī's source for this paragraph is al-Jurjānī, *Sharḥ al-Mawāqif,* VIII, p. 49.

2. That is, that He creates the universe by necessity, not by free choice. He is a necessary agent *(mūjib),* not a free agent *(mukhtār).*

3. The first is true because both antecedent and consequent are true, whereas the second is true because both are false.

Par. 51

1. According to al-Qayṣarī in the introduction to his *Maṭla' Khuṣūṣ al-Kilam,* p. 17, the "thing itself" *(nafs al-amr)* is an expression for God's essential knowledge, which contains the forms of all things whether universal or particular, large or small, in general or in detail, cognitive or concrete. For a more complete explanation of this term, see al-Aḥmadnagarī, *Dustūr al-'Ulamā',* III, p. 370, under *al-mawjūd fī nafs al-amr;* and al-Tahānawī, *Kashshāf,* p. 1403-1404, under *nafs al-amr.*

Par. 52

1. See his *Muntahā al-Madārik,* I, p. 48.

2. Qur'ān, XXV, p. 45.

3. See the tradition reported by Zayd ibn Thābit in the *Musnad* of Aḥmad ibn Ḥanbal, Vol. V, p. 191.

Par. 53

1. That is, if He does not will, He does not act.

Par. 55

1. According to Ibrāhīm al-Kūrānī the statement which follows is quoted from al-Fanārī's *Miṣbāḥ al-Uns.* See *al-Taḥrīrāt al-Bāhirah,* MS Yahuda 5373, fol. 195a; MS Yahuda 4049, fol. 15a.

2. Sayf al-Dīn 'Alī ibn Abī 'Alī al-Āmidī, who died in 631 A.H. See Brockelmann, *Geschichte,* I, p. 494 (393), Supplement I, p. 678. Al-Jāmī's source for al-Āmidī's statement and what follows it in this paragraph and the next is al-Jurjānī's *Sharḥ al-Mawāqif,* III, pp. 183-185. Al-Taftāzānī in his *Sharḥ al-Maqāṣid,* I, p. 96, claims that this statement of al-Āmidī is not to be found in his *Abkār al-Afkār.* I have been unable to find it in either *Abkār al-Afkār* or his *Ghāyat al-Marām fī 'Ilm al-Kalām,* although al-Āmidī deals with the question of the eternal effect in both of these works. See *Abkār al-Afkār, qā'idah* 4, *bāb* 1, *qism* 2, *aṣl* 4, fols. 188a-199a; and *Ghāyat al-Marām,* pp. 258-274.

Par. 58

1. On the question of whether quiddities in themselves are created or not, see al-Aḥmadnagarī, *Dustūr al-'Ulamā',* I, pp. 403-408, under *al-ja'l;* al-Tahānawī, *Kashshāf,* p. 243, under *al-ja'l,* and p. 1316, under *al-māhīyah;* al-Jurjānī, *Sharḥ al-Mawāqif,* III, pp. 40-53; al-Taftāzānī, *Sharḥ al-Maqāṣid,* I, pp. 79-80; al-Ṭūsī, *Risālah,* MS Wetzstein II 1806, fols. 38a-39a; MS Warner Or. 1133, fols. 29a-30b; MS Vat. Arab. 1453, fols. 19a-20a; al-Qūnawī, *al-Risālah al-Mufṣiḥah,* MS Wetzstein II 1806, fols. 23b-25a; MS Warner Or. 1133, fols. 6b-8b; MS Vat. Arab. 1453, fols. 4b-6a; al-Qayṣarī, *Maṭla' Khuṣūṣ al-Kilam,* p. 20; and al-Fanārī, *Miṣbāḥ al-Uns,* pp. 72-73.

Par. 60

1. The source of both this and the following paragraph is al-Jurjānī, *Sharḥ al-Mawāqif,* VIII, pp. 91-92.

2. That is, by so many original witnesses and at each stage of transmission by so many transmitters that neither witnesses nor transmitters could conceivably have agreed together on a falsehood. See al-Aḥmadnagarī, *Dustūr al-'Ulamā',* II, pp. 78-79, under *al-khabar al-mutawātir;* and al-Jurjānī, *al-Ta'rīfāt,* under *al-mutawātir.*

Par. 62

1. The remaining portion of this paragraph is quoted from al-Taftāzānī, *Sharḥ al-Maqāṣid,* II, p. 73.

Par. 64

1. That is, insofar as they exist in themselves rather than in God's knowledge.

2. That is, accidents whose parts do not all exist together at one time, such as motion and sound. See al-Aḥmadnagarī, *Dustūr al-'Ulamā',* II, p. 316, under *al-'araḍ,* III, p. 52, under *al-qārr,* III, pp. 146-148, under *al-kamm;* al-Jurjānī, *al-Ta'rīfāt,* under *al-'araḍ;* al-Tahānawī, *Kashshāf,* pp. 1272-1273, under *al-kamm.*

Par. 65

1. See his *al-Ma'ārif al-'Aqlīyah,* pp. 49-52.

Par. 66

1. Qur'ān, VII, 143.

Par. 67

1. See Ibn ʻArabī, *al-Futūḥāt al-Makkīyah,* III, 95.

2. According to the commentary of Muḥammad Maʻṣūm, f. 181b, *al-mutarjam ʻanhu* should be *al-mutarjim ʻanhu,* that is, the word should be vocalized as the active participle rather than the passive participle.

Par. 68

1. See his *Iʻjāz al-Bayān,* p. 2.

Par. 71

1. Qurʻān, II, 30.

2. Al-Lārī in his *Commentary* identifies this person with Dāwūd al-Qayṣarī. The same passage appears in al-Jāmī's *Tafsīr,* fol. 119a, but again without attribution.

3. This tradition may be found in the *Ṣaḥīḥ* of Muslim, *kitāb al-īmān, bāb maʻrifat ṭarīq al-ruʼyah.* See also Ibn ʻArabī, *Tarjumān al-Ashwāq,* p. 71.

Par. 72

1. See al-Jurjānī, *Sharḥ al-Mawāqif,* VIII, pp. 145-147, for the source of this paragraph as well as the next.

2. The philosophers distinguished between three types of creation: 1) *ibdāʻ,* which they defined as the bringing into existence *(ījād)* of something preceded by neither matter nor time, such as the intellects *(al-ʻuqūl),* 2) *takwīn,* the bringing into existence of something preceded by matter, such as the heavenly spheres *(al-aflāk),* and 3) *iḥdāth,* the bringing into existence of something preceded by time (and consequently by matter also). See, for example, al-Jurjānī, *al-Taʻrīfāt,* under *al-ibdāʻ wa-al-ibtidāʻ, al-iḥdāth,* and *al-takwīn;* al-Tahānawī, *Kashshāf,* p. 134 under *al-ibdāʻ,* p. 1276 under *al-takwīn;* al-Aḥmadnagarī, *Dustūr al-ʻUlamāʻ,* I, p. 17 under *al-ibdāʻ wa-al-ibtidāʻ,* I, p. 45 under *al-iḥdāth,* I, p. 346 under *al-takwīn;* Fakhr al-Dīn al-Rāzī, *Sharḥ al-Ishārāt,* p. 353 *(masʼalah* 7, *namaṭ* 5); al-Ṭūsī, *Sharḥ al-Ishārat,* p. 237 *(namaṭ* 5); and al-Taftāzānī, *Sharḥ al-Risālah al-Shamsīyah,* p. 2. Whether the same distinction is intended here by al-Jurjānī is uncertain.

Par. 73

1. The original version of al-Jāmī's text ends at this point.

Par. 80

1. Al-Jāmī's source for the position of the philosophers given in pars. 80-85

is al-Ṭūsī's *Risālah* to al-Qūnawī. See MS Warner Or. 1133, fols. 31b-33a; MS Wetzstein II 1806, fols. 40a-41a; MS Vat. Arab., fols. 20b-21b.

Par. 81

1. Al-Ṭūsī's scheme may be represented as follows:

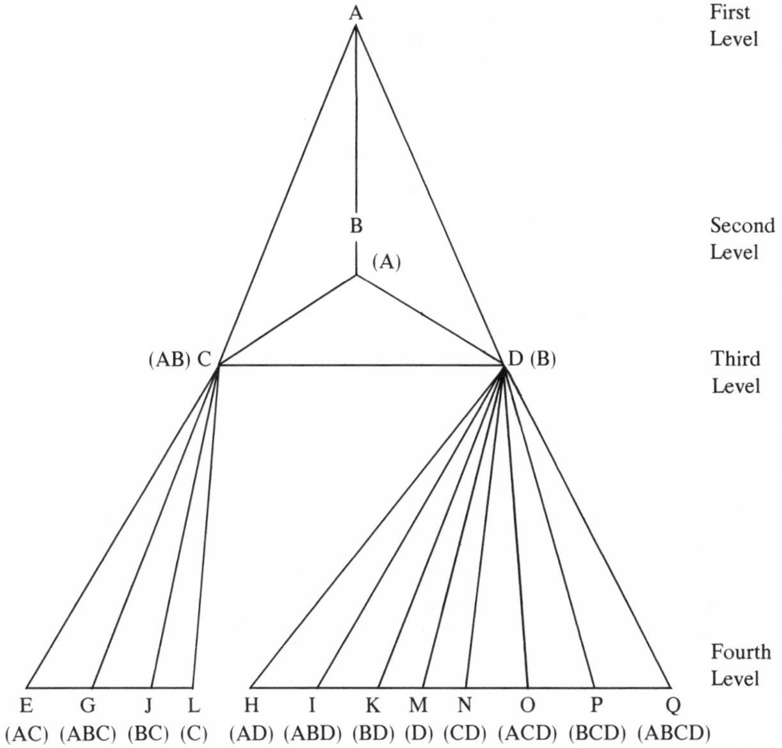

Par. 87

1. The ecstatic angels are those who are immersed in the contemplation of the divine beauty. See al-Kāshānī, *Iṣṭilāḥāt,* pp. 123-124.
2. That is, their material bodies composed of elements.
3. According to the commentary of al-Ḥusaynābādī, the Tablet depends only on the Pen, which is one. See *al-Risālah al-Qudsīyah,* fol. 123b.

Par. 88

1. Namely, the Most Exalted Pen, the ecstatic angels, etc. mentioned in the

preceding paragraph.

Par. 89

1. This quotation may be found in his *Kitāb al-Nuṣūṣ,* pp. 295-296; as well as his *Miftāḥ Ghayb al-Jam' wa-al-Wujūd.* See al-Fanārī's commentary on this latter work entitled *Miṣbāḥ al-Uns,* pp. 69-73. The question of whether general existence is the first emanation is also dealt with in the correspondence between al-Qūnawī and Naṣīr al-Dīn al-Ṭūsī. See al-Qūnawī's *al-Risālah al-Mufṣiḥah,* MS Warner 1133, fols. 8b-11a; MS Wetzstein II 1806, fols. 25a-27a; MS Vat. Arab. 1453, fols 6a-8a; al-Ṭūsī's *Risālah,* MS Werner Or. 1133, fols 30b-31b; MS Wetzstein II 1806, fol. 39a-39b; MS Vat. Arab. 1453, fol. 20a-20b.

2. *Al-a'yān al-thābitah* is the term used by Ibn 'Arabī and his followers for the realities of contingent beings as they exist in God's knowledge. See al-Kāshānī, *Iṣṭilāḥāt,* p. 90, under *al-a'yān al-thābitah,* p. 159, under *al-'ayn al-thābitah;* al-Jurjānī, *al-Ta'rīfāt,* under *al-a'yān al-thābitah;* and al-Jāmī, *Naqd al-Nuṣūṣ,* pp. 12-13.

3. That is, True Existence becomes general existence through attachment to individual essences.

Par. 90

1. Al-Jāmī is referring here to what Ibn 'Arabī and his followers call *al-fayḍ al-aqdas* and *al-fayḍ al-muqaddas.* Through the former the fixed essences and their predispositions are distinguished in God's knowledge, and through the latter they come into existence in the external world. See al-Qaysarī, *Maṭla' Khuṣūṣ al-Kilam,* p. 18; al-Aḥmadnagarī, *Dustūr al-'Ulama',* III, p. 51, under *al-fayḍ al-aqdas* and *al-fayḍ al-muqaddas;* 'Afīfī, *al-Ta'līqāt,* pp. 7-10; and al-Jāmī, *Naqd al-Nuṣūṣ,* pp. 12-13; *Lawā'iḥ,* p. 42 of English translation.

Par. 92

1. That is, those who profess the doctrine of the unity of existence *(waḥdat al-wujūd).*

The
Translation of
al-Jāmī's
GLOSSES
on
AL-DURRAH AL-FĀKHIRAH

1. [par. 5]. One of them[1] took the position that the source of the controversy was in applying the word "existence" *(al-wujūd)* both to the concept of being *(al-kawn)* and to the concept of essence *(al-dhāt).* Thus, those who took the position that it was superadded *(zā'id)* to the essence meant by it "being" *(al-kawn),* whereas those who took the position that it was identical with the quiddity *(al-māhīyah)* meant by it "essence" *(al-dhāt).* Thus, when the question is examined, the controversy disappears. [This argument] is invalidated [by the fact] that if one says that the essence of man is the same as his essence and quiddity, no additional information is conceivably conveyed.

2. [par. 6]. (1) Should you say: The position of the theologians requires that each thing have two existences, that is, the general concept and the portion, and that of the philosophers that it have three existences, that is, the general concept, its portion, and the proper existences. I should say: the theologians replied[1] that [V]what is meant by the portion of the concept of being *(ma'nā al-ḥiṣṣah min mafhūm al-kawn)* is that concept itself together with the particular characteristic of attribution *(khuṣūṣīyat al-iḍāfah),* so that there is no multiplicity at all. The philosophers answered, on the other hand, that the difference [V]is only with respect to the mind *(bi-ḥasab al-'aql),* for in the external world there is not, in the case of man, for example, something which is the quiddity and something else which is existence, much less two existences. Nevertheless, if we supposed existence to be superadded to the quiddity in the external world also, as is the case with the whiteness of snow, that would still not require [two external existences], because either the concept of general [existence] or its portion is a purely mental form *(ṣūrah 'aqlīyah maḥḍah).* [V]Even if this be admitted, the unity of subject and predicate in the external world is necessary, so how could two existences be required for man?

(2) Further consideration is called for, however, for the qualification *(ittiṣāf)* of a quiddity by existence occurs only in the mind *(fī al-'aql),* not in the external world, [v]as has been substantiated in works dealing with this subject. Thus, if the two existences differ in the mind *('aqlan),* it is obvious that the quiddity must have two existences. In answer to this it has been asserted [v]that mental existence *(al-wujūd al-'aqlī)* is of two types: basic existence *(wujūd aṣīl),* like the existence of knowledge *(al-'ilm),* for example, and shadowy existence *(wujūd ẓillī),* like the existence of things known *(al-ma'lūmāt),* and that the difference in the mind between the two existences is only with respect to the second [type of mental existence], not the first. Nevertheless, it is obvious to anyone who is intelligent and informed that to say that the qualification of an external quiddity by external existence occurs only in the mind entails the immediate extinction of external existence upon the extinction of minds *(al-'uqūl).* The absurdity of this is too apparent to be hidden, for it would imply that the Necessary Existent is qualified by external existence only in the mind and that if minds were extinguished He would cease to exist and would not, therefore, be necessarily existent.

(3) Should you say: External existence does not cease with the extinction of minds but remains in view of the knowledge of the Creator *(al-Mūjid);* I should answer: what do you say, then, concerning the existence of the Creator, [v]for its dependence on His knowledge of it is inconsistent with its being necessary? It should be known that what has been said to the effect that the subsistence *(thubūt)* of something in a thing in the external world is preceded by that thing's external existence[2] is valid only with respect to what is other than existence. As for [a thing's] qualification by existence in the external world, this does not depend on a previous existence, but rather requires only that a thing be existent at the time it is qualified [by existence]. Moreover, there is no doubt that a thing does exist when so qualified, and [that it exists] through that very same existence, not through another existence. This is not, moreover, in the same category as exceptions made to logical premisses *(al-muqaddimāt al-'aqlīyah)* since the intellect *(al-'aql)*

makes this judgment in an absolute sense *(muṭlaqan)* only because it is unaware of the particular characteristic *(khuṣūṣīyah)* of existence. When, however, it becomes aware of this characteristic, it no longer applies the judgment universally *(kullīyan),* but only with respect to what is other than existence, for were it to apply it universally, then the qualification of a quiddity by external existence in the mind would depend on the quiddity's [prior] existence in the mind, and its qualification by existence in the mind [would depend in turn] on a still prior existence, and so on. Thus, an endless chain would result, and this, moreover, would not be in the same category as the endless chain which occurs with respect to purely mental entities *(al-umūr al-i'tibārīyah),*[3] for [in the present case] each antecedent *(sābiq)* is something upon which a consequent *(al-lāḥiq)* depends and without which it cannot be realized. This is something to consider.

3. [par. 7]. That is, the general concept *(al-mafhūm al-'āmm)* and the portion *(al-ḥiṣṣah).*

4. [par. 8]. Thus is invalidated what is said to the effect that what is meant by existence is a mental concept *(mafhūm i'tibārī)* which does not exist externally but which is known to everyone, whereas the reality of the Necessary Existent *(ḥaqīqat al-Wājib)* exists [externally] but is not known. It therefore follows that existence is not His reality.[1] However, what is a mental concept and known to everyone is only this [general] concept [of existence] which is extrinsic to the reality of existence *(ḥaqīqat al-wujūd)* not the reality of existence itself.

5. [par. 8]. (1) Let it be known that the meaning of existence *(al-wujūd),* being *(al-kawn),* subsistence *(al-thubūt),* occurrence *(al-ḥuṣūl)* and realization *(al-taḥaqquq),* if the verbal meaning *(al-ma'nā al-maṣdarī)* is intended, is a mental concept *(mafhūm i'tibārī)* and one of the second intelligibles *(al-ma'qūlāt al-thāniyah),*[1] to which nothing in the external world corresponds. It is superadded in the mind to all realities, whether necessary or contingent, in the sense that the intellect can first apprehend them abstracted from existence, and then predicate existence of them, not, however, externally in the sense of there being in the external world something which is the quiddity and

something else which is existence. Existence, moreover, is not predicated of external existents or even mental existents univocally *(muwāṭa'atan)* with the exception of its own portions *(ḥiṣaṣ),* which are individuated through its being attributed to realities. Moreover, the position taken by the philosophers to the effect that the proper existence of the Necessary Existent *(al-wujūd al-khāṣṣ al-wājibī),* which is identical with the essence of the Necessary Existent, is one of its singulars *(fard min afrādihi),* [v]is not true. [v]How can it be true when they themselves explicitly state that it is a second intelligible to which, as stated above, nothing in the external world corresponds?

(2) No rational person doubts that it is impossible for existence in the aforementioned sense to exist, let alone be the very reality of the Necessary Existent, who is the source *(mabdā')* of all existents. How can anyone think that the Ṣūfīs who assert the unity and necessity of existence mean existence in the aforementioned sense?[2] How can objection be made to their assertion of this [doctrine]? One understands from studying what their verifiers say that, in addition to quiddities and existence in the aforementioned sense, there is some other entity because of whose association *(iqtirān)* with quiddities and their being clothed with it, existence in the aforementioned sense comes to inhere in them. This other entity is existence in reality *(ḥaqīqatan).* It is the reality of the Necessary Existent, whereas existence in the aforementioned sense is one of Its effects *(athar min āthārihi)* and a reflection of Its lights. It is self-realized *(mutaḥaqqiq fī nafsihi)* and a realizer *(muḥaqqiq)* of what is other than Itself. It is self-subsistent *(qā'im bi-dhātihi),* and constitutive *(muqawwim)* to what is other than itself. It is not inherent in quiddities, but quiddities, on the contrary, are inherent and subsistent in It in such a manner that impairs neither the perfection of Its sanctity nor the quality of Its majesty. This will be expanded upon later, God willing.

6. [par. 9]. Existence has no real singulars *(afrād ḥaqīqīyah)*[1] as does man, for example, because existence is a single reality having no multiplicity in it. It has singulars only in consideration of its attribution to quiddities, and attribution is a purely mental entity *(amr i'tibārī).* Thus it has no real and distinct

existent singulars *(afrād mawjūdah mutaghāyirah ḥaqīqīyah)* different from the reality of existence.

7. [par. 9]. For it differs in its particulars *(al-juz'īyāt),* although it is a single accident, just as whiteness, for example, differs in its particulars, although that difference does not impair its unity.[1]

8. [par. 9]. The people of God *(ahl Allāh)* took the position[1] that existence, in view of its descent *(tanazzul)* to the planes of created beings *(marātib al-akwān),* and its manifestation *(ẓuhūr)* in the realms of contingency *(ḥaẓā'ir al-imkān),* and in view also of the multiplicity of intermediaries *(kathrat al-wasā'iṭ),* becomes increasingly hidden, and its manifestation and perfections become weaker. As, however, the intermediaries become less, its luminosity *(nūrīyah)* increases, and both its manifestation and the manifestation of its perfections and attributes become stronger. Therefore, its attribution *(iṭlāq)* to the strong is more appropriate *(awlā)* than its attribution to the weak.

9. [par. 10]. The dissimilarity[1] is not in the reality of existence but rather in the manifestation of its properties *(khawāṣṣ),* such as being a cause *(al-'illīyah)* or being caused *(al-ma'lūlīyah),* or strength of manifestation in what is simultaneous in essence *(al-qārr al-dhāt)* and weakness of manifestation in what is successive in essence *(ghayr al-qārr al-dhāt),*[2] just as the dissimilarity between individual humans *(afrād al-insān)* is not in humanity itself *(nafs al-insānīyah)* but rather in accordance with the manifestation of its properties in them. Thus, were that dissimilarity to exclude existence from being identical with the reality of its individuals *(afrād),* then it would also exclude humanity *(al-insān)* from being identical with the reality of its individuals. However, there can be no dissimilarity between the individuals of any other existent thing quite like that between human individuals. Therefore, some of them have become higher in rank and nobler in station than the angels *(al-amlāk),* and others lower in rank and baser in condition than the beasts.

10. [par. 11]. Al-Shaykh Ṣadr al-Dīn al-Qūnawī, may God be pleased with him, said in a passage in which he undertook to argue in the manner of the masters of reason *(arbāb al-naẓar)* in

favor of one of the doctrine *(masā'il)* of this path *(al-ṭarīqah):*[1] "Know that my purpose in mentioning this argument is not to establish the truth of this doctrine for those who may hear this argument nor to disclose my evidence *(mustanad)* for asserting it, since the only evidence and proof *(al-dalīl)* for this as well as other doctrines in my opinion is clear mystical revelation *(al-kashf al-ṣarīḥ)* and true intuition *(al-dhawq al-ṣaḥīḥ).* Indeed, the mention of this argument and others like it occurs for the most part to put at ease those people veiled [from the truth] *(al-maḥjūbīn)* and those whose faith in this path and its masters is weak [V]because of a remainder of uncertainty *(taraddud)* [V]remaining in them."

11. [par. 11]. This was said by 'Ayn al-Quḍāh al-Hamadhānī, may his soul be sanctified, in his *Tamāhīd.*[1] In it he also said:[2] "Do not hasten to deny that which your weak intellect does not perceive. The intellect *(al-'aql)* was created to perceive only certain existents, just as sight *(al-baṣar)* was created to perceive only certain sensibles *(al-maḥsūsāt),* being unable to perceive odors *(al-mashmūmāt),* sounds *(al-masmū'at),* and tastes *(al-madhūqāt).* Similarly, there are many existents which the intellect is unable to perceive. Indeed, those things it does perceive are few and limited in comparison with the multiplicity of existents which it cannot perceive."

12. [par. 12]. Al-Shaykh Ṣadr al-Dīn al-Qūnawī said:[1] "Intellects have a boundary *(ḥadd)* at which they halt insofar as they are limited in their thoughts *(afkār).* They may thus judge impossible many things which, for those possessing intellects unrestricted *(aṣḥāb al-'uqūl al-muṭlaqah)* by such limitations, are possible or even necessary of occurrence, since unrestricted intellects have no boundary at which they halt. On the contrary, they continue to ascend and thus to acquire knowledge from the exalted realms *(al-jihāt al-'alīyah)* and the divine presences *(al-ḥaḍarāt al-ilāhīyah).* In summary, 'That which God openeth unto mankind of mercy none can withhold it; and that which He withholdeth none can release thereafter. He is the Mighty, the Wise.' "[2]

13. [par. 12]. (1) Let it be known that God, the Wise and Bestower, gave to man numerous external and internal faculties

from each of which a certain type of effect results. God's wisdom requires, however, that the scope of these faculties not reach the point at which all the levels of these effects might result. Thus, man's faculty of sight is not sufficient to see everything that can be seen, nor is his faculty of hearing sufficient to hear everything that can be heard, and so forth. Similarly, his intellectual faculty, although the most perfect of his faculties, is not capable of perceiving the realities of things or their states or even divine matters with such certainty that no doubt at all remains.

(2) Is this so surprising when even the philosophers, who claim to have understood all the most difficult questions of metaphysics by the use of the intellect alone, and who maintain that these beliefs of theirs are absolutely certain *(yaqīnīyah),* have been unable, even though they are intelligent and honorable, to substantiate *(taḥqīq)* what is under their very eyes and within the range of their vision, namely, sensible body *(al-jism al-maḥsūs)* and have thus disagreed as to its reality? They have likewise disagreed widely as to the reality of the soul *(al-nafs),* which is the closest thing to them. How can one whose knowledge is such that he knows neither the reality of his soul nor even the reality of his own body *(ḥaqīqat binyatihi),* which he touches with his hand, looks at with his eyes, and, seeking to discover its reality, exerts his greatest effort in contemplating —how can such a one believe, or for that matter anyone else believe, that he has, solely by means of his intellect *('aql)* and reason *(fikr),* understood conclusively the secrets of the modes of the Creator *(asrār aḥwāl al-Ṣāni'),* the Possessor of glory and power, or that he has completely grasped the subtleties of the King and His kingdom?

(3) Often a person with a low level of intelligence and acumen who has little knowledge of things, but who is one of those who do magical tricks, causes strange forms to appear which strike intellects with wonder and leave them baffled as to how to explain them, for no one by means of reason alone is able to comprehend their reality. Have, then, the marvels of God's state and attributes, and the wonders of His creations become simpler and more obvious than the trickery of this

lowly incompetent? Not at all, for even if the unaided intellect can divise proofs for some of them, nevertheless, in the case of many of them, there can be no guidance along the right path except through the instruction of one who is supported by God with obvious miracles *(al-āyāt al-ẓāhirah)* which indicate the truthfulness of his words and the integrity of his acts. How fair-minded was that philosopher who said: "There is no path to certainty in metaphysics, for the maximum goal in this science is merely the acceptance of what is most appropriate and fitting." This is ascribed to the most eminent of the philosophers, Aristotle.

14. [par. 17]. One of the eminent has said:[1] "An intelligible unconditioned by anything at all *(al-ma'qūl lā bi-sharṭ shay' aṣlan)* is called a natural universal *(al-kullī al-ṭabī'ī)*. It becomes a mental universal *(al-kullī al-'aqlī)* when associated with that concept called a logical universal *(al-kullī al-manṭiqī)*. The natural universal, although necessarily associated both in the mind and in the external world with the concepts of universality *(al-'umūm)* and particularity *(al-khuṣūṣ)*, can, nevertheless, be apprehended by the intellect without consideration of what is associated with it. In this respect it exists in the external world, unlike the logical and mental universals, although in the external world it never exists abstracted from the concept of particularity."

15. [par. 18]. (1) Either His existence is: superadded *(zā'id)* to His reality both in the mind and externally, or in the mind only, since the opposite is not intelligible. In this case, if the Necessary Existent is equivalent to the combination [of the reality and existence], it follows that He is compounded both in the mind and externally, or in the mind only; but both of these [conclusions] are absurd with respect to the Necessary Existent, as has been shown in the appropriate place elsewhere *fī mawḍi'ihi)*. If He is equivalent to the substratum *(al-ma'rūḍ)*[1] alone, then He would be in need of something other than Himself in order to exist, namely, His existence. If, on the other hand, He is equivalent to the inherent *(al-'āriḍ)*,[2] and if that inherent is an external existent, then He needs for His existence and continuance *(baqā')* a substratum and this

[need] is incompatible with necessary existence. If, however, the inherent is a mental entity *(amr i'tibārī),* then the Source of Existents *(Mabda' al-Mawjūdāt)* would be nonexistent [externally], and this is absurd.

(2) Or His existence is: identical with Himself both in the mind and externally. In this case this existence is either absolute *(muṭlaq)* or individuated *(muta'ayyin).* If it is absolute the thesis is proven. If, on the other hand, it is individuated, the individuation cannot be intrinsic to Him *(dākhil fīhi),* for then the Necessary Existent would be compounded. Therefore, the individuation must be extrinsic *(khārij).* Thus, the Necessary Existent is a simple entity *(maḥḍummā),* which is existence, and its individuation is an attribute inhering in Him.

(3) Should someone ask: Why is it not possible for Him to be individuated through an individuation which is identical with Him both in the mind and externally, and which cannot be distinguished from Him either in the mind or externally? Then, by analogy with existence, that individuation which is distinguishable from Him in the mind would be the general concept [of individuation] inherent [in Him], or its portion individuated through its annexation to Him, and not the individuation which is identical with Him. [We should answer]: Escape from this difficulty is impossible except through reliance upon mystical revelation and vision *(al-kashf wa-al-mushāhadah),* for, although what you have mentioned is a probability allowed by the intellect, nevertheless mystical revelation and vision testify to the contrary.

16. [par. 19]. We grant that it is identical with it. Nevertheless consideration of its essence in itself is prior to consideration of its being an individuation, and what is antecedent is what is worthy of existence and being a source *(al-mabda'īyah).* Should you say that what is consequent is a concomitant of what is antecedent and cannot be separated from it, I should answer that [v]there is no objection to the inseparability since all aspects of the divine plane *(al-martabah al-ilāhīyah)* are eternal and everlasting, and there is thus no doubt that the real source *(al-mabdā' al-ḥaqīqī)* is the simple essence *(al-dhāt al-maḥḍ).*

17. [par. 20]. Consequently, what is meant by its encompassing *(iḥāṭah)* existents and its expansion *(inbisāṭ)* over them is its appearance in their forms and its manifesting itself in accordance with them, not its being general or universal.

18. [par. 22]. By al-Shaykh Muḥyī al-Dīn [Ibn 'Arabī].[1]

19. [par. 27]. The theologians said that attributes were of three types: completely real attributes *(ḥaqīqīyah maḥḍah),* like blackness, whiteness, and life; real attributes possessing relation *(dhāt iḍāfah),* like knowledge and power; and completely relative attributes *(iḍāfīyah maḥḍah),* like simultaneity *(al-ma'īyah)* and priority *(al-qablīyah),* among which are included negative attributes *(al-ṣifāt al-salbīyah).* With respect to God's essence no change at all is possible in the first type, and any change is possible in the third type. In the second type change is impossible in the attribute itself but is possible in its connection *(ta'alluq).*[1]

20. [par. 28]. The diference between the doctrine of the philosophers and that of the Ṣūfīs in affirming God's attributes is that the philosophers asserted individual unity *(waḥdah shakhṣīyah)* of the Necessary Essence by [considering it] an individuated essence *(dhāt mushakhkhaṣah),* whereas the Ṣūfīs asserted an absolute essential unity *(waḥdah dhātīyah muṭlaqah)* of His essence rather than a particular individual unity *(waḥdah shakhṣīyah juz'īyah).* They also affirmed of His essence attributes which are multiple in the mind only and which are manifestations *(maẓāhir)* of His essence in the concrete world. The philosophers, on the other hand, denied the existence of multiple attributes which are manifestations of His essence, although united with it, because in their view the existence of His essence is individually one, and His essence cannot, therefore, be united with anything else because of the impossibility of validly predicating one of the other.[1]

21. [par. 29]. Namely, 'Ayn al-Quḍāh al-Hamadhānī.[1]

22. [par. 29]. Thus His attributes are relations *(nisab)* and attributions *(iḍāfāt)* which attach to the transcendent essence *(al-dhāt al-muta'āliyah)* with respect to its connections *(muta'alliqāt).*[1]

23. [par. 32]. That is, the active intellect *(al-'aql al-fa''āl).*[1]

24. [par. 33]. That is, the commentator, al-Muḥaqqiq [Nasīr al-Dīn al-Ṭūṣī].

25. [par. 33]. That is, not the form.

26. [par. 33]. That is, upon the consideration of your knowledge of yourself through this form is superimposed *(tarakkaba)* the consideration of your knowledge of this form through itself.

27. [par. 34]. One could say, however, that the condition for the apprehension of something without the occurrence *(ḥudūth)* of the form of that thing is that that thing be the apprehender's self or one of his states *(aḥwāl),* for his self and its states are the closest things to him, and it is thus not improbable that he need no additional form in apprehending them as opposed to those things which are distinct from him.

28. [par. 34]. This calls for further consideration *(fīhi ta'ammul),* however, for the occurrence of a thing to its recipient *(qābil)* is only by inhering *(al-ḥulūl)* and subsisting *(al-qiyām)* in it. This is in contrast to its occurrence to its agent *(fā'il),* for the meaning of its occurrence to its agent can only be its emanation *(ṣudūr)* from it and its realization *(taḥaqquq)* in its presence. Moreover, its occurrence in the first manner is, no doubt, closer to apprehension without an additional form than its occurrence in the second manner. This is something to consider.

29. [par. 35]. It is apparent that this also is a rhetorical *(khiṭābī)* rather than a demonstrative *(burhānī)* argument as is indicated by his saying "if you have concluded . . . , you can conclude . . ." without taking up the question of whether the second [clause] necessarily follows from the first as sound natural intelligence *(al-fiṭrah al-salīmah)* attests [is necessary].[1]

30. [par. 35]. (1) The author of *al-Muḥākamāt* said:[1] "When the commentator [Naṣīr al-Dīn al-Ṭūsī] had won the opinion *(ẓann)*[2] of the theologian[3] in favor of his thesis by means of the foregoing rhetorical premisses, he proceeded to demonstrate[4] his thesis as follows: It has been established both that the First Principle knows His essence and that His essence is the cause of His effect. It has also been established that knowledge of the cause is a cause for knowledge of the effect. It follows from these premisses that the occurrence *(huṣūl)* of the effect is the

same as its being apprehended *(ta'aqqul),* because, the two causes[5] being united *(muttaḥid),* it follows that the two effects[6] are united,[7] and just as the difference between the two causes is in the mind *(fī al-i'tibār)* only, the difference between the two effects is likewise [in the mind only]."

(2) In objection it may be said: We do not admit that if the difference between the two causes is in the mind, it necessarily follows that the difference between the two effects is likewise in the mind. Do you not see that the first intellect through its three aspects *(i'tibārāt)* is the cause of its three effects, namely an intellect, a soul, and a sphere, and that these are without doubt completely distinct from each other *(mutabāyinah)* and hardly united in essence. This should be considered.

31. [par. 36]. Existence [comprises] nothing beyond the essence of the First, those [intellectual] substances, and those things whose forms are impressed in them. God's knowledge of His essence is identical with His essence, [V]and His knowledge of those substances is their existence and their emanation from Him. His knowledge of those things whose forms are impressed in those substances is by means of the presence *(ḥuḍūr)* of those forms which are impressed in them and which are present to them, for those substances are present to God and what is present to something present is also present.[1] Since it is evident, however, that everything other than the First is one of His effects, [V]and His knowledge of His effects is their existence in His presence *('indahu)* and their emanation from Him, what need is there for the mediacy *(tawassuṭ)* of the forms impressed in those substances with respect to His knowledge of all existents? Indeed, He needs this mediacy only with respect to His knowledge of nonexistents *(al-ma'dūmāt).*

32. [par. 37]. For if His knowledge of a certain thing is by means of its form being impressed in the intellectual substances, then it follows that He is in need of those substances with respect to His knowledge of that thing. May God be high exalted above what the evildoers say.

33. [par. 39]. Not[1] in the sense, however, that these aspects originate *(taḥduth)*[2] in God's intellection, may He be exalted above what does not befit Him, but rather that the intellection

of some of them is posterior in rank *(muta'akhkhir al-rutbah)*[3] to that of the others, for all of them are uniformly eternal and everlasting intellections.

34. [par. 40]. These are the cognitions *(al-'ulūm)* which have become many and multiple through the multiplicity of their connections *(muta'alliqāt).*

35. [par. 41]. Khawājah Naṣīr [al-Dīn al-Ṭūsī] in his *Risālah* written in answer to the questions of al-Shaykh Ṣadr al-Dīn al-Qūnawī.

36. [par. 41]. He also said in the glosses to this *Risālah:*[1] "[As for] Him who is exalted above time *(al-muta'ālī 'an al-zamān),* time for Him is a single thing from eternity to everlastingness and equally related to Him. His knowledge encompasses its parts in detail as well as what occurs in its parts one thing after another. It is as if a temporal being were to be likened to someone reading a book. His sight falls on one letter after another, such that one letter has passed by him, another is present before his eyes, and yet another his sight has not yet reached. A being exalted above time, on the other hand, is like someone who has the whole book present before him and knows its arrangement. The First's knowledge of temporal beings *(al-zamānīyāt)* is of this sort."

37. [par. 44]. He said "in a manner close to that of the philosophers" only because the first concomitant *(awwal al-lawāzim)* according to the Ṣūfīs is the cognitive relation *(al-nisbah al-'ilmīyah),* [V]followed by general existence *(al-wujūd al-'āmm),* [V]and finally the individuations which attach to it in view of its expansion *(inbisāṭ)* over quiddities [V]of which the first is the first intellect [V]and what is in its plane, then what follows them, and so on to infinity. According to the philosophers, on the other hand, the first concomitant is the first intellect, then what follows it and so on.

38. [par. 50]. [V]That is, both of them are proper for Him in accordance with varying motives *(al-dawā'ī).*[1] This is not inconsistent with the necessity of His acting [V]when the motive is pure, such that it is impossible for him not to act, nor does it imply that there is no difference between Him and a necessary agent *(al-mūjib),* for the latter acts necessarily by virtue of his

nature *(naẓaran ilā nafsihi),* such that he is absolutely unable to abstain.

39. [par. 50]. It is evident that this agreement between the two parties [v]is only with respect to the expression *(al-'ibārah),* since volition *(al-mashī'ah)* and will *(al-irādah)* in the view of the philosophers are nothing more than the knowledge of the most perfect order *(al-niẓām al-akmal)* [of the universe], so that the meaning of their saying: "If He wills, He acts" is: If the knowledge of the most perfect order occurs to Him, then He brings the universe into existence, and if it does not occur to Him, He does not bring it into existence. The meaning of what the religionists *(al-millīyūn)* say, on the other hand, is: If after knowing the universe He wills its bringing-into-existence, He brings it into existence, and if He does not so will, He does not bring it into existence.

40. [par. 57]. How can it lag behind when His intention *(qaṣd)* necessitates *(mūjib)?* Moreover, there is no doubt that the necessitation *(al-ījāb)* [of something] cannot be conceived without the existence [of the thing necessitated], regardless of whether such necessitation depends on His essence or on one of His attributes, like intention in this instance.

41. [par. 60]. A certain person has said:[1] "The Creator is a speaker *(mutakallim)* and His speech *(kalām)* is eternal. What speech means is to inform someone of what one knows. In this sense the Creator is a speaker since all things are known to God and He can inform mankind of them.

42. [par. 62]. Ibn Sa'īd of the Ash'arites[1] said: "His speech is one in eternity and is not qualified by any one of those five, namely, command *(al-amr),* prohibition *(al-nahy),* narration *(al-khabar),* interrogation *(al-istifhām),* and vocation *(al-nidā'),* for it only becomes one of those in that which does not pass away *(fīmā la yazāl).*[2] Objection was raised against him that these are its species *(anwā'),* [v]so that it cannot exist without them, nor with them either,[3] [v]since a genus cannot exist except within its species. The answer is to deny this with respect to species that occur to a genus in accordance with a connection *(al-ta'alluq).* That is, they are not real species *(anwā' haqīqīyah)* of it, to make necessary what you have mentioned, but rather

mental species *(anwā' i'tibārīyah)* occurring to it only because of its connection to things. [v]Thus it is possible for their genus to exist without them as well as with them." Al-Sayyid al-Sharīf [al-Jurjānī] said: "What Ibn Sa'īd said is not as improbable as they imagined." From *Sharḥ al-Mawāqif.*

43. [par. 63]. (1) The author of *al-Mawāqif*[1] said in one of his treatises: "The word 'meaning' *(al-ma'nā)* is sometimes applied to the signification *(madlūl)* of an utterance *(al-lafẓ)* and sometimes to an entity which subsists in something else. When al-Shaykh al-Ash'arī said that speech is the meaning in the mind *(al-ma'nā al-nafsī),* his colleagues understood him to mean the signification of the utterance only, and that this, in his view, is what is eternal. As for expressions *(al-'ibārāt),* they are called speech only metaphorically *(majāzan),* because they indicate what is speech in reality. Thus they maintained in accordance with al-Ash'arī's position that the utterances were originated and that they were not His speech in reality.

(2) Nevertheless, their understanding of the doctrine of al-Shaykh [al-Ash'arī] in this way leads to a number of erroneous conclusions *(lawāzim fāsidah),* such as the impossibility of declaring someone an unbeliever who denies that what is between the covers of a copy of the Qur'ān is the speech of God even though he knows necessarily from religion that it is the speech of God in reality, or the impossibility of opposing and challenging the real speech of God, or the impossibility of what is recited and preserved being His speech in reality, as well as many other things which are evident to one who is well versed in religious precepts. It therefore becomes necessary to interpret this statement of al-Shaykh [al-Ash'arī] to the effect that he intended the second meaning. The speech of the mind *(al-kalām al-nafsī)*[2] would then in his opinion be something which included both the utterance and its meaning, and which subsisted in the essence of God, was written in the copies of the Qur'ān, was recited by tongues and preserved in hearts, but was, nevertheless, neither the writing, nor the recitation, nor the preservation, all of which are originated.

(3) As for what is said to the effect that the letters and utterances are ordered and in sequence, the answer to that is

that the ordering is only in the pronunciation *(al-talaffuẓ)* owing to the lack of facilitation of the instrument.[3] The pronunciation is, therefore, originated, and the proofs indicating the origination [of His speech] should be interpreted [as indicating] the origination of the pronunciation rather than the origination of what is pronounced. In this way the proofs [for both positions] are reconciled.

(4) Although what we have stated is contrary to the position of our more recent colleagues, [v]nevertheless, its truth becomes evident upon reflection." Al-Muḥaqqiq al-Sharīf [al-Jurjānī] said: "This interpretation of the statement of al-Shaykh [al-Ash'arī] was that chosen by Muḥammad al-Shahrastānī in his book called *Nihāyat al-Aqdām,*[4] and there is no doubt that it is closer to the literal precepts *(al-aḥkām al-ẓāhirīyah)* pertaining to the principles of the religion *(qawā'id al-millah).* From *Sharḥ al-Mawāqif.*

44. [par. 65]. 'Ayn al-Quḍāh al-Hamadhānī said in one of his Persian letters:[1] "God is perfect in essence, complete in attributes. His speech is independent of such organs as the tongue, throat, lips, and palate from which the various letters issue. When I have an intention and wish to make it known to someone, I have need of tongue and letters and sounds in order to convey my intention to his understanding. God, however, has no need for these since any item of knowledge He wishes He places in the heart without the use of letters or sounds. 'He has written faith upon their hearts,'[2] and 'Who teacheth by the pen, teacheth man that which he knew not.'[3] 'The Merciful hath made known the Qur'ān.'[4] Every bit of eternal knowledge which falls to the lot of a heart is the speech of eternity, and its source is the knowledge of eternity, [v]for there is no way of exhausting the knowledge of eternity. 'Say: though the sea became ink for the words of my Lord, verily the sea would be used up before the words of my Lord were exhausted.' "[5]

45. [par. 72]. Al-Shaykh [Ibn 'Arabī] said in the first volume of *al-Futūḥāt* in [the section containing] the questions:[1] "The meaning of acquisition *(al-kasb)* is the connection *(ta'alluq)* of the will of a contingent being with a certain act to the exclusion of any other. The divine power *(al-iqtidār al-ilāhī)* then creates

[that act] at [the moment of] the connection, and that is called acquisition.

NOTES
to the Translation of al-Jāmī's *GLOSSES*

Gloss 1

1. The author of *al-Ṣaḥā'if al-Ilāhīyah,* Shams al-Dīn Muḥammad ibn Ashraf al-Samarqandī (Brockelmann, *Geschichte,* I, p. 615). See al-Taftāzānī, *Sharḥ al-Maqāṣid,* I, p. 52, which is al-Jāmī's source for this gloss.

Gloss 2

1. Al-Jāmī's source for the theologians' reply and the philosophers' answer to it is al-Taftāzānī, *Sharḥ al-Maqāsid,* I, p. 54.

2. This proposition was known as *al-qā'idah al-far'īyah.* See al-Aḥmadnagarī, *Dustūr al-'Ulamā',* I, pp. 374-376, under *thubūt al-shay' lil-shay' far' li-thubūt al-muthbat lahu;* and Kāshif al-Ghiṭā', *Naqd al-Ārā' al-Manṭiqīyah,* pp. 352-368.

3. An endless chain of mental entities was considered possible. See al-Aḥmadnagarī, *Dustūr al-'Ulamā',* I, p. 290, under *al-tasalsul.*

Gloss 4

1. See, for example, p. 15 of 'Alā' al-Dīn al-Bukhārī's famous attack on the *waḥdat al-wujūd* school of Ṣūfism entitled *Fāḍiḥat al-Mulḥidīn wa-Nāṣiḥat al-Muwaḥḥidīn.*

Gloss 5

1. For the definition of second intelligible, see note 1 to par. 19 of the

translation of *al-Durrah al-Fākhirah.*

2. This distinction between the two senses of existence is clearly made by Ṣūfīs of the *waḥdat al-wujūd* school. See, for example, al-Qayṣārī, *Maṭla' Khuṣūṣ al-Kilam,* pp. 5-7; al-Fanārī, *Miṣbāḥ al-Uns,* p. 53; al-Mahā'imī, *Ajillat al-Ta'yīd,* fol. 6a.

Gloss 6

1. For al-Jāmī's source for this gloss, see al-Qayṣarī, *Maṭla' Khuṣūṣ al-Kilam,* p. 9.

Gloss 7

1. That is, the general concept of whiteness remains one even through the individual instances of whiteness differ. The whiteness of snow, for example, is more brilliant than the whiteness of ivory.

Gloss 8

1. Al-Jāmī's source for this gloss is al-Qayṣarī, *Maṭla' Khuṣūṣ al-Kilam,* p. 10.

Gloss 9

1. Al-Jāmī's source is again al-Qayṣarī, *Maṭla' Khuṣūṣ al-Kilam,* p. 10.

2. Quantity *(al-kamm)* can be divided into what is continuous *(muttaṣil),* such as body and time, and what is discrete *(munfaṣil),* such as number. It can also be divided into what is simultaneous *(qārr al-dhāt),* that is, those things whose parts all exist together at one time, such as body, and into what is successive *(ghayr qārr al-dhāt),* or those things whose parts do not all exist together at one time, such as motion and rest. See al-Aḥmadnagarī, *Dustūr al-'Ulamā',* II, p. 316, under *al-'araḍ,* III, p. 52, under *al-qārr,* III, pp. 146-148, under *al-kamm;* al-Jurjānī, *al-Ta'rīfāt,* under *al-'araḍ;* al-Tahānawī, *Kashshāf,* pp. 1272-1273, under *al-kamm;* Ibn Sīnā, *al-Shifā', al-Manṭiq, al-Maqūlāt,* pp. 127-130; al-Taftāzānī, *Sharḥ al-Maqāṣid,* I, pp. 135-136.

Gloss 10

1. I have been unable to find the source of this quotation.

Gloss 11

1. The quotation is actually from his *Zubdat al-Ḥaqā'iq,* pp. 26-27.

2. See his *Zubdat al-Ḥaqā'iq,* p. 50.

Gloss 12

1. I have been unable to locate the source of this quotation.
2. Qur'ān, XXXV, 2.

Gloss 14

1. I have been unable to identify the source of this quotation.

Gloss 15

1. That is, the reality.
2. That is, existence.

Gloss 18

1. See his *Fuṣūṣ al-Ḥikam,* I, p. 181.

Gloss 19

1. E.g. in the object of His knowledge or power.

Gloss 20

1. That is, if the existence of the attributes was not identical with the existence of the essence but only united with it, it would be impossible to predicate the attributes of the essence, because to predicate one thing of another requires that both exist through the same existence.

Gloss 21

1. See his *Zubdat al-Ḥaqā'iq,* pp. 40, 42.

Gloss 22

1. That is, those things to which the attributes, or, in the Ṣūfī view, the essence itself, are connected as, for example, the object of God's knowledge *(al-ma'lūm),* or the object of His power *(al-maqdūr).*

Gloss 23

1. One would expect the gloss to refer to the first intellect *(al-'aql al-awwal)* rather than the active intellect.

Gloss 29

1. In commenting on this section of al-Ṭūsī's *Sharḥ al-Ishārāt* in *al-Muḥākamāt,* p. 441, Quṭb al-Dīn al-Rāzī explains that al-Ṭūsī has followed the common practice of first presenting a rhetorical or dialectical argument in support of a thesis and then following it with a demonstrative argument. Accordingly, the argument quoted in pars. 33-34 is a rhetorical argument, whereas that given in par. 35 is meant to be a demonstrative argument.

Gloss 30

1. See Quṭb al-Dīn al-Rāzī, *al-Muḥākamāt,* p. 443.

2. That is, presumptive knowledge based only on rhetorical or probable premisses.

3. The edition of *al-Muḥākamāt* printed in Istanbul in 1290 reads *muta'allim* (student) instead of *mutakallim* (theologian).

4. See, however, al-Jāmī's comment on this demonstration in the preceding gloss.

5. That is, His essence and His knowledge of His essence.

6. That is, His effect and His knowledge of His effect.

7. This conclusion is apparently based on the premiss that from a single cause only a single effect can result.

Gloss 31

1. That is, the forms are present to the intellectual substances in which they are impressed, and the substances are present to God. Therefore the forms are also present to God.

Gloss 33

1. This entire gloss is a quotation from Ṣadr al-Dīn al-Qūnawī, *Kitāb al-Nuṣūṣ,* p. 275.

2. Reading *annahā taḥduth* as in the 1315 lithograph of *Kitāb al-Nuṣūṣ* rather than *annahu yaḥduth* as quoted by al-Jāmī in this gloss.

3. Rather than posterior in time, for were some of them posterior in time they would be originated rather than eternal.

Gloss 36

1. Al-Ṭūsī's glosses to his *Risālah* are found in MS Vat. Arab. 1453. This particular gloss appears in the margin of fol. 21b.

Gloss 38

1. For the source of this gloss, see al-Taftāzānī, *Sharḥ al-Maqāṣid,* II, p. 59.

Gloss 41

1. I have been unable to identify the source of this quotation.

Gloss 42

1. Perhaps the reference here is to ʻAbd Allāh ibn Saʻīd ibn Kullāb (Sezgin, *Geschichte,* I, p. 599) to whom this position on God's speech is usually attributed. See al-Ashʻarī, *Maqālāt al-Islāmīyīn,* pp. 584-586; al-Āmidī, *Abkār al-Afkār,* fols. 40b, 42b, 44a, 46b; al-Subkī, *Ṭabaqāt al-Shāfiʻīyah,* II, p. 51; van Ess, "Ibn Kullāb und die Mihna," p. 104. ʻAbd Allāh ibn Saʻīd ibn Kullāb, however, died about 240/854 and thus could not have been an Ashʻarite. As al-Jāmī indicates, the entire gloss is taken from al-Jurjānī's *Sharḥ al-Mawāqif* (Vol. VIII, p. 100).

2. That is, in time as opposed to eternity. See al-Aḥmadnagarī, *Dustūr al-ʻUlamā',* III, p. 196, under *mā lā yazāl.*

3. That is, with them as a separate entity rather than as a part of them.

Gloss 43

1. ʻAḍud al-Dīn al-Ījī (Brockelmann, *Geschichte,* II, p. 267, Supplement, II, p. 287). Al-Jāmī's source for this quotation is al-Jurjānī, *Sharḥ al-Mawāqif,* VIII, pp. 103-104.

2. For this concept, see al-Aḥmadnagarī, *Dustūr al-ʻUlamā',* III, p. 134, under *al-kalām al-nafsī;* and Earl Edgar Elder, *A Commentary on the Creed of Islam,* pp. 58-59.

3. The tongue cannot pronounce letters and words all at once but only in sequence. Consequently the pronunciation of letters and words is originated but not the letters and words themselves.

4. Al-Jurjānī is perhaps referring to al-Shahrastānī's apparent support of the Ḥanbalī-Salafī position on God's speech in his *Nihāyat al-Aqdām,* pp. 311-317.

Gloss 44

1. See his *Nāmah-hā,* pp. 145-146.
2. Qur'ān, LVIII, 22.
3. Qur'ān, XCVI, 4-5.
4. Qur'ān, LV, 1-2.
5. Qur'ān, XVIII, 109.

Gloss 45

1. See Ibn 'Arabī, *al-Futūḥat al-Makkīyah,* I, p. 42.

The Translation of al-Lārī's *COMMENTARY* on *AL-DURRAH AL-FĀKHIRAH*

In the name of God, the Merciful, the Compassionate.

1. *Praise be to God, Who became manifest through His essence to His essence:* that is, Who knew His essence through His essence rather than through a knowledge superadded to His essence. This is knowledge in a universal and general manner *('alā wajh kullī jumlī)* and by it the author has alluded to the first individuation *(al-ta'ayyun al-awwal).*

Became individuated in His inner knowledge: that is, became individuated after that as fixed essences *(ta'ayyana ta'ayyunan thubūtīyan)* in His inner knowledge. This is knowledge of particulars *('ilm tafṣīlī)* and by it the author has alluded to the second individuation *(al-ta'ayyun al-thānī).*[1]

The effects of these manifestations being then reflected: that is, His existence was dyed with the qualities *(aḥkām)* and effects *(āthār)* of these manifestations. This is an allusion to the plane of contingency *(martabat al-imkān),* that is, the existence of contingents in the concrete world *(fī al-'ayn).*

Upon His outward aspect: The outward aspect of existence is an expression for pure existence *(al-wujūd al-baḥt)* without consideration of any other thing or without consideration of any other thing along with it, whereas the inner aspect of existence *(bāṭin al-wujūd)* is an expression for the expanse of His knowledge *('arṣat 'ilmihi).*

Such that unity became multiplicity: without any change in the reality of existence *(ḥaqīqat al-wujūd)* or in its real unity or even any change and imperfection in His real attributes, for this multiplicity is a relative multiplicity *(kathrah nisbīyah).*

As you see and behold: that is, either as you see the multiplicity, in which case the meaning is clear, or as you see the unity which has become multiplicity, the meaning in that case being that what you see in actual fact *(fī al-wāqi')* is the unity in the form of multiplicity, whether you realize this or not.

This multiplicity reverted to its original unity: by his divesting himself of the properties and qualities of multiplicities and by their elimination from his view, may God bless him and give him peace, until he reaches that first unity. This is the rank *(al-martabah)* proper to our Prophet, may God bless him and give him peace, and therefore the author did not mention his name.

Who have inherited of this virtue a large portion: that is, have inherited a share and portion of this virtue as his followers *(bi-sabab al-mutāba'ah),* not that they have inherited it in reality, since, as you know, it is proper to the Prophet alone, may God bless him and give him peace.

3. *That there is in existence a necessary existent:* that is, that among existents *(al-mawjūdāt)* there is an existent whose existence is necessary through itself.

For otherwise that which exists would be restricted to contingent being: since what exists is restricted logically to necessary and contingent being.

And consequently nothing would exist at all: that is, nothing at all would be in existence, and this is contrary to actual fact *(al-wāqi').*

This is because contingent being, even though multiple, etc.: This means that the nature of contingent being *(ṭabī'at al-mumkin),* even though it is multiple in its singulars *(muta'addid al-afrād),* is not self-sufficient, etc. In short, contingent being is a species *(naw')* and a reality *(ḥaqīqah)* which does not exist through itself, nor does it bring others into existence. Neither the multiplicity of its singulars nor the claim that they depend one upon the other [for their existence] is of any use here, since we are speaking about the species itself and its realization *(taḥaqquq).*

4. *Both in the mind and externally:* that is, mental existence *(al-wujūd al-dhihnī)* is identical with the mental existent *(al-mawjūd al-dhihnī)* and external existence *(al-wujūd al-khārijī)* is identical with the external existent *(al-mawjūd al-khārijī),* as has been transmitted from them.

This implies that existence is common to proper existences in name only, rather than in meaning, etc.: This calls for further investigation, however, because it is possible for the proper existences of things to be identical with those things, so that each of those things, in this respect, would be a singular of absolute existence *(al-wujūd al-muṭlaq)* and absolute existence would be common in meaning to the proper existences, which are identical with those things.

It might also be imagined that if the existence of a thing were identical with that very thing, this would require that it be necessarily existent on the basis of [the argument] that if the existence of a thing is identical with that thing, then that thing is self-existent *(mawjūd bi-dhātihi),* and that what is self-existent is necessarily existent. Such is not the case, however, because if what is meant by self-existent is something whose essence requires its existence and realization, then we should not admit that if the existence of a thing were identical with that thing it would be self-existent in that sense. On the other hand, if what is meant [by self-existent] is something whose essence is a source of its effects *(mabda' lil-āthār),* then it is admitted [that it is self-existent]. We should not admit, however, that what is self-existent is necessarily existent, because it is possible that its being a source of its effects is the creation of an agent *(maj'ūl li-fā'il),* just as its being qualified by existence is the creation of an agent if it is assumed that existence is superadded *(zā'id).*

Belief concerning something in an absolute sense endures: that is, existence in an absolute sense. *Even though belief as to its particular characteristic ceases:* that is, the particular characteristic of existence. In other words we may believe something to exist but, nevertheless, be uncertain as to whether it is necessarily existent, or is a substance or an accident. The combination of this belief with that uncertainty indicates that existence is a common term with respect to meaning.

And because [*existence*] *is subject to division in meaning:* in that we can say existence is either necessary *(wājibī)* or contingent *(mumkinī).* Other methods of demonstrating the falsity of this position may be found in works dealing with this subject, and one who wishes to examine this question in detail may refer to them.

What they meant by identity was indistinguishability in the external world: He restricted the statement to external existence, although the previous discussion included mental existence as well, since there is no difference between the two existences in what has been mentioned so far. He therefore left the case of mental existence to determination by analogy *(al-muqāyasah).*

5. *The existences of things are these portions:* that is, all existent things including the Necessary Existent. In objection it may be said *(wa-fīhi)* that attributed existence *(al-wujūd al-muḍāf),* insofar as it is attributed [to something], is dependent on that thing's being [already] qualified by existence and being existent. Thus if that thing existed through that existence attributed [to it], a circle would result. Furthermore, attributed [existence] is a purely mental entity *(amr ma'qūl maḥḍ),* and mental entities in their opinion are nonexistent. Qualification *(al-ittiṣāf),* however, is a relation *(nisbah)* whose realization in actuality depends on the realization of its two terms *(al-ṭarafayn).* This would also imply that the existence of the Necessary Existent depended on its apprehension *(al-ta'aqqul)* [by minds]. Furthermore, if the proper existence of a thing consisted of absolute existence together with attribution, then it would have to subsist in that thing, although it is obvious that such a concept does not subsist in that thing, for the meaning of existent is that which has existence, not that which has the existence of that thing.

To all of these [objections] it can be answered that if the cause of the existence of a thing is realized, then that thing becomes such that the intellect *(al-'aql)* abstracts *(yantazi')* from it the concept of existence during apprehension *(al-ta'aqqul),* not that that concept subsists in it in actuality. Thus the meaning of an existent is that which has existence in this sense, that is, that from which existence is abstracted during apprehension. And since this implies the validity of attributing existence to the thing, the [term] attributed existence *(al-wujūd al-muḍāf)* was used as an expression for the thing's existence. This should be considered carefully *(fa-ta'ammal).*

6. *Similar to this are the whiteness of snow and the whiteness of ivory:* If it be said that snow is not really white, as has been

shown in the works dealing with this subject *(kamā buyyina fī mawḍi'ihi),* we should answer that insofar as it is seen as white, it can validly be used as a simile.

[2] *What is meant by the portion of the concept of being is that concept itself together with the particular characteristic of attribution, so that there is no multiplicity at all:* It has been said that the portion must have a particular characteristic *(khuṣūṣīyah)* which tips the scales in favor of *(turajjiḥ)* its attribution to one particular quiddity rather than another, since the absolute concept itself *(nafs al-mafhūm al-muṭlaq)* does not require its attribution to any particular thing. On the contrary, it is equally related to all things. The answer to this is what has already been said with respect to the question of abstraction *(mas'alat al-intizā').*[1]

Is only with respect to the mind, for in the external world there is not something which is the quiddity, etc.: The gist of this is that the multiplicity of existences is only in the mind, whereas the being-in-existence *(mawjūdīyah)* of this existent is not in the mind. Here it may be objected *(wa-fīhi)* that this requires that the quiddity not be qualified by existence, since you have concluded that none of these hypothetical existences is outside the mind. One can answer that whoever says this is denying *(māni'),* that that is his less extensive support *(sanaduhu al-akhaṣṣ),* and that to refute a less extensive support is useless.[2] Nor can the objection be answered by the doctrine of abstraction *(mas'alat al-intizā'),* since that is not the position of the philosophers on the question of existence.[3]

Even if this be admitted, the unity of subject, etc.: that is, even if it be admitted that the general concept and the portion existed externally, they would nevertheless be one, since only particulars have [external] existence, the existence of universals in the external world being identical with the existence of their existent particulars. Thus there would be but one single entity in the external world. What is meant by the predicate *(al-maḥmūl)* is the essential universal *(al-kullī al-dhātī)* and by the subject *(al-mawḍū')* the singular *(al-fard)* existing externally.

As has been substantiated in works dealing with this subject, etc.: where they escaped from the endless chain *(al-tasalsul)* [which would result] if a quiddity were qualified by existence externally, for the subsistence of an attribute in something depends on the existence of that in which it subsists *(thubūt ṣifah li-shay' fara' 'alā wujūd al-muthbat lahu).*[4]

That mental existence is of two types: basic [*existence*] *like the existence of knowledge:* It is as if he had made mental existence *(al-wujūd al-'aqlī)* more general than either existence in the mind *(al-wujūd fī al-'aql),* or the existence of the mind *(al-wujūd lil-'aql),* or of the intelligible *(lil-ma'qūl).* Knowledge does not exist in the mind, nor is it something [merely] conceived *(mutaṣawwar)* or perceived *(mash'ūr bihi).* On the contrary, it exists externally in itself and subsists in the mind and is established in it. Similarly, external existence is not something [merely] conceived but is something which subsists in something conceived when it is conceived. It follows from this that existence exists outside the mind, but that it subsists in conceived and perceived mental entities existing in the mind. This, however, is contrary to [their] position, for it has been demonstrated that existence does not exist except insofar as the question is interpreted according to [the doctrine of] abstraction.

For its dependence on His knowledge of it is inconsistent with its being necessary: Furthermore, His being qualified by knowledge depends on His being qualified by existence. Thus, if His being qualified by existence depended, in turn, on knowledge and His being qualified by it, a circle *(al-dawr)* would result.

7. *Identical with the essence in the case of the Necessary Existent:* that is, the Necessary Existent is one of the singulars of general [existence], unlike contingents, which are not singulars of it but rather things in which its singulars subsist.

8. *Ramification:* The purpose of this is to point out that the position taken by the unitarian Ṣūfīs *(al-Ṣūfīyah al-muwaḥḥidah)*[1] on the question of existence is not inconsistent with the rational intellect *(al-'aql al-naẓarī).*

9. *That existence is predicated by analogy, etc.:* The philosophers used as proof for their position that this concept was

accidental with respect to its singulars of dissimilar realities the fact that it was an analogous term *(mushakhik).* This is therefore an answer to them.

This [*argument*], *however, is refuted by the case of the accident:* Furthermore, with respect to their statement: "nor is their essential attribute one" if what is meant by essential attribute *(al-dhātī)* is the absolute attribute *(al-muṭlaq)* which is sometimes qualified by strength *(al-qūwah)* and sometimes by weakness *(al-ḍu'f),* then it is certainly one as well as essential. However, if what is meant by it is the attribute conditioned *(al-muqayyad)* by strength or weakness, then the multiplicity is admitted. This, however, does not imply the multiplicity of the aforementioned absolute essential attribute *(al-dhātī al-muṭlaq).*

The source of the error here is in imagining that the strong attribute *(al-qawī)* insofar as it is qualified by strength is an essential attribute or that the weak attribute *(al-ḍa'īf)* insofar as it is qualified by weakness is an essential attribute. On the contrary strength is an accidental quality inhering in the essential attribute after its realization within some of its singulars. Similarly weakness is an accidental quality inhering in it in some of its other singulars. Even if it were admitted [that the strong or weak attribute was essential], the unity of the absolute attribute is not inconsistent with its being essential also, for what is essential to an essential attribute is also essential.

Also a difference, etc.: This is either a particular *(naqḍ tafṣīlī)* or a general refutation *(naqḍ ijmālī)*[1] connected specifically with the matter of the quiddity *(māddat al-māhīyah),* that is, the quiddity of measure *(al-miqdār)* differs as between one cubit and two cubits with respect to increase and decrease, although it is one in your opinion as well as in the thing itself *(fī nafs al-amr).*[2]

[5] *Is not true:* since it is obvious that the concept which comes to mind when we say [in Persian] "to exist" *(būdan)* cannot be predicated of the Necessary Existent, nor can the state resulting from this infinitive *(al-ḥāṣil bi-al-maṣdar),*[1] that is, "being-in-existence" *(būdagī).*

How can it be true when they themselves explicitly state that it is a second intelligible: What they explicitly stated was that it was a second intelligible with respect to contingents *(al-mumkināt),* since existence inheres in them in the mind rather than externally. They did not state that it was a second intelligible with respect to the Necessary Existent, since He exists in Himself, not through the inherence of a singular of existence in Him. It is thus possible that with respect to Him it is not a second intelligible. Indeed, one knows intuitively that what is customarily conceived by the word "existence" is not predicated univocally *(muwāṭa'atan)* of Him, as has been mentioned previously.

10. *As long as one does not mean by this:* that is, by his statement "every light and knowledge," a difference in reality, but rather means by it a difference in manifestation *(al-ẓuhūr).*

11. *Of all worldly attachments:* This is an allusion to passing away *(al-fanā')* from bodily human existence.

And the rules of rational thought: This is an allusion to [the fact that] when spiritual human existence *(al-wujūd al-basharī al-rūḥānī)* passes away, then the real passing away *(al-fanā' al-ḥaqīqī),* which does not return its possessor, is realized.

A revealing light: This is the opening up of the eye of insight *('ayn al-baṣīrah).*

At the appearance of a level beyond the level of the intellect: in the sense that the intellect is incapable of perceiving it and attaining it with its rational faculty, not in the sense that the intellect denies it and declares it impossible. This interpretation is supported by his saying later:[1] "The intention [here], however, is merely to eliminate any logical impossibility, etc.," for what the intellect which is free of the taint of the estimation *(al-wahm)* denies and declares impossible is, indeed, impossible. Should you say that this is inconsistent with the quotation from al-Shaykh Ṣadr al-Dīn al-Qūnawī in the gloss to this section[2] where he says: "They may thus judge impossible many things which, for those possessing intellects unrestricted by such limitations, are possible or even necessary of occurrence"; I should answer that his statement: "Intellects have a boundary at which they halt insofar as they are limited in their thoughts" is an allusion to those intellects imprisoned within the confines of rational thought *(al-fikr)* and speculation *(al-naẓar).* The intellect which is imprisoned within the confines of rational thought draws upon the estimative faculty *(al-qūwah al-wahmīyah)* and does not proceed except with assistance from the estimation, as the philosophers have demonstrated at length in works dealing with this subject *(fī mawḍi'ihi)*. Moreover, it is possible for this intellect to be overcome by the estimation at certain times, so that it clings to the premisses of the estimation *(muqaddimāt al-wahm)* and judges some of the mystically revealed truths *(al-kashfīyāt)* to be impossible.[3] Thus, at this stage the intellect is not a pure intellect *('aql khāliṣ)*. However, if it were to purify itself from seeking the judgment of the estimation, it would not judge impossible things which have been substantiated. This is a matter which is agreed upon, and the inconsistency you have mentioned is thus eliminated. We could also answer that what he meant by impossibility was extreme improbability *(ghāyat al-istib'ād)*, that is, that the intellect thinks many things so improbable that it all but declares them impossible.

[10] *Because of a remainder of uncertainty:* in connection with the contents of what was previously affirmed or denied.

Remaining: that is, subsistent *(thābit)*. The word "remaining" is for resemblance *(al-mushākalah)*.[1]

12. *For many of the philosophers and theologians have taken the position that natural universals exist in the external world:* Their position was that the universal human intelligible reality *(al-ḥaqīqah al-'aqlīyah al-insānīyah al-kullīyah)* in itself was not individuated in any external or even mental individuation, but rather became individuated after its realization within its singulars through their individuation, so that within each individuation it was identical with that individuation. Thus in Zayd it is identical with Zayd and is qualified with his characteristic and distinguishing attributes and acts. In 'Amr it is identical with 'Amr and is qualified by his attributes and acts, and likewise in Khālid, although in itself and in conformity with its own essence and reality it is devoid of all of these attributes. Thus, this reality, which is single and absolute in its own plane, is multiple and determined in the planes of its singulars conforming to them rather than to its own essence.

18. *Moreover, if it is absolute, then the thesis is proven:* Should you say: What is absolute in this sense is a natural universal. Therefore, if the thesis is proven that the Source of Existents *(Mabda' al-Mawjūdāt)* is this absolute, then the Necessary Existent *(al-Wājib)* must, in their opinion, be a natural universal, although this is not their position. We should answer: We do not admit that, considered as an absolute, it is a natural universal. On the contrary, it is possible for it to be an existent which is individuated in itself in such a way as to be consistent with *(yujāmi')* all individuations and not reject any specific individuation, as the author substantiated below where he said: "It is evident, etc.,"[1] and in the appended gloss where he said: "Consequently, what is meant, etc."[2]

19. *Then it cannot in itself be individuated:* that is, not be individuated at all, or else be individuated with an individuation external to it. If such were not the case, it would have to be individuated with an individuation which was identical with it. We should then shift the argument to it, for either it would terminate in an individuation which in itself was not individuated, or an endless chain would result. Should you say: If every individuated thing were identical with its individuation, there would not exist multiple entities *(umūr muta'addidah),* so how could an endless chain be imagined? We should answer: There are entities which are multiple through multiplicity conceived in the mind *(ta'addud i'tibārī).* One cannot reply to this that the endless chain would then consist of mental entities *(umūr i'tibārīyah),*[1] because we should then say that being conceived in the mind *(al-i'tibār)* is an attribute of the multiplicity, whereas that which is multiple consists of real [externally existent] entities *(umūr ḥaqīqīyah),* as is evident.

[16] *There is no objection to the inseparability, etc.:* This means that the concomitance *(luzūm)* of an individuation with an absolute essence *(dhāt muṭlaqah)* and the impossibility of this individuation's being separated from it is not inconsistent with *(la yunāfī)* its absoluteness in itself and with respect to its own plane, as is the actual case, in their opinion, with respect to the Transcendent Essence *(al-dhāt al-muta'āliyah),* with which all of the eternal and everlasting individuations are concomitant.

20. *And which the intellect, should it conceive of it in a certain individuation, would be unable to imagine as being common:* Yet neither would its individuation in this manner be such that it would exclude its manifestation in the forms of the universals which exist in the mind and which are true of and predicated of their singulars. Thus, with respect to a certain manifestation it would be a natural universal and with respect to its manifestation in the form of Zayd, for example, be a real [externally existing] particular *(juz'ī ḥaqīqī),* but with respect to its own essence be neither a universal nor a real particular.

21. *Consider this by analogy with the rational soul which pervades the parts of the body:* For example, with respect to its connection with [the organ of] sight, it is manifest in its form and is imbued with its effects and qualities, and with respect to its connection with [the organ of] hearing is imbued with the qualities of hearing. Similarly, with respect to its relationship to the physical faculty *(al-qūwah al-ṭabī'īyah),* it takes nourishment, digests, grows, reproduces, and so forth, and with respect to the physical faculty *(al-qūwah al-nafsānīyah),* it perceives and moves. Further analogies can be drawn from this, for it is a model for the aforementioned absolute essence.

Or even better by analogy with the perfectional rational soul: that is, the perfect *(kāmilah)* [soul]. Choosing the relative adjective *(al-nisbah)* with its suffixed *yā'*[1] is a constant practice of this group because of the elegance and novelty associated with it. The progression implied by the use of the expression "or even better" has several aspects. The first is that the rational soul does not really become manifest in the forms of the parts and faculties of the body, but rather is qualified with a different attribute with respect to each one of them. The second is that the body with all of its parts and faculties is like a single thing, whereas spiritualized bodies *(al-abdān al-mutarawḥinah)* are entities each one of which is separate from the other. The third aspect is that the effects of each one of these [spiritualized bodies] are different from and contrary to the effects of any other. All of these are aspects of the similarity [of the perfectional rational soul] to what is being considered, [namely, the aforementioned absolute essence]. This is thus a closer and more perfect similarity.

23. *Similar to this are the spirits of the perfect:* that is, after death, as is immediately suggested by the way we say: the spirit of so-and-so, and the spirits of those people.[1]

Seeing him: that is, the Truth *(al-Ḥaqq),* may He be praised, *exalted above time and place:* that is above their encompassing [Him], *realized that the relation of all times and places to him was one and the same:* and similar to His relation to all things whether temporal or spatial, abstract or material.

For him to appear in every time and every place: that is, in association with every time and place.

And in any form he desired: even the form of time and place.

24. *Analogy:* This is a perfect analogy, even though there is a difference between the appearance of the form in the mirror and His appearance in His cognitive and concrete places of manifestation *(majālīhi al-'ilmīyah wa-al-'aynīyah),* since He is what constitutes *(maqawwim)* His places of manifestation. Furthermore, He exists in reality, whereas His places of manifestation do not really exist but rather have reflected upon them the light of existence *(nūr al-wujūd),* just as a wall has reflected upon it the reflection of red paper, although the wall itself is not in reality red. As for the aspect of similarity [between them], it is that [both] appear in different forms while [their] unity remains as it was without any change at all, and that [their] appearance in certain [forms] does not prevent [their] appearing in others.

25. *And, in the opinion of their two leaders:* namely, Abū al-Ḥasan al-Ash'arī, who is the leader of the Ash'arites, and Abū al-Ḥusayn al-Baṣrī, the leader of the Mu'tazilites, as was previously mentioned.

And the denial of a partner to Him: with respect to the attributes of lordship *(ṣifāt al-rubūbīyah)* and the qualities of divinity *(nu'ūt al-ilāhīyah),* for such denial has been agreed upon. Nevertheless, the Ṣūfīs hold [in addition] that He has no partner with respect to existence and realization *(al-taḥaqquq).* Thus, the meaning of "There is no god but God" is "There is no existent but God."

In fact, it is impossible to imagine in Him: that is, in absolute existence in the preceding sense by which I mean the reality of real and simple existence *(ḥaqīqat al-wujūd al-basīṭ al-ḥaqīqī)* denuded of all other individuations but individuated in itself in such a way as to be consistent with *(yujāmi')* all individuations although some are exclusive of others.

Is either an existent or attributive existence: The word "or" is merely to give a choice in expression *(lil-takhyīr fī al-'ibārah).*[1]

Which is nothing: either cognitively *('ilman)* or concretely *('aynan).* This is the reality of nonexistence *(al-'adam)* rather than the concept of it which occurs in the mind, for the latter is a mental existent *(mawjūd dhihnī)* included within the aforementioned absolute existent *(al-mawjūd al-muṭlaq)* and is one of the individuations of absolute existence *(al-wujūd al-muṭlaq).* Even if it were assumed to be something, it would nevertheless not share with Him the attributes of lordship.

26. *But is rather His being considered as He is in Himself:* that is, His unity is established *(thābitah)* insofar as His essence is considered as it is in itself and insofar as there is no duality *(ithnaynīyah)* [in it], rather than superadded *(zā'idah).* In other words, unity, like all other attributes, is identical with Him with respect to reality and the thing itself *(nafs al-amr)* but other than He with respect to [mental] consideration *(al-i'tibār)* and intellection *(al-ta'aqqul).*

From which are derived the unity and the multiplicity: This means that they are among the forms of the individuations of this unity, just as the various levels of the sciences *(marātib al-'ulūm)* are forms of the individuations of His knowledge, may He be praised.

Moreover, if it: that is, this [essential] unity. What is meant is that the essence, with respect to this unity, has two aspects *(i'tibārān).*

It is called oneness: as opposed to singleness *(al-wāḥidīyah),* not essential oneness *(al-aḥadīyah al-dhātīyah),* for oneness without qualification *(qayd)* is what is opposed to singleness.

28. *As for the Ṣūfīs, they took the position that God's attributes were identical with His essence with respect to existence*

but other than it with respect to intellection: It might be imagined from the literal meaning of this expression that there is no difference between the position of the philosophers and that of the Ṣūfīs, since it would appear that to differ *(al-taghāyur)* with respect to concept *(bi-ḥasab al-mafhūm)* and to differ with respect to intellection *(bi-ḥisab al-taʿaqqul)* are one and the same. Upon examination, however, the distinction between them is verified, because the difference between essence and attribute with respect to concept is that the two concepts are different, but what they are true of is one and the same, whereas what is meant by difference with respect to intellection in the doctrine of the Ṣūfīs is that just as the concept of the attribute differs from that of the essence, so also does what the attribute is true of differ from what the essence is true of. However, this difference is with respect to intellection and individuational cognitive existence *(al-wujūd al-ʿilmī al-taʿayyunī).*[1] Thus, God's knowledge is one of the individuations of His essence in exactly the same way and without any difference as are separate entities *(al-umūr al-munfaṣilah),* for everything which is other than He is one of His individuations. There is no difference in this respect between attributes and separate entities, for an attribute is only distinguished from other things by a relationship *(nisbah)* and some other characteristic *(khuṣūṣīyah).* Effectuation *(al-taʾthīr),* however, pertains to the essence rather than to the attributes. Thus the source of revelation *(mabdaʾ al-inkishāf)* is His essence, not His attribute.[2] Let this be pondered. God, in respect to being the source of revelation *(mabdaʾīyat al-inkishāf),* is knowledge *(ʿilm),* and in respect to that knowledge He is knowing *(ʿālim).* However, every respect relating to knowledge is realized only in knowledge.[3] Thus, what knowledge is really true of is not His essence but rather His essence in a certain respect,[4] and that is a separate entity *(ghayr)* and contingent. Similarly what "necessary" *(al-wājib)* is true of is not His essence itself but His essence in a certain respect, namely, [in respect to] the attribution of necessity. Thus His essence is the denotation *(miṣdāq)* of "necessary," not what "necessary" is true of. All the other attributes and respects which are predicated of His essence are analogous, for in themselves, and in the plane in which they are themselves, they are neither attribute *(na't),* nor name *(ism),* nor description *(rasm).* This should be remembered. The author stated this clearly in the gloss, where he said: "Thus His attributes are relations, respects, and attributions which attach to the transcendent essence with respect to its connections."[5]

Denied His attributes: The intent of the philosophers is probably the denial of effective attributes *(al-ṣifāt al-mu'aththirah).* Such [effective attributes] are realized neither in the external world nor in intellection *(fī al-ta'aqqul).* You are aware that what is in the intellect is not effective, but that what is effective is the essence as well as some of the effects resulting from the essence. Thus their position is not inconsistent with the doctrine of the Ṣufīs. Let this be understood.

Completely different: that is, different in concrete real existence *(al-wujūd al-ḥaqīqī al-'aynī).*

29. *He also said: "Our essences are imperfect":* This statement appears to be closer to the doctrine of the philosophers. However, what is intended by it is what accords with the doctrine of the Ṣūfīs.

In no way is in need: with respect to His existence or the attributes of His perfection, *of anything:* other than His essence. *Sufficient for everything:* that is, for all things, *with respect to everything:* that is, with respect to everything that befits it by way of existence and its consequents *(tawābi').*

Has no duality in it whatsoever: with respect to actual fact *(al-wāqi')* and real existence. The duality exists only with respect to cognition *(al-'ilm)* and intellection *(al-ta'aqqul).*

30. *All are in agreement:* that is, all of the three groups.

They found no difficulty with respect to the connection of His knowledge, etc.: This means that something superadded to the essence can be supposed by the intellect to be a form corresponding to an external entity, whereas the essence itself cannot. There is thus no difficulty *(ishkāl)* with respect to the mere possibility that His knowledge be connected to the thing known by being a form corresponding to it. As for whether the connection of His knowledge to something originated necessitates its being originated, this is another question.

31. *Apprehends His essence by means of His essence:* that is, not by means of an attribute superadded to His essence.

It follows that He apprehends multiplicity: because knowledge of the complete cause *(al-'illah al-tāmmah)* implies knowledge of the effect *(al-ma'lūl).* The gist *(ḥāṣil)* of the doctrine of al-Shaykh [Ibn Sīnā) is that His knowledge of His essence is identical with His essence and is thus presentational *(ḥuḍūrī),* whereas His knowledge of what is other than He is superadded to His essence and is representational *(ḥuṣūlī)* like the knowledge of contingent beings.[1]

32. *Both an agent and a recipient at the same time:* that is, an agent of something and a recipient of that same thing, for this is impossible in their opinion.

By attributes that are neither relative nor negative: but, on the contrary, real *(ḥaqīqīyah),* although the philosophers limited the attributes to these two.

A substratum for His multiple and contingent effects: some of which are originated. This is impossible in the opinion of the theologians who allow His being a substratum for nonoriginated things.

That His first effect is not distinct: for the first effect would then be [His] knowledge of the first effect, since [His] knowledge of a thing is prior to that thing, whereas the existence of a thing is posterior to [His] knowledge of it.

And that He does not bring into existence anything which is distinct from Him through His own essence directly, etc.: Their position is that the First brings everything into existence through His essence without the mediacy *(tawassuṭ)* of anything in that.

Positions of the philosophers: that is, the doctrines *(masā'il)* of the philosophers.

Plato, who affirmed, etc: after he had affirmed [His] knowledge. This applies also to his statement "and the Peripatetics, who affirmed." The details and substantiation of their doctrines are to be sought from the appropriate works on this subject *(min mawḍi'ihi).*

33. *The commentator then indicated, etc.:* The gist of his position is that His knowledge of His essence and of the first effect is not by means of a form distinct [from Him], whereas His knowledge of other things is by means of forms impressed *(ṣuwar munṭabiʿah)* in the first effect and in the other intellectual substances *(al-jawāhir al-ʿaqlīyah).*

Other than the form of his own essence through which he is what he is: The word "form" is sometimes applied to an entity resembling the source of revelation *(mabdaʾ al-inkishāf),* by which I mean knowledge, or it may be applied to the thing itself at the time it is perceived, and by this I mean the thing known *(al-maʿlūm).* It is this second meaning which is intended here, as is indicated by his saying: "through which he is what he is." It should be understood that the commentator's thesis here is that the knowledge of the First is not by means of the occurrence of a form in Him, and that it is possible for Him, on the contrary, to know a thing either by means of that very thing or through the occurrence of a form not inhering in Him. He supports this with apparently presumptive premisses *(muqaddimāt ẓannīyah ẓāhirīyah)* which conclude with his saying: "The foregoing have been presented."[1] He then specifies the thesis and presents it in detail by stating that God knows His essence through His essence and knows the first effect through the essence of the first effect and by means of its presence *(ḥuḍūr)* and occurrence *(ḥuṣūl)* to Him. He knows all other existents through the occurrence of their forms in the intellects *(al-ʿuqūl).* This, however, is also a rhetorical rather than a demonstrative method producing, as it were, a certain conviction *(iqnāʿ).* It should be known that the word "form" in construct [with "his own essence"] gives the illusion of duality *(tuwahhim al-ithnaynīyah)* as between essence and form, and, if the matter were not obvious, it would have been better and clearer to say: Just as an apprehender in perceiving his own essence does not require a form other than his own essence, but on the contrary apprehends his essence through his essence. . . .

By means of a form which you have imagined or brought to mind: that is, by means of a form which you have generated originally, or which you have brought to mind after the thing perceived is no longer present.[2]

Indeed, the only things that double are your considerations, etc.: That is, you [originally] had one consideration, which was your knowledge of your essence. This doubled, and there occurred to you another consideration, namely, your knowledge of the form of your essence. We have already shown that the form of the essence is only a word and that no form is [really] there. If what is meant by "form" is [the essence] insofar as it is a form, that is, the essence with the qualification of being known *(ma' waṣf al-ma'lūmīyah),* then there is still no form in that sense. The correct way of exemplifying this, [by analogy to] the knowledge of a human, is with the form which emanates from someone when he apprehends something different from himself. The order of composition *(sawq al-tarkīb)* also requires this.[3] It would, therefore, be more correct to say: Indeed, the only things that double are your considerations connected with that thing[4] and that form.

Only: that is, not [connected] with the form of some other entity after that. This is what is meant by the author's statement in the gloss: "That is, not the form."[5]

Or by way of superimposition: [This must be understood] in conjunction with "double," according to the context. That is, your considerations double or are superimposed [one upon the other]. The word "or" is merely to give a choice in expression *(lil-takhyīr fī al-'ibārah).*[6]

If such is your situation with respect to what emanates from you with the participation of something besides yourself: although what emanates from you does not really emanate from you but only apparently does so. This, however, is still another reason for the remoteness.[7]

34. *Is not inferior to its occurrence to its recipient:* that is, the proximity *(qurb)* of the thing to its agent is not less *(anqaṣ)* than its proximity to its recipient insofar as it occurs to it.

Therefore, the essential effects: that is, those which have no intermediary whatsoever between them and their agent.

Of the Apprehender and Agent through His essence: ["through His essence" is] connected with both "Apprehender" and "Agent."

Occur: that is, it is possible for them to occur to Him, because the premisses imply only the possibility of that. For this reason he undertook to prove it again by saying: "The foregoing having been presented. . . ."[1] Up to that point he had made clear only that his thesis, namely, that God is a knower without the inherence of a form in Him, is something rationally possible. The remainder [of his argument] consists of characterizing *(tashkhīṣ)* the nature *(kayfīyah)* of the thesis in specific terms *('alā al-ta'yīn)* and demonstrating it.

[31]a. *And His knowledge of those substances is their existence and their emanation from Him. His knowledge of those things whose forms are impressed in those substances is by means of the presence of those forms which are impressed in them:* It should be understood that the forms of all the other intellectual substances are impressed in the first effect, that is, the first intellect. Thus, the First knows them by means of these forms, just as He knows the other things whose forms are inscribed *(al-murtasimah)* in the [intellectual] substances. It is apparent from his position[1] that God's knowledge of the first substance is its existence and its emanation from Him, and that His knowledge of the other caused existents *(al-mawjūdāt al-ma'lūlah)* is by means of the impressed forms, since there is no necessity for asserting such a point of view *(i'tibār)* except in the case of the first emanation *(al-ṣādir al-awwal)* even though the literal meaning of al-Ṭūsī's expression: "Since the intellectual substances, etc."[2] is conducive to what the author has mentioned.

35. *The existence of the first effect is thus identical with the First's apprehension of it:* What follows from the premisses is that the first effect is known to God through itself, not through an additional form. Then, since it is necessary that there be to whatever is qualified by being known a certain existence and occurrence, if not in intellection then externally, it is established that the first effect in its external existence and occurrence[1] is present to Him. Thus its occurrence in the external world and God's apprehension of it are one and the same. It is thus established that the existence of the first effect is identical

with God's apprehension of it. However, since the thesis was the specification *(ta'yīn)* and characterization *(tashkhīṣ)* of [God's] apprehension, it would have been more appropriate to say: The First's apprehension of it is identical with its existence.[2]

Then, since everything is caused by God either with or without an intermediary *(wāsiṭah),* we say: This proof implies that His knowledge of all existents is identical with their existence. This is so because the First together with the first effect is the cause of the second effect, and the First's knowledge of His essence and of the first effect is the cause of His knowledge of the second effect. Then, just as there is no difference between the two causes, so also there is no difference between the two effects, and so on up to the last effect.

[31]b. *And His knowledge of His effects is their existence in His presence:* that is, as implied by al-Ṭūsī's proof, as we mentioned above, although al-Ṭūsī did not make this claim except in the case of the first effect. So keep in mind what is intended.

37. *Because those intellectual substances are contingent, they are therefore originated:* The word "originated" is the predicate of *anna.*[1] His meaning is that they are originated through essential origination *(al-ḥudūth al-dhātī)* and known prior to their existence by priority according to rank *(qablīyah bi-ḥasab al-martabah),* and what is prior *(al-sābiq)* cannot in any way be identical with what is posterior *(al-masbūq).*

As [God's] active and eternal knowledge: that is, the source of [His] action, which includes the giving of existence *(i'ṭā' al-wujūd).*

And with particulars in a universal manner also: in accordance with what is well known and apparent from his position.

And which is prior to the existence of things: that is, according to rank.

With respect to the most noble of His attributes: namely, [His] knowledge.

Otherwise, it would have been impossible to give them existence: because [God], the Knowing and Wise, gives to whoever is deserving what he deserves in accordance with His wisdom.

Thus His giving depends on His knowledge.

Is valid only if they: that is, the multiple entities.

If, on the other hand, they are identical with Him: as in the opinion of the unveiled *(al-makshūfīn)* who say: There is nothing in existence except a single individual *('ayn wāḥidah).* These are the verifying Ṣūfīs *(al-ṣūfīyah al-muḥaqqiqūn),* who assert the unity of existence *(waḥdat al-wujūd),* may God sanctify their souls.

In reality, however, He is neither subsistent, nor is He a substratum: This means, then, that the secret as to why subsistence *(al-ḥulūl)* is not impossible is that, in reality, there is no real quality of being subsistent *(ḥāllīyah)* or being a substratum *(maḥallīyah),* but rather, a single really existent reality which is seen as subsistent and as a substratum, as a substance and as an accident, as abstracted [from matter] *(mujarrad),* as completely material and as pure fantasy. In reality, no multiplicity or change hovers around its real and essential unity. It is now as it was. Neither adoration nor really being adored, neither real pleasure nor real pain, whether they be transitory as in this world or everlasting as in the next, is incompatible with it. Nor are real and actual proximity, distance, union, and separation, as you see and observe with all their characteristics *(al-khuṣūṣīyāt)* occurring in the universe *(al-'ālamīn),* incompatible [with it].

40. *This is analogous to what has been said, etc.:* Genus and difference exist through one existence at the level of the specific quiddity *(al-māhīyah al-naw'īyah),* and knowledge of the quiddity is in reality knowledge of the genus and difference but of a sort in which the genus is not distinguished from the difference and neither of them is distinguished from the species. Nevertheless the relation of this knowledge, as it exists in the mind, to the species, genus and difference is [one] reality without differentiation *(min ghayr tafāwut).* Both [genus and difference] have another existence, also in the mind, of a different sort, in which the genus and difference are distinguished. Their two existences are then different from the existence of the species.[1] The foregoing is a perfect analogy *(naẓīr tāmm)* to the essence of the Truth in the doctrine of the unitarian Ṣūfīs

(al-ṣūfīyah al-muwaḥḥidah), according to which His effects are His modes *(shu'ūnāt)* and aspects *(i'tibārāt)* which are fused *(al-mundamijah)* in His essence without being distinguished at the level of His essential unity. This is contrary to the position of the philosophers, according to which the Truth's effects are really separate entities *(aghyār)* and substances distinct from His essence, may He be praised and exalted above what does not befit Him. The analogy is thus not entirely applicable to their position.

41. *How can they deny, etc.:* They also said: [God's] decision *(al-qaḍā')* is equivalent to [His] knowledge of things and their states as a whole *(ijmālan)* in the world of intellects *('ālam al-'uqūl),* whereas [His] decree *(al-qadar)* is the equivalent of [His] knowledge of them in particular *(tafṣīlan)* in the world of souls *('ālam al-nufūs)* and encompasses the characteristics of substances and attributes as well as the characteristics of qualifications *(al-quyūd)* and conditions *(al-sharā'iṭ)* insofar as such particularization and characterization are possible. Primary providence *(al-'ināyah al-ūlā)* is the First's knowledge [both] as a whole and in particular and encompasses what is in both worlds *(al-'ālamayn)*[1] exactly. This is an unequivocal assertion of [His] knowledge of particulars as particulars.

They also made the relation to Him of [*all*] *times, past, future, and present, a single relation, etc.:* A temporal existent *(al-mawjūd al-zamānī)* is situated in present time *(zamān al-ḥāl),* so that it lies between two sides, one of which is the past and the other the future, for the present is between the past and the future. As for that which is abstracted from time *(al-mujarrad 'an al-zamān),* since time is not an envelope for it, it is not situated in the present, but on the contrary is self-realized *(mutaḥaqqiq bi-nafsihī)* outside of time, and the past and future do not lie on either side of it. Thus the relation of the three times to it, insofar as it is outside of time, is a single relation just like the relation to it of all other existents separate from it. One cannot, therefore, say with respect to it that some things have passed it by and others have not yet occurred to it. This is quite apparent. When those immersed [in time and space] *(al-mutawaghghilūn)* claimed that knowledge of temporal things *(al-zamānīyāt),* specifically insofar as they are temporal, could only be conceived if the knower were also temporal, they imagined that [his] knowledge of what is in past time, for example, insofar as it is so, depends on a past time's being realized with respect to him. Such is not the case, however. On the contrary it depends only on the realization of a past time, even though with respect to something other than he. Thus, on the basis of their erroneous claim, they further claimed that whoever denies temporality of the Truth denies as well His knowledge of particulars. This is the reason the philosophers are accused of this.[2] Thus they forced upon the philosophers what they did. This should be understood.

44a. *The gist of this is that He knows:* that is, the gist of the two doctrines taken together, for the first doctrine indicates the first way [of knowing] and the second doctrine the second way.

Absentational knowledge of them prior to their existence: by priority of essence and rank *(qablīyah dhātīyah martabīyah).*

[37] *Followed by general existence:* that is, the essence known as absolute and pure receptivity *(al-qābilīyah al-maḥḍah al-muṭlaqah).* This is the first individuation *(al-ta'ayyun al-awwal).*[1] Should you say: The first individuation in this case is the cognitive relation *(al-nisbah al-'ilmīyah);* we should answer: Yes. However, general existence is the first of the separate individuations *(al-ta'ayyunāt al-munfaṣilah),* since the cognitive relation is one of the attributes of [God's] essence.

Of which the first is the first intellect: that is, of which the first is the quiddity of the first intellect, namely, that existent which in the language of the philosophers is called the first intellect.

And finally the individuations which attach to it: which are in the world of ideas and realities *('ālam al-ma'ānī wa-al-ḥaqā'iq).* This is the second individuation *(al-ta'ayyun al-thānī).*

And what is in its plane: like the ecstatic angels *(al-malā'ikah al-muhayyamah),* the perfect men *(al-kummal),* and others. This will be taken up in the substantiation of the emanation of multiplicity from unity.

44b. *I should answer yes:* This is to affirm [the limitation of His knowledge by the second way] to the present *(al-ḥālīyah),* although not in the sense imagined by the questioner and which caused him to object, but rather in the sense indicated by the author's statement: "since [all] times are the same in relation to Him as well as present with Him, as has just been mentioned."

In relation to Him are present: that is, the relation of all existents to Him is similar to the relation of existents in the present to a temporal existent *(al-mawjūd al-zamānī).*

46. *Our mere knowledge of what can possibly emanate from us:* namely, [our] external, voluntary acts. It should be known that we first conceive the act and then, successively, judge it to be good, find we have an inclination towards its occurrence, determine to bring about its occurrence, and finally move the [appropriate] organ. The act then emanates, and its effect is realized. As for the conception of the act, it flows from the Effusive Principle *(al-Mabda' al-Fayyāḍ)* without our choosing, as does also our knowledge of the goodness of its occurrence. However, that knowledge and belief is called choice *(ikhtīyār),* and that act thus emanates from this choice of ours. In that respect it is called voluntary, although in reality all of that is realized only through the Effusive Principle and exists only through His bringing it into existence without our having control over any part of it. On the contrary, we are only substrata for the occurrence *(jarayān)* of these entities *(al-umūr),* including the act, from the Real Agent *(al-Fā'il al-Ḥaqīqī).* Thus, our choice is in reality compulsion *(jabr).* This, however, is only a summary substantiation of the question of compulsion and choice, for a detailed substantiation requires a lengthy exposition inappropriate for this chapter.

Is what follows upon [*our*] *desire which, in turn, stems from* [*our*] *knowledge of the goal:* The author meant by "desire" inclination towards the act's occurrence, as we have mentioned. For this reason he made it stem from the knowledge of the goal, which is the knowledge of the goodness of the act. By inclination he meant the determination to cause [the act] to occur, and for that reason he made it stem from desire.

47. *For it:* that is, the benefit, *is a purpose and goal:* What results from an act is called a goal *(ghāyah),* considering that the act terminates with it. It is called a final cause *('illah ghā'īyah),* however, considering that the belief that it will result from the act serves as a motive for bringing about the occurrence of the act. It is in this latter respect that a goal is unanimously considered impossible with respect to the Creator, may He be praised.

48. *He does not possess a state similar, etc.:* nor a state resembling muscular power, etc.

Emanates from Him through the essence alone: It might be imagined from this that the essence takes the place of these things. However, what is to be understood from his statement: "They make His essence and His knowledge together, etc." is that it is the cognitive relation *(al-nisbah al-'ilmīyah)* which takes their place. Thus, "the essence alone" is to be taken in a more general sense than one which excludes or includes consideration of any other matter with it.

49. *But with respect to intellection:* as was mentioned with respect to knowledge itself and all of its aspects.[1]

50a. *All of the religionists:* that is, those who believe in one of the divine religions or creeds.

[38] *That is, both of them are proper for Him in accordance with varying motives, etc.:* What is to be understood from the totality of his argument is that the difference between the position of the theologian and that of the philosopher is that in the view of the philosopher action is a concomitant *(lāzim)* of the Creator's essence. This is based on its being a concomitant of His volition *(al-mashī'ah),* which, in turn, is a concomitant of His essence, for the concomitant of a concomitant is a concomitant. Such is not the case in the view of the theologian, for he does not make the basis *(mustanad)* of action a concomitant of His essence. This presents a difficulty, however, because, in the view of the theologians His action is a concomitant of His will *(al-irādah),* for they said: If He wills, He acts, and His will must be concomitant with Him, for it is an attribute of perfection *(ṣifat kamāl),* and its nonexistence would be an imperfection *(naqṣ).* Therefore, if it were possible for

will to be separated from Him, imperfection would be possible [for Him]. This, however, is absurd *(muḥāl),* for just as imperfection is absurd with respect to Him, so also is the possibility of imperfection absurd. Thus, if will is concomitant, then the action concomitant with it is also concomitant. Therefore, the nonexistence of the action is impossible in the thing itself *(fī nafs al-amr).* It is apparent, then, that the difference between the theologian and the philosopher consists solely in affirming or not affirming will [of God]. Should it be said that God's action is not concomitant with His will, because His will is eternal, but is rather concomitant with the connection of His will *(ta'alluq al-irādah),* so that the meaning of "if He wills" is "if His will connects"; we should answer by shifting the argument to the connection of His will and asking whether it is a perfection or an imperfection. It cannot be an imperfection, nor, if it is a perfection, can there be any possibility of its not existing. Moreover, one cannot say that it is possible for it to be neither a perfection nor an imperfection, because we should then say that if it were not a perfection then God's action would of necessity be vanity *('abath),* for if His action were good, then its source[1] would be a perfection. Thus, clearly stated, the real difference between the three positions is that in the view of the theologian both the occurrence of the action from God and its nonoccurrence are proper in the thing itself, whereas in the view of the philosopher and the Ṣūfīs the nonexistence of God's action is not proper in the thing itself. Nevertheless the Ṣūfīs affirmed will of God, attributed His action to His will, and made His will a necessary cause of His action. They therefore said that He was a free agent *(mukhtār),* since a free agent is one who acts through will. The philosophers, on the other hand, did not affirm will of Him, but made His action attributable to His knowledge. They therefore made Him a necessary agent *(mūjib)* rather than a free agent, since a free agent must possess will. Thus, the Ṣūfīs agree with the theologians in affirming free choice and agree with the philosophers on the concomitance *(luzūm)* of action with Him and the impossibility of His not acting. They differ from the theologians in that the latter allow the nonexistence of action in actuality *(bi-ḥasab al-wāqi'),* and from the philosophers in that the philosophers do not affirm will [of God] nor make action attributable to it.

When the motive is pure: The gist of this is that if the knowledge of the benefit, which is the motive for action, connects, then the action is necessary and its nonexistence impossible with respect to that motive. However, the nonexistence of the action is possible in itself *(fī nafs al-amr)* because of the possibility of the nonexistence of that motive and the possibility of the existence of some other motive. In summary, the attributes of the Creator are eternal, and their connections *(ta'alluqāt)* are originated and contingent. They are not necessitated by [God's] essence, for [God's] essence necessitates neither the existence of action nor its nonexistence. It is apparent that there is no need [to mention] this, for what is immediately understood by what is proper or not proper is what is so with respect to itself *(bi-ḥasab nafs al-amr),* for what is possible with respect to itself can be necessary with respect to something else. The author mentioned all this, however, only for greater clarity.

50b. *Except that the philosophers took the position:* as opposed to the theologians, [in whose view] His will is not concomitant with His essence. This is the implication *(muqtaḍā)* of the author's argument, and you are aware of what it contains. Accordingly his statement: "Thus the antecedent of the first hypothetical proposition, etc." is a corollary *(tafrī')* of the philosopher's position [only].

[39] *Is only with respect to the expression, etc.:* It is possible that its meaning is: "If that from which the effect of will results[1] is realized from Him, He acts. If it is not realized, He does not act." In this case the agreement would be with respect to meaning *(bi-ḥasab al-ma'nā).*

51. *And free choice in bringing the world into existence:* This is the emanation of action from Him through knowledge, wisdom *(ḥikmah),* and will, even though all of these are concomitant with His essence, and He is a necessary agent *(fā'il mūjib)* in this respect and in the sense of the action's being concomitant with Him. Nevertheless, His choice is not like the choice of humans, nor is it like the compulsion *(jabr)* of humans

in the sense that He would be an agent compelled to act *(fā'il majbūr 'alā al-fi'l).*

His command is one: that is, His essential command.

Thus wavering and the possibility of two different decisions are inapplicable to Him: because each of these would imply plurality, multiplicity, and manifoldness, may His essence be exalted above that, and because free choice is one of the essential entities which are realized in the plane of His essential unity.

Compulsion and free choice as these are understood by humans: that is, being compelled to act *(al-majbūrīyah fī al-fi'l)* in the sense of action occurring from someone whether he wills it or not, and wavering between two things, as previously mentioned.[1]

What actually occurs: that is, whatever occurs, from whomever it occurs, and in whatever manner it occurs, *is necessary:* for it is what is known and realized in the expanse of His knowledge *(fī 'arṣat 'ilmihi).* Anything else is impossible for the possibility of its not occurring is something imagined only by him who wavers [between two choices].

52. *And that it was possible for Him that He not will, so that it would not appear:* that is, not willing is possible for Him. It is obvious that the meaning of the verse [from the Qur'ān] does not indicate this, nor does his explanation of it. For this reason the author undertook to interpret it as he did.

Nor is decisive choice as mentioned above: with respect to the Creator.

[*Serves*] *either to deny the compulsion imagined by weak intellects:* The justification *(tawjīh)* for this is that what is introduced by "that,"[1] although his statement "so that it would not appear" is dependent upon it, is the subject *(fā'il)* of "it was possible" with the meaning: it was affirmed. Thus the meaning is: The dependence of the nonappearance of the world on His not willing was affirmed of Him. Its meaning thus reverts to: If He did not will, the action would not appear, and serves to emphasize it. The emphasis is an exageration of the denial of the imagined compulsion, particularly in the use of an expression indicating the possibility of the nonexistence of the world as a result of His not willing.

"And if He willed He would have made it still": The meaning of his statement: "If He does not will He does not act"[2] is, according to custom: If He wills not to act. Thus His saying: "If He willed He would have made it still" has no other meaning than this.

Or [to show] that God: that is, the existence of the world has nothing to do with His essence or His essential perfection, for He is accompanied by His perfection whether the world exists or not. Thus his statement: "It was possible for Him [that He not will]", that is, in view of His independent essence, or, as we should say, the possibility of the nonexistence of the world as a result of His not willing, implies the independence of His essence from the world. Instead of mentioning what was implied *(al-lāzim),* as intended, he mentioned what implied it *(al-malzūm).*

53. *In affirming a will superadded:* that is, in intellection *(fī al-ta'aqqul).*

55. *They allowed the dependence of an eternal effect on a free agent:* in the sense that His action is in accordance with His will, even though His will is concomitant with His essence and His action is concomitant with His will, as was previously mentioned, not in the sense affirmed by the theologian, for [in that sense] an eternal effect cannot rationally depend on a free agent.

Even though He is a free agent: in the sense mentioned a number of times previously.

56. *Something existing through a prior existence:* that is, prior to the intention of bringing [it] into existence.

58. *Rather than in accordance with Himself:* that is, the Manifest *(al-Mutajallī).*

Imperfection, then, attaches to the attributes: not in the thing itself *(fī nafs al-amr),* nor with respect to real existence *(al-wujūd al-ḥaqīqī),* but with respect to appearance *(al-ẓuhūr)* and imaginary existence *(al-wujūd al-khayālī).*

59. *Either ascribes these attributes to God as imperfect:* like the theologians, *or else denies them of Him completely:* like the philosophers. *May God be high exalted above what the evildoers:* of both groups, *say.*

60. *And that all that:* that is, what is predicated as the source *(mabda')* of each of these respectively, namely, command, prohibition, and narration, *is among the divisions of speech:*[1] according to the language, since, according to it, saying *(al-qawl)* is included among them.[2] Even more explicit than this is the fact that the prophets used the expression "God said." It is as if the author, may his soul be sanctified, did not mention this because saying *(al-qawl)* has widespread and well-known metaphorical meanings other than speech *(al-kalām)*.[3]

61. *One of them rejecting the minor premiss of the second syllogism:* These were the pious ancestors *(al-salaf al-ṣāliḥ),* may God be pleased with them all.

And the other rejecting the major premiss: and admitting its minor premiss. These are the Ḥanbalites, who say: God's speech consists of these letters and they subsist in His essence and are eternal. It is evident that the denial of the major premiss is unjustified *(ghayr muwajjah),* because what is successive *(al-ghayr al-qārr)* must have originated parts, otherwise it would not be successive. Indeed, it must, while existing, have a nonexistent part which is yet to come [into existence].

Each group rejecting one of the two premisses of the first syllogism: One group rejected the minor premiss of the first syllogism. These are the Mu'tazilites, who say: His speech consists of originated sounds and letters which do not subsist in His essence but are, on the contrary, created in something else, such as the Preserved Tablet *(al-Lawḥ al-Maḥfūẓ).* Another group rejected the major premiss. These are the Karrāmites, the followers of Abū 'Abd Allāh al-Karrām al-Sijistānī, who say: His speech consists of sounds and letters subsisting in His essence. May God be exalted above what the evildoers say.

In the manner mentioned above: that is, one group rejecting the minor premiss and the other the major.

[42] *So that it cannot exist without them:* that is, without any of them, *nor with them either:* with all of them. This point, however, is open to question *(fīhi baḥth),* for a genus exists within all of its species at one and the same time.

Since a genus cannot exist, etc.: This is the proof for our statement: "So that it cannot exist without them."

Thus it is possible for their genus to exist: that is, what was only considered a genus, not that it is a real genus *(jins ḥaqīqī).*

62. *Rather than in the thing named:* that is, the thing expressed *(al-mu'abbar 'anhu).*

[43] *Nevertheless, its truth becomes evident upon reflection:* and one realizes that it is the truth which corresponds to actual fact *(al-wāqi'),* so that his differing from the position of our latter-day colleagues does no harm. Moreover, one realizes that in reality he agrees with our latter-day colleagues even though it appears that he differs. This is the probable interpretation of his statement *(muḥtamal al-kalām).* His intent, however, is unknown.

63. *With respect to their being known to God, are eternal:* and are also an attribute of His according to the position of the theologians.

All the other expressions and significations of created beings: and, indeed, all objects of knowledge *(al-ma'lūmāt),* whether existent, nonexistent, or intermediate between the two *(al-ḥāl).*[1] What is intended is that His speech, with respect to its particular characteristic *(khuṣūṣīyah),* and in view of its being His speech, is an eternal attribute, although in view of the forms through which it is known *(ṣuwar ma'lūmīyatihā),* it is not the source of instruction *(mabda' al-ifhām).*

Which rests on a leg: He has, as it were, compared the two premisses of a proof with two legs upon which it [might be said to] rest. His meaning is that there is not [even one] premiss of a proof for establishing it, much less two. On the other hand [he may have intended] *sāq* as derived from *sawq,* [meaning to propound], as to propound a proof in various ways. His meaning would then be: There is no proof to demonstrate it no matter how it is propounded. In either case his purpose is to stress his denial [of the existence of any proof].

64. *If it is equivalent to this attribute then its nature is obvious:* with respect to being eternal or originated. However, its being pronounced, written, and designated *(mushār ilayh)* would then be enigmatical.

Then there is no doubt that their subsisting in God is only in consideration of the form through which they are known, and that therefore it is not an attribute in itself: although this is not characteristic solely of these expressions and meanings, as was previously mentioned[1] and needs no further mention here.

As for the object of [*His*] *knowledge:* that is, the expressions and significations with respect to themselves rather than with respect to the forms through which they are known. There is no doubt that their significations with respect to their being significations of them are of the class of substances known to the Truth *(al-Ḥaqq),* since their being known through expressions is not the same as their being known to the Truth absolutely. Thus, the meaning of his statement below, "As for their significations," cannot be with respect to their being significations of them or objects of knowledge or concepts of them, for otherwise the division into substances and other than substances would not be proper, since, in this respect, they are accidents only.

As for their significations: that is, the things themselves not with respect to their being significations or ojbects of knowledge, for with respect to their being known to the Truth, their nature has already been mentioned, and with respect to their being known to created being *(al-makhlūq),* they are an attribute of created being. Moreover, if the meaning intended were with respect to their being significations and objects of knowledge, then in that respect they would be of the category of accidents, and the division [into substances and accidents] would not be proper.[2]

So how can they subsist in Him: eternally. The first is obvious, because is is impossible for substances to subsist [in anything]. As for the second, it is because successive entities *(al-amr al-ghayr al-qārr)* are originated, so how could they subsist eternally [in God]?

65a. *What the Ṣūfīs have to say:* that is, what some of the Ṣūfīs have to say. Some of this [the author] has mentioned in the text *(al-aṣl)* and some in the glosses *(al-ḥawāshī).*

[44] *For there is no way of exhausting the knowledge of eternity:* and, therefore, speech, which is sequential *(mutarattib),* does not end. This means that each time He imparts

information, further imparting of information can be imagined and is an object of His power. Thus it never happens that the imparting of information ceases.

65b. *God's attributes, however, do not define His essence:* because He is individuated through Himself *(muta'ayyin bi-dhātihī)* and no individuation particularizes *(yu'ayyin)* Him at all, for everything which an individuation particularizes is contingent and compound *(murakkab)* in its essence.

And consequently they are not: that is, having learned that the speech of the Creator is not like the speech of human beings *(al-ādamī),* you should know that it is one of the aspects *(i'tibārāt)* of His knowledge, for His knowledge is a source of His informing *(mansha' li-i'lāmihi)* and is, in this respect, speech. [The author] asserted this below[1] when he said: "and spoke to him with the knowledge of His essence."

66. *Thus, the Creator's speech:* with the meaning of the gerund *(al-maṣdar),* that is, His speaking *(takallum),* for there is a lack of preciseness *(musāmaḥah)*[1] in the statement.

67. *You will see clearly that the speech of God is that which is recited, heard, and pronounced:* in the world of forms and similitude *('ālam al-ṣuwar wa-al-mithāl)* and in a form and similitude befitting His state. One should know that all the levels of speech, even the speech of inanimate beings *(al-jamādāt),* are levels of God's speech, but in accordance with the planes of His manifestations *(tajalliyāt)* and descents *(tanazzulāt)* as required by the doctrine of unification *(mas'alat al-tawḥīd).* As for the particular characteristic *(al-khuṣūṣīyah)* subsistent in the Qur'an by which it is attributed to God and specifically associated with Him, it is that the Qurān is speech which befits His state and which no one speaking a language of its genus can imitate. The reason it did not appear in the world of sense and visibility *('ālam al-ḥiss wa-al-shahādah)* in a human manifestation *(fī maẓhar al-bashar)* is that in this world speech befitting His state is impossible. Should you say: If this type of speech appeared in a human manifestation *(fī maẓhar al-basharīyah),* then the purpose behind the sending down *(inzāl)* of the Qur'ān, namely, its inimitability *(i'jāz)*[1] by created beings, would be lost. I should answer: On the contrary, it is

possible for it to be inimitable in other than this manifestation, by analogy with the inimitable acts *(al-af'āl al-mu'jizah)* emanating from the Prophet.[2] It is obvious, however, that inimitability in the first and actual way, is more perfect and substantial.

69. *That the speech which is an attribute of God is none other than His relating and pouring forth:* This is apparent from what was said by al-Imām Ḥujjat al-Islām [al-Ghazālī][1] and by a certain person, namely, [Dāwūd] al-Qayṣarī.[2]

Moreover, the books sent down composed: up to: *Thus the two syllogisms:* This is apparent from what was said by al-Shaykh al-Kabīr [Ibn 'Arabī][3] and al-Shaykh Ṣadr al-Dīn al-Qūnawī,[4] and by al-Qayṣarī as well since what he said includes an exposition of both meanings [of speech]. One should note that [the author's] statement: "which have appeared through the mediacy of [God's] knowledge," up to: "Thus the two syllogisms," is to explain the statement of al-Shaykh Ṣadr al-Dīn al-Qūnawī, which is not clear.

71. *In both the world of similitude and that of sense:* except that what befits His state becomes manifest only in the world of similitude and not in the world of sense, as has been pointed out.

72. *God's custom is to bring power and choice into existence in a man, etc.:* Thus a man is [himself] created and is also a substratum for other creations *(makhlūqāt)* which are carried out upon him through God's power and action. However, some of these are created posteriorly to the creation of others, not in the sense of essential necessitating posteriority *(ba'dīyah dhātīyah istilzāmīyah),* but rather in the sense of coincidental customary posteriority *(ba'dīyah 'ādīyah ittifāqīyah).*[1] Thus, God first creates in a man knowledge in its different degrees, then will, power, and finally the act. None of this is from the man himself. How could it be when he in himself is nothing! What an excellent doctrine is held by the theologians on this question and how objectionable is the doctrine of the philosophers and that of the Mu'tazilites! for the philosophers determined upon necessitating causation *(al-sababīyah al-mustalzimah)* whereby it is impossible for an effect not to result, and the Mu'tazilites determined upon generation *(al-tawlīd)* on the part of man.

As for the verifying Ṣūfīs, the mirrors of their hearts were illumined by virtue of the verse: "Now We have removed from thee thy covering,"[2] so that they saw in existence neither the man nor what is carried out upon him. Indeed, they saw only a real, simple, and single essence *(dhāt wāḥidah basīṭah ḥaqīqīyah)* appearing in the form of the man and in the form of what is carried out upon him, but in such a way that this appearing *(al-zuhūr)* and manifesting *(al-iẓhār)* does not change its unitary essence *(dhātahu al-aḥadīyah).* This is what they said after the secret of the Reality of Realities *(Ḥaqīqat al-Ḥaqā'iq)* and the Substance of Substances *(Hayūlā al-Hayūlayāt)* was revealed [to them]. How great is our merit by merely having their discourse on our lips, even though we have no conception of its meaning, to say nothing of having realized its content. We take refuge in God from error in articulating their discourse, either on purpose or inadvertantly, as well as from denying their discourse, and being deprived of the joy of hearing it. Praise be to God for His favor, as is due Him and befits Him.

75. *Even though He is exalted above composition:* that is, exalted, in their view, above composition with respect to His essence, for, although they assert composition and multiplicity [of Him] with respect to His attributes, they, nevertheless, do not take that multiplicity into account when considering the emanation of acts [from Him].

78. *It is apparent that the true position:* that is, it is apparent from the philosophers' proofs by virtue of their being presumptive *(ẓannīyah)* and convincing *(iqnā'īyah)* and from the theologians' proofs inasmuch as they [contain] unfounded premisses *(muqaddimāt wāhiyah).* However, in actuality, [the proofs for the true position] are real and certain in the author's view. How could they not be, when this has been agreed upon by the Ṣūfīs and revealed to them, and the author's knowledge concerning them is certain.

83. *Moreover, if we go beyond these levels to the fifth and sixth:* and consider the relation in both directions *(ilā al-jānibayn),* as mentioned above,[1] although for infinity [to result] it is sufficient to consider the relation in one direction only,

since the levels are infinite in the sense that they do not come to an end.

84. *Its intellect:* that is, the intellect of some sphere, namely, the second sphere from the [First] Principle. It is possible that the possessive pronouns qualifying "matter" and "soul" similarly [refer to some sphere] in order to be in agreement with the pronoun qualifying "intellect." On the other hand it is possible that they convey [a sense of] specificity as [would be the case] with the pronoun [in the expression] "its level," that is, the level of that thing.[1] We have brought this up only because the first intellect brought into existence the form, matter, and soul of the first sphere but not, however, its intellect, since it itself is its intellect. On the contrary, according to their doctrine, it brought into existence the intellect of the second sphere. It should be known that they said that God brought the first intellect into existence, and that the first intellect brought the first sphere into existence along with its matter, its form and its rational soul, which directs it, as well as the second intellect. Then the second intellect brought its sphere into existence both materially and formally, as well as the soul of its sphere and the intellect of the third sphere, and so on up to the tenth intellect. Then the tenth intellect created the four elements and the three generations *(al-mawālīd al-thalāthah)*[2] with all their many species, souls, and faculties, and so on as God willed.

This is what they said, and most people have interpreted their words literally to the effect that there is an agent and cause other than God, may He be exalted above what does not befit Him. However, al-Muḥaqqiq al-Dawwānī has demonstrated in an essay[3] he wrote to explain the meaning of the following verse by al-Ḥāfiz al-Shīrāzī:[4]

> Said our Pīr: On the pen of creation passed no error.
> On his pure, error-covering sight praise be.

that their real position is that there is no agent in existence except God. He has explained this clearly and whoever desires certainty [on this point] should refer to this essay. Indeed, what they meant by the intellect's bringing something into existence was its having a role *(madkhalīyah)* in bringing that thing into existence. The author's[5] words, however, cannot be restricted to either interpretation and are valid in any case. This should be considered carefully. Nevertheless, some of his expressions towards the end of what he has to say indicate what the substantiation [of this] is.[6]

They presented this by means of analogy: and conjecture *(takhmīn)* not by way of demonstration and certainty. Nevertheless, they made it conform to their axioms *(qawā'id)* and doctrines *(masā'il),* since most of their doctrines are conjectural *(takhmīnī)* and presumptive *(ẓannī).*

85. *These aspects are not hypothetical:* That is, they are not purely hypothetical.

NOTES
to the Translation of al-Lari's *COMMENTARY*

Par. 1

1. For al-Jāmī's description of the first and second individuations, see his *Naqd al-Nuṣūṣ,* pp. 8-12.

Gloss 2

1. See the commentary on par. 5.

2. In the handbooks on the art of disputation *(ādāb al-baḥth)* denial *(man'),* opposition *(mu'āraḍah),* and refutation *(naqḍ)* are listed as the three methods by which objection to a thesis may be made. In denial the objector denies one of the premisses used by the defender in proving his thesis. The objector may do this either with or without a support *(sanad),* and the support may be coextensive *(musāwī),* less extensive *(akhaṣṣ,* more specific), or more extensive (*a'amm,* more general). See al-Ījī, *Ādāb al-Baḥth;* Ṭāshkubrīzādah, *Ādāb al-Baḥth wa-al-Munāẓarah;* and Sāchaqlīzādah, *al-Risālah al-Waladīyah,* pp. 89-89. See also note 3 to par. 9 of the translation of *al-Durrah al-Fākhirah.*

In the present case, the objector is denying the premiss of the philosophers that some quiddities are external existents by arguing as follows:

> No (things which have only mental existences) are (external existents).
> All (quiddities) are (things which have only mental existences).
> Therefore, no (quiddities) are (external existents).

The minor premiss is the objector's less extensive support. To deny the minor premiss by claiming that some quiddities are not things which have only mental existences is uselsss, since one cannot argue from this that some quiddities are external existents.

3. The position of the philosophers was that universals existed externally within their particulars. See, for example, Ibn Sīnā, *al-Shifā', al-Ilāhīyāt,* pp. 202-212; al-Kātibī, *al-Risālah al-Shamsīyah,* p. 11 of English translation, p. 6 of Arabic text; and al-Urmawī, *Maṭāli' al-Anwār,* p. 53. The theologians, on the other hand, held that universals existed only in the mind. See al-Taftāzānī's *Sharḥ al-Risālah al-Shamsīyah,* pp. 46-47; Quṭb al-Dīn al-Rāzī's *Lawāmi' al-Asrār,* pp. 55-56; and particularly his *Risālat Taḥqīq al-Kullīyāt,* which deals with the method by which the intellect abstracts universals from the mental forms of particulars.

4. For this axiom, see note 2 to the translation of gloss No. 2. An endless chain of mental existences would, however, be possible. See note 3 to the translation of gloss No. 2.

Par. 8

1. That is, those Ṣūfīs professing the doctrine of the unity of existence *(waḥdat al-wujūd).*

Par. 9

1. For these forms of objection, see note 3 to par. 9 of the translation of *al-Durrah al-Fākhirah.*

2. For the expression "in the thing itself," see note 1 to par. 51 of the translation of *al-Durrah al-Fākhirah.*

Gloss 5

1. *Al-ḥāṣil bi-al-maṣdar* is the state or quality which results from an action and subsists in the agent or recipient of that action, such as, being knowledgeable *('ālimīyah),* being known *(ma'lūmīyah),* being in movement *(mutaḥarrikīyah),* being in existence *(mawjūdīyah).* See al-Aḥmadnagarī, *Dustūr al-'Ulama,* III, p. 273, under *al-maṣdar.*

Par. 11

1. See *al-Durrah al-Fākhirah,* par. 12.

2. See gloss No. 12.

3. For the judgment of the estimation, see note 1 to par. 12 of the translation of *al-Durrah al-Fākhirah.*

Gloss 10

1. *Al-mushākalah* is one of the figures of the art of *badī'.* It consists of expressing a concept by a word other than the usual word in order to maintain

a resemblance between it and another word in the sentence. In this case "remaining" *(bāqī)* is used instead of "established" *(thābit)* because of its resemblance with "remainder" *(baqīyah)*. See al-Qazwīnī, *Talkhīṣ al-Miftāḥ*, p. 352-354; and al-Aḥmadnagarī, *Dustūr al-'Ulamā'*, III, p. 271, under *al-mushākalah.*

Par. 18

1. See *al-Durrah al-Fākhirah,* par. 20.
2. See gloss No. 17.

Par. 19

1. And, therefore, not be impossible. See note 3 to the translation of gloss No. 2.

Par. 21

1. That is, choosing *kamālī,* the relative adjective formed by suffixing *yā'* to *kamāl* (perfection), rather than *kāmil,* the customary word for "perfect."

Par. 23

1. All of the manuscripts insert the commentary on gloss No. 42. at this point and again later in its proper place immediately following the commentary on par. 61. Two of the manuscripts, Yahuda 3872 and 'Aqā'id Taymūr 393, have marginal notes indicating that the commentary on this gloss is out of place.

Par. 25

1. That is, one may choose either the expression "an existent" or "attributive existence," since the two have almost the same meaning. According to al-Fanārī in his *Misbāḥ al-Uns,* p. 53, *al-wujūd al-iḍafī* is the equivalent of the expression *al-mawjūdīyah.*

Par. 28

1. That is, the difference exists not only in human minds but also in the plane of God's cognitive manifestation *(majlā 'ilmī),* mentioned above in the commentary on par. 24.
2. That is, God is not in need of the attribute of knowledge in order that things be revealed to Him. His essence is sufficient for that. See *al-Durrah al-Fākhirah,* par. 27.
3. The translation of this, as well as the preceding sentence, is based on

my own proposed rewording given in the notes to the Arabic text.

4. That is, in respect to being the source of revelation.

5. See gloss No. 22.

Par. 31

1. For the difference between *'ilm ḥuḍūrī* and *'ilm ḥuṣūlī,* see al-Tahānawī, *Kashshāf,* pp. 1056-1057, under *al-'ilm.*

Par. 33

1. See *al-Durrah al-Fākhirah,* par. 35, as well as note 1 to the translation of gloss No. 29.

2. Literally, "after its absence from the thing perceived."

3. Since the example al-Ṭūsī presents in this paragraph is that of a human who apprehends something other than himself, and it is only in the following paragraph that al-Ṭūsī cites the example of a human who apprehends his own essence.

4. Rather than, as stated by al-Ṭūsī, "with your essence." It should be noted that two of the manuscripts of *al-Durrah al-Fākhirah,* Yahuda 5373 and Warner Or. 997(1), substitute *bi-dhālika* (with that) for *bi-dhātika* (with your essence). On the other hand, the 1290 Istanbul edition of al-Ṭūsī's *Sharḥ* reads *bi-dhātika.*

5. See gloss No. 25.

6. Since "to double" and "to be superimposed" mean approximately the same thing in this context.

7. That is, the remoteness of your situation from that of an apprehender with respect to what emnates solely from his own essence; or perhaps the remoteness meant is the remoteness of the analogy.

Par. 34

1. See *al-Durrah al-Fākhirah,* par. 35.

Gloss 31 a

1. That is, al-Ṭūsī's position.

2. See *al-Durrah al-Fākhirah,* par. 36.

Par. 35

1. Rather than through an additional form.

2. Rather than: "The existence of the first effect is thus identical with the First's apprehension of it."

Par. 37

1. The unvocalized Arabic text of this sentence is ambiguous. The predicate of *anna* could just as well be *masbūqah* (preceded), or *ma'lūmah* (known). The respective translations would then be: "because those intellectual substances are contingent and originated, they are therefore preceded by . . ." and "because those intellectual substances are contingent, originated, and preceded by . . . , they are therefore known."

Par. 40

1. The Arabic text has *al-jins* (genus), which is surely an error.

Par. 41

1. For the distinction between *qaḍā', qadar,* and *'ināyah* according to the philosophers, see al-Ṭūsī, *Sharḥ al-Ishārāt,* p. 337; and Quṭb al-Dīn al-Rāzī, *al-Muḥākamāt,* pp. 446-447.
2. That is, that God does not know particulars.

Gloss 37

1. See al-Jāmī's *Lawā'iḥ,* p. 16, flash 17, where the first individuation is defined as *qābilīyat-i maḥḍ,* which Whinfield translates as simple potentiality. Al-Kāshānī, in his *Iṣṭilāḥāt,* p. 165, equates the first individuation with *al-qābilīyah al-ūlā.*

Par. 49

1. See the commentary on par. 28.

Gloss 38

1. That is, the connection.

Gloss 39

1. That is, His will, in the view of the theologians, and His knowledge, in the view of the philosophers.

Par. 51

1. See *al-Durrah al-Fākhirah,* par. 51.

Par. 52

1. That is, "that He not will."

2. See *al-Durrah al-Fākhirah,* par. 50.

Par. 60

1. A fivefold division of speech is mentioned in gloss No. 42, and in al-Jurjānī's *Sharḥ al-Mawāqif,* VIII, pp. 99-100.

2. A marginal notation at this point in Yahuda 3872 and 'Aqā'id Taymūr 393 reads in translation: "That is, among the three divisions, namely, command, prohibition, and narration."

3. See, for example, al-Aḥmadnagarī, *Dustūr al-'Ulamā',* III, p. 101, under *al-qawl.*

Par. 63

1. For the meaning of *ḥāl* as used here, see al-Tahānawī, *Kashshāf,* pp. 359-360, under *al-ḥāl.*

Par. 64

1. See *al-Durrah al-Fākhirah,* par. 63.

2. The point al-Lārī seems to be making here is that significations with respect to their being significations exist only as mental forms and are therefore accidents. Since al-Jāmī has divided them into both substances and successive accidents, he must mean by significations the actual concrete things themselves corresponding to the mental forms which are signified by the verbal expressions. If this is so, however, it is hard to explain why in his commentary on *As for the object of His knowledge,* al-Lārī says that their significations with respect to their being significations of them are of the class of *substances* known to God. For the meaning of *madlūl,* see al-Aḥmadnagarī, *Dustūr al-'Ulamā',* III, p. 283 under *al-ma'nā.*

Par. 65b

1. See *al-Durrah al-Fākhirah,* par. 66.

Par. 66

1. For the meaning of *musāmaḥah,* see: al-Jurjānī, *al-Ta'rīfāt,* under *al-tasāmuḥ;* al-Aḥmadnagarī, *Dustūr al-'Ulamā',* III, p. 255 under *al-musāmaḥah,* I, p. 291 under *al-tasāmuḥ;* al-Tahānawī, *Kashshāf,* p. 639 under *al-tasāmuḥ.*

Par. 67

1. That is, its rendering them incapable of imitating it.

2. The objection being made here appears to be that were the Qur'ān a manifestation of God's speech at the human level, that is, in the world of sense and vision, it would not be inimitable and, consequently, would not be an indication of the veracity of the Prophet. The answer given by al-Lārī is that the Qur'ān might still be inimitable even if manifested in the world of sense and vision just as certain other acts of the Prophet, such as the splitting of the moon, were inimitable even though manifested in the world of sense and vision.

Par. 69

1. See *al-Durrah al-Fākhirah,* par. 66.
2. See *al-Durrah al-Fākhirah,* par. 71.
3. See *al-Durrah al-Fākhirah,* par. 67.
4. See *al-Durrah al-Fākhirah,* par. 68.

Par. 72

1. For the varieties of priority and posteriority, see: al-Tahānawī, *Kashshāf,* pp. 1213-1215, under *al-taqaddum;* al-Aḥmadnagarī, *Dustūr al-'Ulamā',* I, pp. 334-338, under *al-taqaddum;* and al-Jurjānī, *Sharḥ al-Mawāqif,* VI, pp. 269-274. The point al-Lārī is making is that a man's act, although posterior to his knowledge, will, and power, is not an effect of these human attributes but is rather an effect of God's knowledge, will, and power.

2. Qur'ān, L, 22.

Par. 83

1. That is, the lower levels with respect to the higher, and the higher levels with respect to the lower, in the manner mentioned in par. 83 of *al-Durrah al-Fākhirah.*

Par. 84

1. Al-Lārī's meaning here seems to be that the pronouns qualifying "matter" and "soul" refer either to some unspecified sphere, like the pronoun qualifying "intellect," or to the specific level *(martabah)* of those things emanating from the first intellect which include the second intellect as well as the form, matter, and soul of the first intellect.

2. That is, the mineral, vegetable, and animal orders generated from the four elements—fire, air, water, and earth.

3. See Dānish Pazhūh, *Fihrist,* Vol. III, Part 1, p. 452; Vol. III, Part 4, p. 2248.

4. *Dīwān.* Ed. Brockhaus, No. 237, Vol. II, p. 158. The translation is based on that of H. Wilberforce Clarke, Vol. I, p. 428.

5. That is, al-Jāmī, who, as has been mentioned, is quoting al-Ṭūsī.

6. Al-Lārī seems to be referring to what al-Jāmī (al-Ṭūsī) says in par. 85.

LIST OF WORKS AND ARTICLES CITED

'Afīfī, Abū al-'Alā'. *al-Ta'līqāt 'alā Fuṣūṣ al-Ḥikam.* (Volume two of 'Afīfī's edition of Ibn 'Arabī's *Fuṣūṣ al-Ḥikam.)* Cairo, 1365/1946.

Afnan, Soheil Muhsin. *A Philosophical Lexicon in Persian and Arabic.* Beirut, 1969.

Ahlwardt, Wilhelm. *Verzeichnis der arabischen Handschriften der königlichen Bibliothek zu Berlin.* Ten volumes. Berlin, 1887-1899.

al-Aḥmadnagarī, 'Abd al-Nabī ibn 'Abd al-Rasūl. *Jāmi' al-'Ulūm al-Mulaqqab bi-Dustūr al-'Ulamā'.* Four volumes. Hyderabad, 1329-1331.

d'Alverny, Marie Thérèse. "Anniyya-Anitas," in *Mélanges offerts à Etienne Gilson.* Paris/Toronto, 1959. Pp. 59-91.

al-Āmidī, Sayf al-Dīn 'Alī ibn Abī 'Alī. *Abkār al-Afkār.* MS Petermann, I, 233, Staatsbibliothek Preussischer Kulturbesitz, Berlin.

———. *Ghāyat al-Marām fī 'Ilm al-Kalām.* Ed. Ḥasan Maḥmūd 'Abd al-Laṭīf. Cairo, 1391/1971.

Arberry, Arthur John. *Classical Persian Literature.* London, 1958.

al-Ash'arī, Abū al-Ḥasan 'Alī ibn Ismā'īl. *Maqālāt al-Islāmīyīn wa-Ikhtilāf al-Muṣallīn.* Ed. Hellmut Ritter. 2nd ed. Wiesbaden, 1963. (Bibliotheca Islamica 1.)

Bābur Pādshāh Ghāzī, Ẓahīr al-Dīn Muḥammad. *Bābur-nāma.* English trans. Annette Susannah Beveridge. Reprint. New Delhi, 1970.

Bacharach, Jere. "The Dinar Versus the Ducat," in *International Journal of Middle East Studies,* 4, 1: 77-96.

al-Baghdādī, Ismā'īl Bāshā ibn Muḥammad Amīn ibn Mīr Salīm. *Hadīyat al-'Ārifīn, Asmā' al-Mu'allifīn wa-Āthār al-Muṣannifīn.* Two volumes. Istanbul, 1951-1955.

———. *Īḍāḥ al-Maknūn fī al-Dhayl 'alā Kashf al-Ẓunūn.* Two volumes. Instanbul, 1364/1945-1366/1947.

Belin, M. "Notice Biographique et Littéraire sur Mir Ali-Chîr-Névâii," in *Journal Asiatique,* Cinquième série, 17 (1861): 175-256, 281-375. (Pp. 300-375 contain extracts from *Khamsat al-Mutaḥayyirīn* translated into French.)

Brockelmann, Carl. *Geschichte der arabischen Litteratur.* 2nd ed. Two volumes. Leiden, 1943-1949. Three supplements. Leiden 1937-1942.

Browne, Edward Granville. *A Literary History of Persia.* Four volumes. Cambridge, 1902-1924.

al-Bukhārī, 'Alā' al-Dīn Muḥammad ibn Muḥammad. *Fāḍiḥat al-Mulḥidīn wa-Nāṣiḥat al-Muwaḥḥidīn.* Printed in *Majmū'at Rasā'il fī Waḥdat al-Wujūd,* Istanbul, 1294, pp. 2-47, where it is entitled *Risālah fī Waḥdat al-Wujūd* and attributed to Sa'd al-Dīn al-Taftāzānī.

Catalogue of the Arabic Manuscripts in the Library of the India Office. Vol. 2. Four parts. Oxford, 1930-1940.

Dānish Pazhūh, Muḥammad-taqī. *Fihrist-i Kitābkhānah-i Ihdā'ī-i Āqā-i Sayyid Muḥammad Mishkāt bih Kitābkhānah-i Dānishgāh-i Tihrān.* Vol. 3. Five parts. Tehran, 1332-1338 (Intishārāt-i Dānishgāh-i Tihran 169, 181, 299, 303, 533.)

Dārā Shikūh, Muḥammad. *Safīnat al-Awliyā'.* Cawnpore, 1884.

Dozy, Reinhart P.A. *Supplément aux dictionnaires arabes.* 2nd ed. Paris/Leiden, 1927.

Drewes, Gerardus W.J. "Sech Joesoep Makasar," in *Djawa,* No. 2, (1926): 83-88.

Ecker, Jacobus. *Gâmii de Dei Existentia et Attributis Libellus "Stratum Solve!" sive "Unio Pretiosus."* Pars Prior. Prolegomena una cum Capitibus Selectis in Latinum Sermonem Translatis. Bonn, 1879.

Edwards, Edward. *A Catalogue of the Persian Printed Books in the British Museum.* London, 1922.

Elder, Earl Edgar. *A Commentary on the Creed of Islam.* Sa'd al-Dīn al-Taftāzānī on the Creed of Najm al-Dīn al-Nasafī. New York, 1950.

Encyclopedia of Islam. 2nd ed. Vol. 1. Leiden/London, 1960.

Ethé, Hermann. *Catalogue of the Persian Manuscripts in the*

Library of the India Office. Two volumes. Oxford, 1903-1937.

al-Fanārī, Shams al-Dīn Muḥammad ibn Ḥamzah. *Miṣbāḥ al-Uns bayn al-Ma'qūl wa-al-Mashhūd fī Sharḥ Miftāḥ Ghayb al-Jam' wa-al-Wujūd.* Tehran, 1323. (Commentary on *Miftāḥ al-Ghayb* of Ṣadr al-Dīn al-Qūnawī.)

al-Fārābī, Abū Naṣr Muḥammad ibn Muḥammad ibn Ṭarkhān. *Kitāb al-Alfāẓ.* Ed. Muḥsin Mahdī. Beirut, 1968.

———. *Kitāb al-Ḥurūf.* Ed. Muḥsin Mahdī. Beirut, 1970.

al-Farghānī, Sa'īd al-Dīn Muḥammad ibn Aḥmad. *Muntahā al-Madārik.* Two volumes. [Cairo], 1293. (Commentary on *al-Qaṣīdah al-Tā'īyah* of Ibn al-Fāriḍ.)

Farīdūn Beg, Aḥmad ibn 'Abd al-Qādir. *Munsha'āt al-Salāṭin.* Two volumes. Istanbul, 1274-1275.

Fihris al-Khizānah al-Taymūrīyah. Four volumes. Cairo 1367/1948-1369/1950.

Frank, Richard M. "The Origin of the Arabic Philosophical Term *Annīyah,"* in *Cahiers de Byrsa* 6 (1956): 181-201.

al-Ghazālī, Abū Ḥāmid Muḥammad ibn Muḥammad. *al-Ma'ārif al-'Aqlīyah.* Ed. 'Abd al-Karīm al-'Uthmān. Damascus, 1383/1963.

Gibb, Hamilton A.R. and Kramers, Johannes Hendrik. *Shorter Encyclopedia of Islam.* Leiden/London, 1953.

Goichon, Amélie Marie. *Lexique de la langue philosophique d'Ibn Sīnā.* Paris, 1938.

Ḥāfiẓ, Shams al-Dīn Muḥammad al-Shīrāzī. *Dīwān.* Ed. Hermann Brockhaus. Three volumes. Leipzig, 1854-1860.

———. *The Dīvān-i-Ḥāfiẓ.* Trans. H. Wilberforce Clarke. Two volumes. Calcutta, 1891.

al-Hamadhānī, 'Ayn al-Quḍāh 'Abd Allāh ibn Muḥammad. *Nāmah-hā.* Ed. 'Alī-naqī Munzawī and 'Afīf 'Usayrān. Tehran, 1969.

———. *Zubdat al-Ḥaqā'iq,* in *Muṣannafāt-i 'Ayn al-Quḍāh Hamadhānī.* Ed. 'Afīf 'Usayrān. Vol. 1, Tehran, 1341/1962. (Intishārāt-i Dānishgāh-i Tihrān 695.)

al-Ḥasanī, 'Abd al-Ḥayy ibn Fakhr al-Dīn. *Nuzhat al-Khawāṭir wa-Bahjat al-Masāmi'.* Seven volumes. Hyderabad, 1350/1931-1378/1959.

Ḥikmat, 'Alī Aṣghar. *Jāmī.* Tehran, 1320/1942.

al-Ḥillī, al-'Allāmah Jamāl al-Dīn al-Ḥasan ibn Yūsuf ibn 'Alī ibn al-Muṭahhar. *Kashf al-Murād fī Sharḥ Tajrīd al-I'tiqād.* [Tehran], 1352. (Commentary on *Tajrīd al-'Aqā'id* of Naṣīr al-Dīn al-Ṭūsī.)

Hitti, Philip K., Faris, Nabih Amin, and 'Abd al-Malik, Buṭrus. *Descriptive Catalogue of the Garrett Collection of Arabic Manuscripts in the Princeton University Library.* Princeton, 1938.

al-Ḥusaynābādī, Ibrāhīm ibn Ḥaydar ibn Aḥmad al-Kurdī. *al-Risālah al-Qudsīyah al-Ṭāhirah bi-Sharḥ al-Durrah al-Fākhirah.* MS 9276, Dār al-Kutub al-Ẓāhirīyah, Damascus, fols. 89b-124b.

Ibn 'Arabī, Muḥyī al-Dīn Muḥammad ibn 'Alī. *Fuṣūṣ al-Ḥikam.* Ed. Abū al-'Alā' 'Afīfī. Two volumes. Cairo, 1365/1946.

———. *al-Futūḥāt al-Makkīyah.* Four volumes. Cairo, 1329.

———. *Tarjumān al-Ashwāq.* Ed. and trans. Reynold A. Nicholson. London, 1911.

Ibn Ḥanbal, Aḥmad. *Musnad.* Six xolumes. Cairo, 1313.

Ibn Sīnā, Abū 'Alī al-Ḥusayn ibn 'Abd Allāh. *al-Ishārāt wa-al-Tanbīhāt.* Ed. Sulaymān Dunyā. Four parts. Cairo, 1957-1960.

———. *al-Shifā', al-Ilāhīyāt.* Eds. al-Ab Qanawātī and Sa'īd Zāyid. Cairo, 1380/1960.

———. *al-Shifā', al-Manṭiq, al-Burhān.* Ed. Abū al-'Alā' 'Afīfī. Cairo, 1375/1956.

———. *al-Shifā, al-Manṭiq, al-Madkhal.* Eds. al-Ab Qanawātī, Maḥmūd al-Khuḍayrī, and Fu'ād al-Ahwānī. Cairo, 1371/1952.

———. *al-Shifā', al-Manṭiq, al-Maqūlāt.* Eds. Maḥmūd Muḥammad al-Khuḍayrī, al-Ab Qanawātī, Aḥmad Fu'ād al-Ahwānī, and Sa'īd Zāyid. Cairo, 1378/1959.

al-Ījī, 'Aḍud al-Dīn 'Abd al-Raḥmān ibn Aḥmad. *Ādāb al-Baḥth.* Printed in *Majmū' al-Mutūn al-Kabīr.* Cairo, 1368/1949.

Ivanow, Wladimir. *Concise Descriptive Catalogue of the Persian Manuscripts in the Collection of the Asiatic Society of*

Bengal. Calcutta, 1924. (Bibliotheca Indica 240.)

Ivanow, Wladimir and Hosain, M. Hidayat. *Catalogue of the Arabic Manuscripts in the Collection of the Royal Asiatic Society of Bengal.* Vol. 1. Calcutta, 1939. (Bibliotheca Indica 250.)

al-Jāmī, Nūr al-Dīn ʻAbd al-Raḥmān ibn Aḥmad. *al-Durrah al-Fākhirah fī Taḥqīq Madhhab al-Ṣūfīyah wa-al-Mutakallimīn wa-al-Ḥukamā' al-Mutaqaddimīn.* Printed at the end of *Asās al-Taqdīs fī ʻIlm al-Kalām* by Fakhr al-Dīn al-Rāzī, pp. 247-296. Cairo, 1328.

———. *Haft Awrang.* Ed. Āqā Murtaḍā. Tehran, 1337.

———. *Lawā'iḥ.* Ed. and trans. E.H. Whinfield and Mīrzā Muḥammad Ḳazvīnī. London, 1928. (Oriental Translation Fund, New series, 16.)

———. *Nafaḥāt al-Uns min Ḥaḍarāt al-Quds.* Ed. Mahdī Tawḥīdī Pūr. Tehran, 1337.

———. *The Nafahátal-ons min hadharát al-qods, or the lives of the Soofis.* Eds. Gholám ʻIisa, ʻAbd al Hamíd, and Kabír al-Dín Ahmad. With a biographical sketch of the author by W. Nassau Lees. Calcutta, 1858-1859.

———. *Naqd al-Nuṣūṣ fī Sharḥ Naqsh al-Fuṣūṣ.* Bombay, 1307. (A commentary on *Naqsh al-Fuṣūṣ,* an abridgement by Ibn ʻArabī of his *Fuṣūṣ al-Ḥikam.*)

———. *Risālah fī al-Wujūd.* Ed. and trans. Nicholas Heer. Published as "Al-Jāmī's *Treatise on Existence"* in *Islamic Philosophical Theology,* edited by Parviz Morewedge. Albany, 197 .

———. *Sharḥ Fuṣūṣ al-Ḥikam.* (A commentary on Ibn ʻArabī's *Fuṣūṣ al-Ḥikam.)* Printed in the margin of ʻAbd al-Ghanī al-Nābulusī's *Sharḥ Jawāhir al-Nuṣūṣ fī Ḥall Kalimāt al-Fuṣūṣ.* Two volumes. Cairo, 1304-1323.

———. *Tafsīr al-Qur'ān.* MS Yahuda 1308, Robert Garrett Collection, Princeton University Library, fols. 15b-137b.

al-Jurjānī, al-Sayyid al-Sharīf ʻAlī ibn Muḥammad. *Ḥāshiyah ʻalā Sharḥ al-Maṭāliʻ.* Istanbul, 1303. (A gloss on *Lawāmiʻ al-Asrār fī Sharḥ Maṭāliʻ al-Anwār* of Quṭb al-Dīn al-Rāzī.)

———. *Ḥāshiyat Sharḥ al-Tajrīd.* MS 865 [988H], Robert

Garrett Collection, Princeton University Library. (A gloss on the commentary of Maḥmūd al-Iṣbahānī on *Tajrīd al-'Aqā'id* of Naṣīr al-Dīn al-Ṭūsī.)

———. *Sharḥ al-Mawāqif.* Eight volumes. Cairo, 1325/1907. (A commentary on *al-Mawāqif fī 'Ilm al-Kalām* of 'Aḍud al-Dīn al-Ījī.)

———. *al-Ta'rīfāt.* Cairo, 1357/1938.

al-Kāshānī, Kamāl al-Dīn 'Abd al-Razzāq. *Iṣṭilāḥāt al-Ṣūfīyah.* Printed in the margin of his *Sharḥ Manāzil al-Sā'irīn.* [Tehran], 1315.

al-Kāshī, Ghiyāth al-Dīn Jamshīd ibn Mas'ūd. See Kennedy, Edward Stewart.

Kāshif al-Ghiṭā', 'Alī ibn Muḥammad Riḍā ibn Hādī. *Naqd al-Ārā' al-Manṭiqīyah wa-Ḥall Mushkilātihā.* Al-Najaf, 1383.

al-Kāshifī, Fakhr al-Dīn 'Alī ibn al-Ḥusayn al-Wā'iẓ al-Ṣafī. *Rashaḥāt-i 'Ayn al-Ḥayāt.* Cawnpore, 1911-1912.

al-Kātibī, Najm al-Dīn 'Alī ibn 'Umar. *al-Risālah al-Shamsīyah fī al-Qawā'id al-Manṭiqīyah.* Ed. and trans. A. Sprenger. Calcutta, 1854. (Bibliotheca Indica 88, Appendix 1.)

Kennedy, Edward Stewart. *The Planetary Equatorium of Jamshīd Ghiyāth al-Dīn al-Kāshī.* Princeton, 1960.

al-Kūrānī, Ibrāhīm ibn Ḥasan. *al-Amam li-Īqāẓ al-Himam.* Hyderabad, 1328.

———. *al Taḥrīrāt al-Bāhirah li-Mabāḥith al-Durrah al-Fākirah.* MS Yahuda 5373, fols. 185b-199a; and MS Yahuda 4049, Robert Garrett Collection, Princeton University Library.

al-Lāhawrī, Ghulām-Sarwar ibn Ghulām-Muḥammad ibn Raḥīm Allāh. *Khazīnat al-Aṣfiyā'.* Two volumes. Lucknow, 1290/1873.

al-Laknawī, Abū al-Ḥasanāt Muḥammad 'Abd al-Ḥayy. *al-Fawā'id al-Bahīyah fī Tarājim al-Ḥanafīyah.* Cairo, 1324.

al-Lārī, Raḍī al-Dīn 'Abd al-Ghafūr. *Khātimah.* Appended to his *Ḥāshiyah-i Nafaḥāt al-Uns.* MS Or. 218, British Museum, fols. 151b-175b.

Lees, William Nassau. "Biographical Sketch of the Mystic Philosopher and Poet Jami." English preface to al-Jāmī's *The Nafahátal-ons min hadharát al-qods.* Calcutta, 1858-1859.

Le Strange, Guy. *The Lands of the Eastern Caliphate.* Cambridge, 1930.

Loth, Otto. *A Catalogue of the Arabic Manuscripts in the Library of the India Office.* London, 1877.

al-Mahā'imī, 'Alā' al-Dīn 'Alī ibn Aḥmad. *Ajillat al-Ta'yīd fī Sharḥ Adillat al-Tawḥīd.* MS Yahuda 4601, Robert Garrett Collection, Princeton University Library. (A commentary by the author on his own work, *Adillat al-Tawḥīd.)*

Mingana, Alphonse. *Catalogue of the Arabic Manuscripts in the John Rylands Library in Manchester.* Manchester, 1934.

Morewedge, Parviz, editor. *Islamic Philosophical Theology.* Albany, 197 .

Muḥammad Ma'ṣūm ibn Mawlānā Bābā al-Samarqandī, Abū al'Iṣmah. *al-Farīdah al-Nādirah fī Sharḥ al-Durrah al-Fākirah.* MS 1364 (Delhi, 1841), India Office Library, London.

al-Munāwī, 'Abd al-Ra'ūf. *al-Kawākib al-Durrīyah fī Tarājim al-Sādah al-Ṣūfīyah.* MS Fayḍ Allāh 1509, Istanbul.

Munzawī, 'Alī-naqī. *Fihrist-i Kitābkhānah-i Ihdā'ī-i Āqā-i Sayyid Muḥammad Mishkāt bih Kitābkhānah-i Dānishgāh-i Tihrān.* Two volumes. Tehran, 1330-1332. (Intishārāt-i Dānishgāh-i Tihrān 123, 168.)

Muslim ibn al-Ḥajjāj, Abū al-Ḥusayn. *al-Jāmi' al-Ṣaḥīḥ.* Eight volumes. Istanbul, 1329-1333.

al-Nabhānī, Yūsuf ibn Ismā'īl. *Jāmi' Karāmāt al-Awliyā'.* Two volumes. Cairo, 1381/1962.

al-Nābulusī, 'Abd al-Ghanī ibn Ismā'īl. *Sharḥ Jawāhir al-Nuṣūṣ fī Ḥall Kalimāt al-Fuṣūṣ.* Two volumes. Cairo, 1304-1323. (A commentary on the *Fuṣūṣ al-Ḥikam* of Ibn 'Arabī.)

Nawā'ī, Mīr 'Alī-Shīr. *Khamsat al-Mutaḥayyirīn.* See Belin, M.

Nicholson, Reynold Alleyne. *Studies in Islamic Mysticism.* Cambridge, 1921.

Pertsch, Wilhelm. *Die arabischen Handschriften der herzoglichen Bibliothek.* Five volumes. Gotha, 1878-1892.

Pickthall, Mohammed Marmaduke. *The Meaning of the Glorious Koran.* New York: New American Library, 1953.

al-Qayṣarī, Dāwūd ibn Maḥmūd. *Maṭla' Khuṣūṣ al-Kilam fī Ma'ānī Fuṣūṣ al-Ḥikam.* Tehran, 1299. (A commentary on the *Fuṣūṣ al-Ḥikam* of Ibn 'Arabī.)

al-Qazwīnī, Jalāl-al-Dīn Muḥammad ibn 'Abd al-Raḥmān. *Talkhīṣ al-Miftāḥ.* Ed. 'Abd al-Raḥmān al-Barqūqī. Cairo, 1322/1904. (An abridgement of the third part of al-Sakkākī's *Miftāḥ al-'Ulūm.*)

al-Qūnawī, Ṣadr al-Dīn Muḥammad ibn Isḥāq. *I'jāz al-Bayān fī Ta'wīl Umm al-Qur'ān.* Hyderabad, 1368/1949.

———. *Kitāb al-Nuṣūṣ.* Printed at the end of al-Kāshānī's *Sharḥ Manāzil al-Sā'irīn.* [Tehran], 1315.

———. *Miftāḥ Ghayb al-Jam' wa-al-Wujūd.* Printed in the margin of Shams al-Dīn al-Fanārī's commentary on the same work entitled *Miṣbāḥ al-Uns bayn al-Ma'qūl wa-al-Mashhūd fī Sharḥ Miftāḥ Ghayb al-Jam' wa-al-Wujūd.* Tehran, 1323.

———. *al-Risālah al-Hādiyah.* MS Wetzstein II 1806, fols. 46a-61b, Staatsbibliothek Preussischer Kulturbesitz, Berlin; MS Warner Or. 1133, fols. 42b-51a, University of Leiden Library (incomplete at end); MS Vat. Arab. 1453, fols. 25b-41b, Bibliotheca Vaticana.

———. *al-Risālah al-Mufṣiḥah.* MS Wetzstein II 1806, fols. 9b-34b, Staatsbibliothek Preussischer Kulturbesitz, Berlin; MS Warner Or. 1133, fols. 2b-21b, University of Leiden Library; MS Vat. Arab. 1453, fols. 1b-14b, Bibliotheca Vaticana.

al-Qur'ān al-Karīm. Eds. Muḥammad 'Alī Khalaf al-Ḥusaynī, Ḥifnī Nāṣif, Naṣr al-'Ādilī, Muṣṭafā 'Ināni, Aḥmad al-Iskandarī. 2nd ed. Cairo: Dār al-Kutub al-Miṣrīyah, 1371/1952.

al-Qūshjī, 'Alā' al-Dīn 'Alī ibn Muḥammad. *Sharḥ al-Tajrīd.* Tabriz(?), 1307. (A commentary on *Tajrīd al-'Aqā'id* of Naṣīr al-Dīn al-Ṭūsī.)

al-Rāzī, Fakhr al-Dīn Muḥammad ibn 'Umar. *Sharḥ al-Ishārāt.* (A commentary on *al-Ishārāt wa-al-Tanbīhāt* of Ibn Sīnā.) Printed in the margin of al-Ṭūsī's *Sharḥ al-Ishārāt.* [Istanbul], 1290.

al-Rāzī, Quṭb al-Dīn Muḥammad ibn Muḥammad. *Lawāmi' al-Asrār fī Sharḥ Maṭāli' al-Anwār.* Istanbul, 1303. (A commentary on *Maṭāli' al-Anwār* of Sirāj al-Dīn al-Urmawī.)

———. *al-Muḥākamāt.* [Istanbul], 1290. (A gloss on the commentaries of Fakhr al-Dīn al-Rāzī and Naṣīr al-Dīn al-Ṭūsī on Ibn Sīnā's *al-Ishārāt wa-al-Tanbīhāt.)*

———. *Risālat Taḥqīq al-Kullīyāt.* MS Warner Or. 958(21),

fols. 67b-71b, University of Leiden Library.

———. *Taḥrīr al-Qawā'id al-Manṭiqīyah fī Sharḥ al-Risālah al-Shamsīyah.* Two volumes. Cairo, 1323/1905. (A commentary on Najm al-Dīn al-Kātibī's *al-Risālah al-Shamsīyah.)*

Sabzawārī, Hādī. *Sharḥ Ghurar al-Farā'id.* Eds. Mehdi Mohaghegh and Toshihiko Izutsu. Tehran, 1348/1969.

Sāchaqlīzādah, Muḥammad al-Mar'ashī. *al-Risālah al-Waladīyah.* Cairo, 1329.

Sachau, Eduard and Ethé, Hermann. *Catalogue of the Persian, Turkish, Hindustani and Pushtu Manuscripts in the Bodleian Library.* Part One. The Persian Manuscripts. Oxford, 1889.

Sām Mīrzā, Abū al-Naṣr. *Tuḥfah-i Sāmī.* Ed. Waḥīd Dastgirdī. Tehran, 1314/1936.

al-Sanhūtī, Yāsīn ibn Ibrāhīm. *al-Anwār al-Qudsīyah fī Manāqib al-Sādah al-Naqshabandīyah.* Cairo, 1344.

Sayılı, Aydın. *The Observatory in Islam.* Ankara, 1960.

Sezgin, Fuat. *Geschichte des arabischen Schriftums.* Vol. 1. Leiden, 1967.

al-Shahrastānī, Muḥammad ibn 'Abd al-Karīm. *Nihāyat al-Aqdām fī 'Ilm al-Kalām.* Ed. Alfred Guillaume. Oxford, 1931.

Sharḥ al-Durrah al-Fākhirah. MS 1125 (Ar. 640), Asiatic Society, Calcutta. (An anonymous commentary on al-Jāmī's *al-Durrah al-Fākhirah.)*

al-Shawkānī, Muḥammad ibn 'Alī. *al-Badr al-Ṭāli' bi-Maḥāsin Man ba'd al-Qarn al-Sābi'.* Two volumes. Cairo, 1348.

Storey, Charles Ambrose. *Persian Literature. A Bio-bibliographical Survey.* Two volumes. London, 1927-1958.

al-Subkī, Tāj al-Dīn 'Abd al-Wahhāb ibn Taqī al-Dīn. *Ṭabaqāt al-Shāfi'īyah al-Kubrā.* Six volumes. Cairo, 1324.

al-Ṭabarī, Abū Ja'far Muḥammad ibn Jarīr. *Jāmi' al-Bayān fī Tafsīr al-Qur'ān.* Thirty volumes. Būlāq, 1323-1329.

al-Tādhifī, Muḥammad ibn Yaḥyā. *Qalā'id al-Jawāhir fī Manāqib al-Shaykh 'Abd al-Qādir.* Cairo, 1331.

al-Taftāzānī, Sa'd al-Dīn Mas'ūd ibn 'Umar. *Risālah fī Waḥdat al-Wujūd.* See al-Bukhārī, 'Alā' al-Dīn.

———. *Sharḥ al-Maqāṣid.* Two volumes. Istanbul, 1277. (The commentary of the author on his *al-Maqāṣid fī 'Ilm al-Kalām.)*

———. *Sharḥ al-Risālah al-Shamsīyah.* Istanbul, 1312. (A commentary on *al-Risālah al-Shamsīyah* of Najm al-Dīn al-Kātibī.)

Tagirdzhanov, A.T. *Opisanie Tadzhikskikh i Persidskikh Rukopisei Vostochnogo Otdela Biblioteki LGU.* Vol. 1. Leningrad, 1962.

al-Tahānawī, Muḥammad ʻAlī ibn ʻAlī ibn Muḥammad Ḥāmid. *Kashshāf Iṣṭilāḥāt al-Funūn.* Ed. A. Sprenger. Calcutta, 1278/1861.

Ṭalas, Muḥammad Asʻad. *al-Kashshāf ʻan Makhṭūṭāt Khazā'in Kutub al-Awqāf.* Baghdad, 1372/1953.

Ṭāshkubrīzādah, ʻIṣām al-Dīn Aḥmad ibn Muṣṭafā. *Ādāb al-Baḥth wa-al-Munāẓarah.* Printed in *Majmūʻ al-Mutūn al-Kabir.* Cairo, 1368/1949.

———. *al-Shaqā'iq al-Nuʻmānīyah fī ʻUlamā' al-Dawlah al-ʻUthmānīyah.* Printed in the margin of Ibn Khallikān's *Wafayāt al-Aʻyān wa-Anbā' Abnā' al-Zamān.* Two volumes. Būlāq, 1299.

al-Ṭūsī, Naṣīr al-Dīn Muḥammad ibn Muḥammad. *Risālah.* MS Warner Or. 1133, fols. 22a-39a, University of Leiden Library; MS Vat. Arab. 1453, fols. 14b-25b, Bibliotheca Vaticana (with al-Ṭūsī's glosses); MS Wetzstein II 1806, fols. 34b-45b, Staatsbibliothek Preussischer Kulturbesitz, Berlin. (Letter in which al-Ṭūsī answers the questions put to him by Ṣadr al-Dīn al-Qūnawī in his *al-Risālah al-Mufṣiḥah.)*

———. *Sharḥ al-Ishārāt.* [*Istanbul*], 1290. (A commentary on Ibn Sīnā's *al-Ishārāt wa-al-Tanbīhāt.)*

al-Urmawī, Sirāj al-Dīn Maḥmūd ibn Abī Bakr. *Maṭāliʻ al-Anwār.* Printed in the margin of Quṭb al-Dīn al-Rāzī's commentary on it entitled *Lawāmiʻ al-Asrār fī Sharḥ Maṭāliʻ al-Anwār.* Istanbul, 1303.

van Ess, Josef. "Ibn Kullāb und die Miḥna." *Oriens* 18-19 (1965-1966): 92-142.

Voorhoeve, Petrus. *Handlist of Arabic Manuscripts in the Library of the University of Leiden and Other Collections in the Netherlands.* Leiden, 1957.

al-Ziriklī, Khayr al-Dīn. *al-Aʻlām.* 2nd ed. Ten volumes. Cairo, 1373/1954-1378/1959.

GLOSSARY OF TERMS

Terms are listed under their Arabic roots in the following general order: verbs, *maṣdars,* other nouns, participles, adjectives. *Nisbah* adjectives, however, are listed immediately following the word from which they are derived. *Maṣdars* and participles which retain their verbal meaning are included under the listing of the verb. Expressions consisting of more than one word are cross-listed under each word. Following the glossary of Arabic terms are a half dozen Persian terms.

The abbreviations DF, Ḥ, and Sh stand respectively for *al-Durrah al-Fākhirah,* al-Jāmī's *Ḥawāshī* (Glosses), and al-Lārī's *Sharḥ* (Commentary). The numerals following DF refer to the numbers of the paragraphs; those following Ḥ to the numbers of the gloss. A second numeral within parentheses after a gloss number refers to a paragraph of that gloss. Numerals following Sh refer to the sections of the *Sharḥ,* each of which has been numbered to correspond with the number of the paragraph of *al-Durrah al-Fākhirah* with which it deals. Numerals in square brackets after Sh, on the other hand, refer to those sections of the *Sharḥ* which deal with the *Ḥawāshī,* and which have also been correspondingly numbered.

' - b - d

azalan wa-abadan, eternally and everlastingly. DF 51, 63.

min al-azal ilā al-abad, from eternity to everlastingness. Ḥ 36.

abadī, everlasting. DF 58. Ḥ 16, 33. Sh [16], 37.

' - th - r

athar (āthār), effect. DF 1, 56, 75, 76, 77, 80, 81, 83, 84. Ḥ 5(2), 13(1). Sh 1, 4, 21, 46, [39].

' - th - r (continued)

athar qadīm, eternal effect. DF 54, 55. Sh 55.
aththara (ta'thīr), to effect. DF 57, 72, 74.
ta'thīr, efficacy. Sh 28.
mu'aththir, effective; cause. DF 27, 75, 76. Sh 28, 84.
al-ṣifāt al-mu'aththirah, effective attributes. Sh 28.

' - kh - r

ahl al-ākhirah, the people of the Hereafter. DF 71.
ta'akhkhara, to be posterior. DF 31.
ta'akhkhur, posteriority. DF 55.
muta'akhkhir, posterior. Ḥ 33.
al-muta'akhkhirūn, recent [philosophers or theologians]. DF 41. Ḥ 43(4).
muta'akhkhirū al-aṣḥāb, our latter-day colleagues. Sh [43].

' - d - m

ādamī, human being. DF 65. Sh 65b.

' - z - l

azal, eternity. Ḥ 42, 44.
azalan wa-abadan, eternally and everlastingly. DF 51, 63.
min al-azal ilā al-abad, from eternity to everlastingness. Ḥ 36.
azalī, eternal. DF 57, 58, 62. Ḥ 16, 33, 44. Sh [16], 64.
al-'ilm al-azalī al-fi'lī, [God's] active and eternal knowledge. DF 37.

' - ṣ - l

aṣīl, basic. DF 64.
wujūd aṣīl, basic existence. Ḥ 2(2).

' - l - f

mu'allaf, composed. DF 61.

' - l - h

ahl Allāh, the people of God. Ḥ 8.
ilāhī, divine. DF 20, 66, 70. Sh 50a.
al-Dhāt al-Ilāhīyah, the Divine Essence. DF 91.
al-ḥaḍarāt al-ilāhīyah, the divine presences. Ḥ 12.
al-ikhtiyār al-ilāhī, divine choice. DF 51.

’ - l - h (continued)

al-‘ilm al-ilāhī, divine knowledge. DF 91.
al-iqtidār al-ilāhī, divine power. Ḥ 45.
al-martabah al-ilāhīyah, the divine plane. Ḥ 16.
umūr ilāhīyah, divine matters. Ḥ 13(1).
al-ilāhīyāt, metaphysics. Ḥ 13(2), 13(3).
nu‘ūt al-ilāhīyah, the qualities of divinity. Sh 25.

’ - m - r

amr (umūr), thing, entity, matter. DF 30, 32, 37, 38, 40, 46, 51, 55, 58, 63, 67. Ḥ 2(1), 5(1), 5(2), 27, 43(1), 43(2). Sh [2], 11, 19, 21, 28, 33, 34, 37, 46, 48, 51.
amr basīṭ, simple entity. DF 40.
amr dhihnī, mental entity. Sh[2].
amr ghayr qārr, successive entity. Sh 64.
amr i‘tibārī, mental entity. (See trans. of DF, par. 8, n. 2). DF 8, Ḥ 2(3), 6, 15(1). Sh 19.
amr khārijī, external entity. Sh 30.
amr ma‘qūl, mental entity. Sh 5.
umūr ilāhīyah, divine matters. Ḥ 13(1).
umūr wujūdīyah, existential entities. DF 87.
umūr wujūdīyah ‘aynīyah, concrete, existential entities. DF 85, 86.
bi-ḥasab nafs al-amr, with respect to itself, with respect to the thing itself. Sh [38].
fī nafs al-amr, in the thing itself, in itself (See trans. of DF, par. 51, n.1). DF 51. Sh 9, 26, [38], 58.
amara, to command. DF 60, 62, 63.
amr, command. DF 51. Ḥ 42. Sh 51, 60.

’ - m - l

ta’ammala (ta’ammul), to consider, reflect upon, ponder. Ḥ 2(3), 28, 30(2), 43(4). Sh 5, 28, 84.
fīhi ta’ammul, further consideration [of this matter] is called for. Ḥ 2(2), 28.

’ - n - n

annīyah, individual existence (See trans. of DF, par. 22, n.3). DF 22, 65.

' - n - f
ṣūrah mustafāḍah musta'nafah, newly effused form. DF 35.

' - h - l
ahl al-ākhirah, the people of the Hereafter. DF 71.
ahl al-ḥaqq, the people of truth. DF 62.
ahl Allāh, the people of God. Ḥ 8.
ahl al-naẓar min al-falāsifah, the rationalist philosophers. DF 89.
ahl al-sunnah, people of the approved way. DF 45.

' - w - l
ālah, instrument. DF 66, 76, 77.
al-Awwal, the First. DF 31, 32, 35, 38, 40, 45, 83, 84. Ḥ 31, 36. Sh 32, 33, 35.
al-Awwal al-Ḥaqq, the True First. DF 45.
al-Awwal al-Wājib, the Necessarily Existent First. DF 36.
al-Mabda' al-Awwal, the First Principle. DF 77, 78, 79, 81, 85, 86. Ḥ 30(1).
al-Wāḥid al-Awwal, the One First [Being]. DF 81.
awwalīyah, priority. DF 87.
ta'wīl, interpretation. Sh 52.

' - w - n
ān, time. DF 22. Sh [42].

' - w - y
āyah, miracle. Ḥ 13(3).

b - ḥ - t
al-wujūd al-baḥt, pure existence. Sh 1.

b - ḥ - th
fīhi baḥth, this calls for further investigation, this is open to question. Sh 4, [42].

b - d - '
mabda', source, principle, origin. DF 40, 78, 85. Ḥ 5(2), 16. Sh 4, 60.
al-Mabda' al-Awwal, the First Principle. DF 77, 78, 79, 81, 85, 86. Ḥ 30(1). Sh 84.
al-Mabda' al-Fayyāḍ, the Effusive Principle. Sh. 46.

b - d - ' (continued)

mabda' al-ifhām, the source of instruction. Sh 63.
mabda' al-inkishāf, the source of revelation. Sh 28, 33.
Mabda' al-Mawjūdāt, the Source of Existents. DF 18. Ḥ 15(1). Sh 18.
al-Mabda' al-Wāḥid, the One Principle. DF 84.
mabda'īyah, being a source. Ḥ 16.
mabda'īyat al-inkishāf, being the source of revelation. Sh 28.
ibtada'a 'an, to originate from. DF 86.

b - d - r

mutabādir, immediately understood. Sh [38].

b - d - '

abda'a (ibdā'), to create (See trans. of DF, par. 72, n.2). DF 37, 72.
mubtadi', innovator. DF 29.

b - d - n

badan, body. Sh 21.
abdān mutarawḥinah, spiritualized bodies. Sh 21.
abdān 'unṣurīyah, elemental bodies (See trans. of DF, par. 87, n.2). DF 87.

b - d - h

bi-al-badīhah, intuitively. Sh [5].

b - r - '

al-Bārī, the Creator. DF 50, 65. Ḥ 41. Sh 47, [38], 52, 65b.

b - r - z - kh

barzakh, intermediate world. DF 69, 70.

b - r - h - n

barhana, to demonstrate. Ḥ 30(1).
burhān (barāhīn), proof, demonstration. DF 9, 11, 12, 14, 25. Sh 84.
burhānī, demonstrative. Sh 33.
dalīl burhānī, demonstrative argument. Ḥ 29.

b - s - ṭ

basīṭ, simple. DF 75, 76, 77. Sh 72.

b - s - ṭ (continued)

amr basīṭ, simple entity. DF 40.
al-wujūd al-basīṭ al-ḥaqīqī, real and simple existence. Sh 25.
inbasaṭa 'alā, to expand over. DF 20, 90.
inbisāṭ, expansion. DF 90, 91, 92. Ḥ 17, 37.
nisbah inbisāṭīyah, relation of expansion. DF 91.

b - sh - r

maẓhar al-bashar, human manifestation. Sh 67.
maẓhar al-basharīyah, human manifestation. Sh 67.
al-wujūd al-basharī al-jismānī, bodily human existence. Sh 11.
al-wujūd al-basharī al-rūḥānī, spiritual human existence. Sh 11.

b - ṣ - r

baṣar, sight. Ḥ 11. Sh 21.
al-qūwah al-baṣarīyah, the faculty of sight. Ḥ 13(1).
baṣīr, seer. DF 66.
'ayn al-baṣīrah, the eye of insight. Sh 11.
abṣara (ibṣār), to see. Ḥ 13(1).

b - ṭ - l

buṭlān, falsity, absurdity. DF 4, 23. Ḥ 2(2). Sh 4.
bāṭil, absurd. Ḥ 15(1).
abṭala (ibṭāl), to nullify, refute. DF 37. Sh [2].

b - ṭ - n

bāṭin, internal. Ḥ 13(1).
bāṭin al-wujūd, the inner aspect of existence. Sh 1.
fī bāṭin 'ilmihi, in His inner knowledge. DF 1. Sh 1.
al-quwā al-bāṭinah, the internal faculties. DF 21.

b - q - y

baqā', continuance. Ḥ 15(1).

b - ' - th

bā'ith, motive. Sh 47.

b - ' - d

ba'uda, to be improbable. Ḥ 27.

b - ʿ - d (continued)

baʿdīyah ʿādīyah ittifāqīyah, coincidental customary posteriority. Sh 72.

baʿdīyah dhātīyah istilzāmīyah, essential necessitating posteriority. Sh 72.

baʿīd, improbable. Ḥ 42.

istabʿada (istibʿād), to think improbable. DF 11, 12, 14. Sh 11.

b - ʿ - ḍ

tabʿīḍ, partition. DF 10.

b - y - n

mubāyin, distinct, separate. DF 31, 32, 35. Ḥ 27.

mutabāyin, completely distinct (See trans. of DF, par. 14, n. 3). DF 14. Ḥ 30(2).

t - b - ʿ

tābiʿah (tawābiʿ), consequent. Sh 29.

bi-al-tabʿīyah, as a consequence. DF 68.

t - r - k

taraka (tark), to abstain [from an act, from creation]. DF 50. Ḥ 38.

t - m - m

tāmm, perfect. Sh 23, 40, 67.

ʿillah tāmmah, complete cause. DF 85.

al-kamāl al-tāmm, complete perfection. DF 50.

th - b - t

thabata, to be proven, established, affirmed; to subsist. DF 3, 18. Ḥ 15(2), 30(1). Sh [2], 18, 35, 52.

thubūt, subsistence. Ḥ 2(3), 5(1). Sh [2].

taʿayyana taʿayyunan thubūtīyah, to become individuated as fixed essences. Sh 1.

thābit, subsistent, established. Sh [10], 26, 67.

al-aʿyān al-thābitah, the fixed essences (See trans. of DF, par. 89, n. 2). DF 89, 90.

al-kawākib al-thābitah, the fixed stars. DF 85.

athbata (ithbāt), to establish, prove, demonstrate; to affirm,

th - b - t (continued)

to affirm the existence of. DF 12, 17, 20, 25, 28, 29, 30, 31, 47, 48, 49, 50, 51, 53, 54, 55, 60, 63, 64, 77, 78, 85, 88. Ḥ 20. Sh [10], 34, [38], 55, 63, 84.

al-muthbat lahu, thing in which something subsists. Sh [2].

th - l - th

al-thulthīyah, thirdness. DF 80.

th - n - y

thanawī, dualist. DF 29.
ithnaynīyah, duality. DF 25, 29. Sh 26, 29, 33.
istithnā', exception. Ḥ 2(3).

j - b - r

jabr, compulsion. DF 51, 52. Sh 46, 51, 52.
majbūr, compelled. Sh 51.
majbūrīyah, being compelled. Sh 51.
jabarūt, power. DF 66.

j - r - d

mujarrad, abstract, abstracted, unconnected. DF 89. Ḥ 5(1), 14. Sh 23, 37.
mujarrad 'an al-zamān, abstracted from time. Sh 41.
arwāḥ mujarradah, abstracted spirits, spirits abstracted [from matter]. DF 87.
tajarrud, immateriality, abstraction [from matter]. DF 71.

j - z - '

juz' (ajzā'), part. DF 13, 16, 40, 61. Sh 21, 61.
juz'ī, particular, singular, individual. DF 9, 14, 20, 24, 36, 37, 41, 64. Ḥ 7, 20. Sh 20, 41.
al-juz'īyāt al-zamānīyah, temporal particulars. DF 42.
'alā wajh juz'ī, in a particular manner. DF 39.
tajzi'ah, division, partition. DF 10.

j - z - m

jazama, to judge, conclude, decide. DF 57.
al-ikhtiyār al-jāzim, decisive choice. DF 52.

j - s - m

al-jism al-maḥsūs, sensible body. Ḥ 13(2).

al-wujūd al-basharī al-jismānī, bodily human existence. Sh 11.

j - ʻ - l

jaʻl, creation. DF 16.

majʻūl, created, creation. Sh 4.

al-māhīyāt al-ghayr al-majʻūlah, uncreated quiddities (See trans. of DF, par. 58, n. 1). DF 58.

j - l - l

jalāl, majesty. DF 67. Ḥ 5(2).

j - l - w

majlā (majālī), manifestation, place of manifestation. DF 1, 58, 59, 69, 70. Sh 1, 24.

majlā ʻaynī, concrete place of manifestation. Sh 24.

majlā ʻilmī, cognitive place of manifestation. Sh 24.

tajallā (tajallī), to become manifest, to manifest oneself. DF 1, 58, 67, 71. Ḥ 17. Sh 58.

tajallī, manifestation. DF 67. Sh 67.

tajallī mithālī, similative manifestation. DF 71.

al-Mutajallī, the Manifest. DF 58. Sh 58.

j - m - d

jamād, inanimate being. Sh 67.

j - m - ʻ

jamaʻa bayn, to combine. DF 55.

jamʻan wa-furādā, collectively and individually. DF 39, 43.

aḥadīyat jamʻ jamīʻ ṣifātihi wa-asmāʼihi, the oneness of the aggregate of all His attributes and names. DF 74.

al-jamʻīyah, concentration. DF 11.

maẓharīyat al-ism al-jāmiʻ, the manifestation of the comprehensive name [of God] (See trans. of DF, par. 21, n.1). DF 21.

majmūʻ, sum total, combination. DF 16, 40, 47. Ḥ 15(1).

jāmaʻa, to be harmonious with, in harmony with, consistent with. DF 20. Sh 18, 25.

j - m - ʿ (continued)

ijmāʿ, concensus. DF 60.

j - m - l

fī al-jumlah, in general. DF 17.

ʿalā wajh kullī jumlī, in a universal and general manner. Sh 1.

ijmālan, as a whole. DF 40. Sh 41.

ijmālan wa-tafṣīlan, as a whole and in particular. DF 43.

naqḍ ijmālī, general refutation (See trans. of DF, par. 9, n.3). Sh 9.

j - m - h - r

al-jumhūr, all, the majority. DF 26.

jumhūr al-mutakallimīn, the majority of theologians. DF 5, 25.

j - n - s

jins (ajnās), genus. DF 6, 15, 16, 62. Ḥ 42. Sh 40, [42], 67.

j - w - d

al-jūd, liberality. DF 50.

j - w - z

jāza (jawāz), to be possible. DF 46, 55, 77. Ḥ 15(3), 19, 42. Sh 4, [5], 18, 30, 33, [38], 84.

jawāz, possibility. DF 75, 76. Sh 30, 34.

majāzan, metaphorically. Ḥ 43(1).

majāzī, metaphorical. Sh 60.

jawwaza, to allow, to believe possible. DF 55, 75, 78, 79, 80, 85, 86. Ḥ 15(3). Sh 32, [38].

j - w - h - r

jawhar (jawāhir), substance. DF 6. Ḥ 31. Sh 4, 37.

al-jawhar al-awwal, the first substance. Sh [31] a.

al-jawāhir al-ʿaqlīyah, the intellectual substances. DF 36, 37. Ḥ 32. Sh 33, [31] a.

ḥ - j - j

ḥujjah (ḥujaj), proof. DF 12, 25.

ḥ - j - b

al-maḥjūbūn, those veiled [from the truth]. Ḥ 10.

ḥ - j - b (continued)

al-maḥjūbūn 'an al-ḥaqq, those veiled from the truth. DF 37.

ḥ - d - d

ḥadda, to define. DF 65.
ḥadd (ḥudūd), definition. DF 65.

ḥ - d - th

ḥadatha, to originate. DF 44. Ḥ 33.
ḥudūth, occurrence, origination. Ḥ 27, 43(3). Sh 30, 61, 64.
al-ḥudūth al-dhātī, essential origination. Sh 37.
ḥādith, originated. DF 37, 56, 57, 61. Ḥ 43(2), 43(3). Sh 30, 32, 37, [38], 61.
ḥādithah (ḥawādith), event. DF 41, 76.
ḥadīth, tradition. DF 52.
ḥadīth al-taḥawwul, tradition of the transformation (See trans. of DF, par. 71, n. 3). DF 71.
aḥdatha (iḥdāth), to originate (See trans. of DF, par. 72, n. 2). DF 72.

ḥ - r - f

ḥarf (ḥurūf), letter. DF 62, 67, 69, 71. Ḥ 36, 43(3), 44. Sh 61.
ḥurūf al-lafẓ, spoken letters. DF 67.
ḥurūf al-raqm, written letters. DF 67.

ḥ - r - k

ḥarakah, movement. DF 55.
ḥarraka, to move, cause to move. Sh 21, 46.

ḥ - s - s

'ālam al-ḥiss, the world of sense. DF 71.
'ālam al-ḥiss wa-al-shahādah, the world of sense and visibility. Sh 67.
mukālamah ḥissīyah, sensible speech. DF 71.
al-ḥawāss al-ẓāhirah, the external senses. DF 21.
maḥsūs, sensible. Ḥ 11.
al-jism al-maḥsūs, sensible body. Ḥ 13(2).

ḥ - ṣ - ṣ

ḥiṣah (ḥiṣaṣ), portion. DF 5, 6, 7. Ḥ 2(1), 3,5(1), 15(3). Sh [2].

ḥ - ṣ - r

ḥaṣara, to limit. DF 12.

inḥiṣār, limitation, restriction. DF 3, 21. Sh 3.

ḥ - ṣ - l

ḥaṣala, to occur. DF 34, 36, 89. Ḥ 39, 42. Sh 25, 33, 34, 41.

ḥuṣūl, occurrence, existence. DF 34, 36, 57, 73. Ḥ 5(1), 28, 30(1), 40. Sh 33, 35, 47.

ḥuṣūlī, representational (See trans. of Sh, par. 31, n. 1). Sh 31.

ḥāṣil, gist, summary. DF 6, 31, 44. Sh 3, [2], 26, 31, 33, 44a, [38].

al-ḥāṣil bi-al-maṣdar, state resulting from an infinitive (See trans. of Sh, par. [5], n. 1). Sh [5].

ḥaṣṣala (taḥṣīl), to bring into existence. DF 57.

ḥ - ḍ - r

ḥuḍūr, presence, being present, attendance. DF 43, 44. Ḥ 31. Sh 33.

ḥuḍūrī, presentational (See trans. of Sh, par. 31, n. 1). Sh 31.

al-ḥaḍarāt al-ilāhīyah, the divine presences. Ḥ 12.

ḥāḍir, present. DF 41, 44. Ḥ 31, 36. Sh 35.

istaḥḍara, to bring to mind. DF 33.

ḥ - ẓ - r

ḥaẓā'ir al-imkān, realms of contingency. Ḥ 8.

ḥ - f - ẓ

al-Lawḥ al-Maḥfūẓ, the Preserved Tablet. Sh 61.

ḥ - q - q

ḥaqq, truth. DF 33, 37, 65. Sh 33, 35, [43].

al-Ḥaqq, the Truth. DF 37, 43, 52, 58, 74, 87. Ḥ 33, 44. Sh 23, 40, 41, 64.

al-Awwal al-Ḥaqq, the True First. DF 45.

ahl al-ḥaqq, the people of truth. DF 62.

ḥ - q - q (continued)

fī ḥaqq, with respect to. DF 51, 65. Sh 47, [38].

al-Wāḥid al-Ḥaqq, the True One. DF 24.

al-Wujūd al-Ḥaqq, the True Existence. DF 26, 74, 87, 89, 90.

ḥaqīqah (ḥaqā'iq), reality, real quiddity (See trans. of DF, par. 2, n. 1). DF 2, 6, 8, 10, 12, 14, 15, 16, 18, 21, 22, 25, 31, 37, 65, 67, 87, 90. Ḥ 4, 5(1), 5(2), 6, 9, 13(1), 13(2), 13(3), 15(1), 43(4). Sh 1, 3, 10, 12, 25, 26, 37, 40.

Ḥaqīqat al-Ḥaqā'iq, the Reality of Realities. Sh 72.

al-ḥaqā'iq al-kawnīyah, mundane realities. DF 91.

ḥaqīqatan, in reality, really. DF 27. Ḥ 5(2), 43(1), 43(2). Sh 1, 6, 21, 24, 28, 34.

'ālam al-ma'ānī wa-al-ḥaqā'iq, the world of ideas and realities. Sh [37].

bi-al-ḥaqīqah, in reality. DF 44. Sh 40.

bi-ḥasab al-ḥaqīqah, in reality. Sh [43].

fī al-ḥaqīqah, in reality. DF 27, 37, 70, 89, 90. Sh 37, 46.

mukhtalif al-ḥaqīqah, with a dissimilar reality. DF 6, 7. Sh 9.

muttafiq al-ḥaqīqah, with the same reality. DF 6.

ḥaqīqī, real. DF 8, 77, 78. Ḥ 6, 16, 42, 43(2). Sh 1, 19, 20, 32, 37, 40, [42], 72, 78.

al-Fā'il al-Ḥaqīqī, the Real Agent. Sh 46.

al-fanā' al-ḥaqīqī, real passing away. Sh 11.

al-ṣifāt al-ḥaqīqīyah, real attributes [of God]. DF 41, 45, 77. Ḥ 19.

al-wāḥid al-ḥaqīqī, what is really one. DF 78, 79, 80, 91.

al-wujūd al-basīṭ al-ḥaqīqī, real and simple existence. Sh 25.

al-wujūd al-ḥaqīqī, real existence. Sh 29, 58.

al-wujūd al-ḥaqīqī al-'aynī, concrete real existence. Sh 28.

ḥaqqaqa (taḥqīq), to verify, substantiate, demonstrate. DF 38. Ḥ 2(2), 13(2). Sh 18, 28, 32, [37], 46, [38], 84.

muḥaqqiq, verifier. (See trans. of DF, par. 5, n. 1). DF 5, 10, 13, 26, 44. Ḥ 5(2), 24, 43(4). Sh 33, 84.

al-Ṣūfīyah al-muḥaqqiqūn, the verifying Ṣūfīs. DF 49, 78, 86. Sh 37, 72.

muḥaqqiq, realizer. Ḥ 5(2).

muḥaqqaq, substantiated. Sh 11.

ḥ - q - q (continued)

taḥaqqaqa (taḥaqquq), to be realized. DF 15, 21, 90, 91. Ḥ 2(3). Sh 5, 28, 41, 46, [39], 51.

taḥaqquq, realization. DF 14, Ḥ 5(1), 28. Sh 3, 4, 5, 9, 12, 25, 41, 72.

mutaḥaqqiq bi-nafsihi, self-realized. Sh 41.

mutaḥaqqiq fī nafsihi, self-realized. Ḥ 5(2).

ḥ - k - m

ḥakama (ḥukm), to judge, conclude, determine upon; to predicate. DF 28, 35, 42. Ḥ 2(3), 5(1), 12, 29. Sh [2], 11, 46, 72.

ḥukm (aḥkām), quality, characteristic, nature. DF 24, 64, 68, 89. Sh 1, 21, 64.

ḥukm, decision, judgment. DF 51. Sh 11.

ḥukm (aḥkām), precept. Ḥ 43(2), 43(4).

ḥukman, qualitatively. DF 56.

ḥikmah, wisdom. Ḥ 13(1). Sh 37, 51.

al-Ḥakīm, the Wise. Ḥ 13(1). Sh 37.

ḥakīm (ḥukamā'), philosopher. DF 2, 6, 12, 25, 27, 31, 32, 37, 40, 44, 45, 48, 49, 50, 53, 54, 75, 78, 79, 80, 88, 89. Ḥ 2(1), 5(1), 20, 37, 39. Sh [2], 9, 28, 29, 32, 40, 41, [37], [38], 50b, 59, 72, 78.

al-ḥukamā' al-mutaqaddimūn, the early philosophers. DF 2.

ḥ - l - l

ḥalla fī (ḥulūl), to subsist in, inhere in. DF 32, 34, 35, 76. Ḥ 28.

ḥulūl, inherence, subsistence. Sh 34, 37.

ḥāll, subsistent, inherent. DF 34, 37, 39, Sh 33, 37.

al-ḥāllīyah, quality of being subsistent. DF 37. Sh 37.

maḥall (maḥāll), substratum, place. DF 32, 34, 37, 39, 58, 59, 72. Sh 32, 37, 46, 72.

al-maḥallīyah, quality of being a substratum. DF 37. Sh 37.

ḥ - m - l

ḥamala (ḥaml), to interpret; to predicate. Ḥ 43(2). Sh [2], [5], 28, 84.

maḥmal, interpretation. Ḥ 43(4).

ḥ - m - l (continued)

ḥaml, predication. DF 15. Ḥ 20.
maḥmūl, predicate. Ḥ 2(1). Sh [2].
maḥmūl 'alā, predicated of. Ḥ 5(1). Sh 20.
iḥtamala, to be probable. Sh 28.
iḥtimāl, probability. Ḥ 15(3).
'alā al-iḥtimāl, to the point of probability. DF 17.
muḥtamal al-kalām, probable interpretation of the statement. Sh [43].

ḥ - w - j

iḥtāja (iḥtiyāj), to need, be in need. DF 39, 46. Ḥ 15(1), 27, 31, 32, 44.

ḥ - w - ṭ

aḥāṭa bi (iḥāṭah), to encompass; to grasp. DF 20, 44, 45, 68. Ḥ 13(2), 17, 36. Sh 23, 41.
muḥīṭ, all-encompassing. DF 12.

ḥ - w - l

ḥāl (aḥwāl), situation, state, mode. DF 33. Ḥ 13(1), 13(2), 13(3), 27. Sh 41, 67, 71.
ḥāl, intermediate state between existence and nonexistence (See trans. of Sh. par. 63, n. 1). Sh 63.
ḥāl, present. DF 41. Sh 41, 44b.
zamān al-ḥāl, present time. Sh 41.
ḥālī, present, presently existing. DF 44.
ḥālah, state. DF 48. Sh 48.
ḥālah nafsānīyah, psychical state. DF 46.
al-mawjūdāt al-ḥālīyah, presently existing things. DF 44.
al-ḥālīyah, the present. Sh 44 b.
aḥāla, to declare impossible. Sh 11.
muḥāl, impossible, absurd. DF 32, 36, 56. Sh 47, [38], 51.
taḥawwul, transformation. DF 14, 20.
ḥadīth al-taḥawwul, tradition of the transformation (See trans. of DF, par. 71, n. 3). DF 71.
istaḥāla (istiḥālah), to be impossible. DF 50, 53. Ḥ 12. Sh [38].
istiḥālah, impossibility. DF 12, 37. Sh 11, 37, [38].
mustaḥīl, impossible. Sh 11, 72.

ḥ - w - l (continued)

mustaḥīl al-wujūd, impossible of existence. DF 51.

ḥ - y - y

ḥayāh, life. Ḥ 19.

ḥ - y - th

min ḥayth huwa huwa (hiya hiya), as he is in himself. DF 26. Sh 28.

min ḥayth hādhihi al-ḥaythīyah, in this respect. Sh 64.

min hādhihi al-ḥaythīyah, in this respect, from this aspect. DF 13.

kh - b - r

khabar, narration. Ḥ 42.

al-Khabīr, the Well-Informed. DF 43.

akhbara, to inform, narrate. DF 60, 62, 63, 67.

ikhbār, narration. Sh 60.

kh - d - sh

khadasha, to invalidate. Ḥ 1.

kh - r - j

khārij 'an, external to, extrinsic to, outside of. DF 5, 6, 7, 18. Ḥ 4, 15(2), Sh 19, 41.

khārijan, outside the mind, externally, in the external world. DF 4, 5, 20, 78. Ḥ 15(1), 15(2), 15(3).

bi-ḥasab al-khārij, externally, outside the mind, in the external world. DF 49. Ḥ 2(1), 2(3), 5(1), Sh [2], [5].

fī al-khārij, externally, in the external world. DF 4, 12, 19. Ḥ 2(1), 2(2), 4, 5(1), 14. Sh [2], 28, 35.

fī khārij al-'aql, outside the mind. Sh [2].

fī khārij al-dhihn, outside the mind. Sh [2].

khārijī, external, in the external world. DF 4, 8, 20, 37. Ḥ 2(2), 5(1), 15(1). Sh 12, 35, 46.

amr khārijī, external entity. Sh 30.

mawjūd khārijī, external existent. Sh 4.

al-wujūd al-khārijī, external existence. Ḥ 2(2), 2(3). Sh 4, [2].

akhraja, to exclude. Ḥ 9.

kh - ṣ - ṣ

khuṣūṣ, particularity, specific nature. Ḥ 14. Sh 9, 41.

khuṣūṣīyah, characteristic, particular characteristic. DF 4, 40, 74. Ḥ 2(1). Sh 4, [2], 28, 37, 41, 63, 64, 67.

khāṣṣ, proper. Sh 1.

al-wujūd al-khāṣṣ, proper existence (See trans. of DF, par. 4, n. 3). DF 4, 7, 8, 25. Sh 4, 5.

al-wujūd al-khāṣṣ al-wājibī, the proper existence of the Necessary Existent. Ḥ 5(1).

al-sanad al-akhaṣṣ, more specific (less extensive) support (See trans. of Sh, par. [2], n. 2). Sh [2].

khāṣṣah (khawāṣṣ), property. Ḥ 9. Sh 1.

makhṣūṣ, characteristic (adj.). Sh 12.

makhṣūṣ bi, limited to, peculiar to. DF 44.

khaṣṣaṣa (takhṣīṣ), to characterize, to associate specifically with. Sh 41, 67.

ikhtaṣṣa bi (ikhtiṣāṣ), to be proper to, be restricted to. DF 42, 63. Sh 1, 84.

kh - ṭ - ṭ

khaṭṭ, calligraphy. DF 67.

kh - ṭ - b

khiṭābī, rhetorical. Sh 33.

dalīl khiṭābī, rhetorical argument. Ḥ 29.

muqaddimah khiṭābīyah, rhetorical premiss. Ḥ 30(1).

mukhāṭab, person addressed [by God]. DF 63, 68.

kh - l - l

akhalla, to impair. Ḥ 5(2), 7.

ikhtalla (ikhtilāl), to be defective. DF 12.

kh - l - ṣ

khāliṣ, pure, Sh 11.

takhallaṣa, to purify oneself. Sh 11.

kh - l - f

khālafa, to contradict, to differ from, to oppose. DF 32, 49, 53, 78, 79. Ḥ 43(4). Sh [38], [43].

mukhālif, different from. Sh 21.

khilāf al-wāqiʿ, contrary to fact. Sh 3.

kh - l - f (continued)

takhallafa (takhalluf), to lag behind. DF 57, 73. Ḥ 40.

ikhtalafa (ikhtilāf), to differ, be different or dissimilar; to disagree. DF 6, 7, 8, 10, 20, 21, 24, 57, 70. Ḥ 7, 13(2). Sh 9, 10.

ikhtilāf, controversy. Ḥ 1.

mukhtalif, different, dissimilar. DF 51, 80. Sh 24.

mukhtalif al-ḥaqīqah, with a dissimilar reality. DF 6, 7. Sh 9.

kh - l - q

khalaqa (khalq), to create. DF 73. Ḥ 11. Sh 72, 84.

khalq, created beings, humans. DF 51, 66. Sh 51, 67.

khāliq, creator. DF 55.

khalqī, created. DF 20.

makhlūq, created, created being. DF 55, 63, 72, 87. Sh 61, 64, 72.

kh - m - n

takhmīn, conjecture. Sh 84.

takhmīnī, conjectural. Sh 84.

kh - y - r

khayr, good. Sh [38].

fayaḍān al-khayr, the effusion of good. DF 45.

khayrīyah, being good, goodness. Sh 46.

al-takhyīr fī al-'ibārah, to give a choice in expression (See trans. of Sh, par. 25, n. 1). Sh 25, 33.

ikhtiyār, choice, free choice, choosing. DF 51, 54, 55, 72. Sh 46, [38], 51.

al-ikhtiyār al-jāzim, decisive choice. DF 52.

al-ikhtiyār al-ilāhī, divine choice. DF 51.

ikhtiyārī, voluntary. DF 72, 74. Sh 46.

mukhtār, free agent. DF 54, 55, 56. Sh [38].

fā'il mukhtār, free agent. DF 54, 55.

kh - y - l

khayāl, fantasy. Sh 37.

al-wujūd al-khayālī, imaginary existence. Sh 58.

takhayyala, to imagine. DF 25.

d - kh - l

dākhil fī, intrinsic to, included within. DF 5, 7, 18. Ḥ 15(2). Sh 25.

madkhal, role, influence. DF 46, 47, 72, 74.

madkhalīyah, role. Sh 84.

d - r - j

mundarij taḥt, subsumed under. DF 6.

d - r - k

adraka (idrāk), to perceive, apprehend. DF 12, 33, 57, 59. Ḥ 11, 12, 13(1). Sh 11, 21, 33.

mudrak, thing perceived. Sh 33.

d - ʻ - w

dāʻī (dawāʻī), motive. Ḥ 38. Sh [38].

iddaʻā (iddiʻā), to claim. DF 41. Sh 3, [31] b.

istadʻā, to require. Sh [2].

d - q - q

daqīqah (daqā'iq), subtlety. DF 66. Ḥ 13(2).

d - l - l

dalla ʻalā (dalālah), to prove, indicate, attest to, signify. DF 17, 20, 62, 63. Ḥ 43(1), 43(3). Sh 4, 44, 52, 84.

dalīl (dalā'il, adillah), proof, demonstration; indication. DF 4, 12, 13, 17, 60, 63, 78. Ḥ 10, 13(3), 43(3). Sh 33, 35, [31]b, [42], 63, 78.

dalīl burhānī, demonstrative argument. Ḥ 29.

dalīl khiṭābī, rhetorical argument. Ḥ 29.

madlūl, signification. DF 63, 64. Ḥ 43(1). Sh 64.

istadalla (istidlāl), to prove, demonstrate. DF 12, 51. Sh [2], 9, 34.

d - m - j

mundamij, fused. Sh 40.

d - w - r

dawr, circle. Sh 5, [2].

dh - h - b

dhahaba ilā, to take the position, to affirm. DF 5, 8, 11,

dh - h - b (continued)
12, 17, 28, 50, 54, 61, 62, 72, 75, 78, 92. Ḥ 1, 5(1), 8. Sh 8, 9, 12.
madhhab (madhāhib), position, doctrine. DF 2, 4, 6, 32, 41, 46, 74, 77, 88. Ḥ 2(1). Sh [2], 18, 28, 32, 33, [31] a, 37, 40, [38], 50b, 63, 84.

dh - h - n
dhihnan, in the mind, mentally. DF 4, 5, 20. Ḥ 15(1), 15(2), 15(3).
bi-ḥasab al-dhihn, in the mind. Ḥ 5(1).
fī al-dhihn, in the mind. Sh [2], 20, 25, 40.
fī khārij al-dhihn, outside the mind. Sh [2].
dhihnī, mental. DF 20, 37. Ḥ 5(1). Sh 12.
amr dhihnī, mental entity. Sh [2].
mawjūd dhihnī, mental existent. Sh 4, 25.
al-wujūd al-dhihnī, mental existence. Sh 4, 40.

dh - w
dhāt (dhawāt), essence; self; substance. DF 1, 3, 4, 5, 7, 14, 19, 20, 24, 26, 27, 28, 29, 30, 31, 32, 33, 34, 35, 37, 38, 39, 40, 43, 45, 46, 47, 48, 49, 50, 51, 53, 55, 57, 64, 65, 70, 74, 77, 84, 87. Ḥ 1, 5(1), 16, 19, 20, 22, 26, 27, 30(1), 30(2), 31, 40, 43(2), 44. Sh 1, 3, 4, 12, 18, [16], 21, 26, 28, 29, 30, 31, 32, 33, 35, 40, 41, [37], 48, [38], 50b, 51, 52, 55, 61, 64, 65b, 72, 75.
al-Dhāt al-Ilāhīyah, the Divine Essence. DF 91.
al-Dhāt al-Muta'āliyah, the Transcendent Essence. Sh [16].
dhātuhu al-aḥadīyah, [God's] unitary essence. DF 52. Sh 72.
dhawāt al-'ālam, essences of the universe. DF 41.
aḥadī al-dhāt, one in essence. DF 51.
mawjūd bi-dhātihi, self-existent. Sh 4.
qārr al-dhāt, simultaneous in essence (See trans. of Ḥ, No. 9, n. 2). Ḥ 9.
al-qiyām bi-al-dhāt, self-subsistence. DF 32.
al-Wājib li-Dhātihi, the Necessary Existent in Himself. DF 2, 55.
al-Wāḥid al-Qā'im bi-Dhātihi, the Self-Subsistent One.

dh - w (continued)
DF 31.
dhātī, essential, essential attribute. DF 7, 9, 40. Sh 9, 37, 51.
al-ʿadam al-dhātī, essential nonexistence. DF 37.
al-aḥadīyah al-dhātīyah, essential oneness. DF 26.
baʿdīyah dhātīyah istilzāmīyah, essential necessitating posteriority. Sh 72.
al-ḥudūth al-dhātī, essential origination. Sh 37.
ʿillah dhātīyah, essential cause. DF 40.
al-iṭlāq al-dhātī, essential absoluteness. DF 43.
al-kamāl al-dhātī, essential perfection. Sh 52.
qablīyah dhātīyah martabīyah, priority of essence and rank. Sh 44a.
kullī dhātī, essential universal. Sh [2].
maʿlūl dhātī, essential effect. DF 34.
al-maʿīyah al-dhātīyah, essential coextension. DF 43.
martabat waḥdatihi al-dhātīyah, the plane of His essential unity. Sh 51.
waḥdah dhātīyah, essential unity. DF 78. Ḥ 20.

dh - w - q
dhawq, intuition. DF 28. Ḥ 10.
madhūqāt, tastes. Ḥ 11.

r - b - b
rabb (arbāb), master. Ḥ 10.
arbāb al-naẓar, masters of reason. Ḥ 10.
rubūbīyah, lordship. DF 66.
nuʿūt al-rubūbīyah, the attributes of lordship. Sh 25.
ṣifāt al-rubūbīyah, the attributes of lordship. DF 65.

r - t - b
rutbah, plane, rank. DF 88. Ḥ 9, 33, 37.
martabah (marātib), stage, plane, level, rank. DF 20, 58, 59, 66, 71, 74, 81, 82, 83, 86, 91. Ḥ 9, 13(1), 13(3). Sh 1, 11, 12, [16], 26, 40, 67, 83, 84.
martabat al-ījād, the stage of bringing-into-existence. DF 3, 87.
martabat al-imkān, the plane of contingency. Sh 1.

r - t - b (continued)

al-martabah al-jāmiʿah bayn al-ghayb wa-al-shahādah, the the plane linking the invisible and visible worlds. DF 68.

al-martabah al-ilāhīyah, the divine plane. Ḥ 16.

martabat waḥdatihi al-dhātīyah, the plane of His essential unity. Sh 51.

marātib al-akwān, the planes of created beings. Ḥ 8.

bi-ḥasab al-martabah, according to rank. Sh 37.

qablīyah bi-ḥasab al-martabah, priority according to rank. Sh 37.

qablīyah dhātīyah martabīyah, priority of essence and rank. Sh 44a.

rattaba (tartīb), to arrange. DF 51.

tartīb, arrangement. DF 45.

silsilat al-tartīb, chain of succession [of causes and effects]. DF 44.

tarattaba, to be ranked, ordered. DF 31, 61. Ḥ 43(3).

mutarattib, sequential. Sh [44].

tarattaba ʿalā (tarattub), to result from, depend on. DF 27, 91. Ḥ 13(1). Sh 37, 47, [39], 72.

r - j - ḥ

rajjaḥa, to tip the scales in favor. Sh [2].

tarajjaḥa, to preponderate. DF 51.

r - d - d

taraddada (taraddud), to waver, to be irresolute, be uncertain. DF 51. Ḥ 10. Sh 4, 51.

r - s - m

rasama, to describe. DF 65.

rasm (rusūm), description. DF 65. Sh 28.

irtasama (irtisām), to be inscribed. DF 51. Sh [31].

r - f - ʿ

irtafaʿa (irtifāʿ), to be absent, to become extinct, to be eliminated. DF 73. Ḥ 2(2), 2(3). Sh 1, 11.

r - q - m

raqm, script. DF 67. Ḥ 44.

ḥurūf al-raqm, written letters. DF 67.

r - q - y

taraqqī, progression. Sh 21.

r - k - b

tarkīb, composition. DF 75. Ḥ 15(1). Sh 75.
tarkīb, superimposition. Sh 33.
sawq al-tarkīb, order of composition. Sh 33.
murakkab, composed, compound. DF 71. Sh 65b.
tarakkaba, to be compound. DF 18. Ḥ 15(2).
tarakkaba (tarakkub), to be superimposed. DF 33. Ḥ 26. Sh 33.

r - w - ḥ

rūḥ, spirit. DF 23. Sh 23.
arwāḥ mujarradah, abstracted spirits, spirits abstracted from matter. DF 87.
'ālam al-arwāḥ, the world of spirits. DF 71.
al-wujūd al-basharī al-rūḥānī, spiritual human existence. Sh 11.
tarawḥana (tarawḥun), to be, become spiritualized (See trans. of DF, par. 21, n. 2). DF 21.
abdān mutarawḥinah, spiritualized bodies. Sh 21.

r - w - d

arāda, to will. DF 66, 69. Ḥ 39. Sh 51.
irādah, will. DF 27, 29, 45, 47, 48, 49, 51, 53, 57, 58, 68, 69, 72, 74. Ḥ 39, 45. Sh [38], 50b, [39], 51, 55, 72.
murīd, willing. DF 27, 45.
murād, willed, thing willed, object of will. DF 29, 51, 57.

z - m - n

zamān (azminah), time. DF 23, 41, 44, 55, 56. Ḥ 36. Sh 23, 41.
zamān al-ḥāl, present time. Sh 41.
zamān māḍī, past time. Sh 41.
mujarrad 'an al-zamān, abstracted from time. Sh 41.
muta'ālī 'an al-zamān, exalted above time. DF 23. Ḥ 36.
al-mutawaghghilūn fī al-makān wa-al-zamān, those immersed in space and time. DF 23, 42.
zamānī, temporal, temporal being. DF 37, 41, 42. Ḥ 36.

z - m - n (continued)
Sh 23, 41.
al-zamānīyāt, temporal things. Sh 41.
al-juz'īyāt al-zamānīyah, temporal particulars. DF 42.
mawjūd zamānī, temporal existent. Sh 41, 44b.

z - w - l
fīmā lā yazāl, in that which does not pass away (See trans. of Ḥ, no. 42, n. 2). Ḥ 42.

z - y - d
ziyādah, increase. Sh 9.
zā'id 'alā, superadded to, additional to. DF 5, 7, 8, 20, 26, 27, 30, 38, 39, 45, 47, 49, 51, 53, 55, 65. Ḥ 1, 2(1), 5(1), 15(1), 27, 28. Sh 1, 4, 26, 30, 31, 35.

z - y - f
zayyafa (tazyīf), to invalidate. DF 12.

s - ' - l
sā'il, questioner, objector. Sh 44 b.
mas'alah (masā'il), proposition, doctrine, question. DF 12. Ḥ 10. Sh 5, [2], 8, 32, 46, 67, 72, 84.

s - b - b
sabab (asbāb), cause, reason. DF 38, 40. Sh 34.
al-sababīyah al-mustalzimah, necessitating causation. Sh 72.

s -b - q
sabaqa, to be prior to, to precede. DF 37, 55, 57, 88, 91.
sabq, priority. DF 55.
sābiq, previous, prior, antecedent. Ḥ 2(3), 16. Sh 37.
masbūq. preceded, posterior. DF 37, 44, 54. Ḥ 2(3). Sh 37.

s - r - r
sirr (asrār), secret; reason. DF 66, 68. Sh 67, 72.

s - r - y
sarā (sarayān), to pervade. DF 21.

s - l - b
salbī, negative. DF 32.
al-ṣifāt al-salbīyah, the negative attributes. Ḥ 19.

s - l - s - l

tasalsala (tasalsul), to result in an endless chain. DF 19. Ḥ 2(3). Sh [2], 19.

silsilat al-tartīb, chain of succession [of causes and effects]. DF 44.

s - l - f

al-salaf al-ṣāliḥ, the pious ancestors. Sh 61.

s - l - m

sallama, to admit, grant. Ḥ 2(1), 16, 30(2). Sh 4, [2], 9, 18, 61.

s - m - ḥ

musāmaḥah, lack of preciseness. (See trans. of Sh, par. 66, n. 1). Sh 66.

s - m - ʻ

samiʻa, to hear. DF 66. Ḥ 13(1).

samʻ, hearing. Sh 21.

al-qūwah al-samʻīyah, the faculty of hearing. Ḥ 13(1).

samīʻ, hearer. DF 66.

masmūʻāt, sounds. Ḥ 11.

s - m - w

ism (asmāʼ), name [of God]. DF 2, 74. Sh 28.

maẓharīyat al-ism al-jāmiʻ, the manifestation of the comprehensive name [of God] (See trans. of DF, par. 21, n. 1). DF 21.

aḥadīyat jamʻ jamīʻ ṣifātihi wa-asmāʼihi, the oneness of the aggregate of all His attributes and names. DF 74.

al-nisab al-asmāʼīyah, the nominal relations. DF 91.

sammā, to call, name. DF 67. Ḥ 14.

al-musammā, thing named. DF 62.

s - n - n

ahl al-sunnah, people of the approved way. DF 45.

s - n - d

al-sanad al-akhaṣṣ, more specific (less extensive) support (See trans. of Sh, par. [2], n. 2). Sh [2].

s - n - d (continued)

asnada (isnād), to ascribe, attribute. DF 59. Sh [38].
istanada (istinād), to depend on, rely on. DF 54, 55, 75, 76, 77, 80. Ḥ 15(3), 40. Sh 3, 55.
mustanad, evidence, basis. DF 11. Ḥ 10. Sh [38].

s - w - q

sāqa (sawq), to propound [a proof]. Sh 63.
sawq al-tarkīb, order of composition. Sh 33.

s - w - y

'alā al-sawīyah, equal. Sh [2].
mutasāwī, same, equal, identical. DF 23, 41, 44.
mutasāwī al-nisbah, equally related. DF 41. Ḥ 36.

s - y - r

al-kawākib al-sayyārah, the planets. DF 85.

sh - ' - n

sha'n (shu'ūn, shu'ūnāt), matter, thing, mode. DF 23, 43, 45, 58. Ḥ 13(3). Sh 37, 40.

sh - b - h

shubhah (shubah), objection. DF 12.
tashābuh, similarity. DF 65.

sh - kh - ṣ

shakhṣ (ashkhāṣ), individual, particular, singular. DF 14.
waḥdah shakhṣīyah, individual unity. Ḥ 20.
shakhkhaṣa (tashkhīṣ), to characterize. Sh 34, 35.
mushakhkhaṣ, individuated. Ḥ 20.
tashakhkhuṣ, individuation. DF 19.

sh - r - ḥ

al-shāriḥ al-muḥaqqiq, the learned commentator [Naṣīr al-Dīn al-Ṭūsī]. DF 32.

sh - r - dh - m

shirdhimah, small group. DF 30.

sh - r - ṭ

sharṭ (shurūṭ), condition. DF 34, 43, 55, 76, 87.
lā bi-sharṭ shay', unconditioned by anything. Ḥ 14.

sh - r - ṭ (continued)
sharīṭah (sharāʼiṭ), condition. DF 73, 77. Ḥ 17. Sh 41.
sharṭīyah, hypothetical proposition. DF 50, 52, 53.

sh - r - k
shirk, polytheism. DF 28.
sharīk, partner [of God]. DF 25. Sh 25.
shāraka, to share with. Sh 25.
mushārakah, participation. DF 33.
ishtaraka (ishtirāk), to be common to. DF 4, 20, 89. Sh 4.
mushtarik fī, having in common. DF 6.
mushtarak bayn, common to. DF 5, 6, 20, 89. Sh 4.

sh - ʻ - b
tashaʻʻub, manifoldness. Sh 51.

sh - ʻ - r
shuʻūr, awareness. DF 46, 48.
mashʻūr bihi, perceived. Sh [2].
al-Ashʻarīyah, the Ashʻarites. DF 75.
al-Ashāʻirah, the Ashʻarites. DF 77.

sh - q - q
shiqq, alternative [of a disjunctive proposition]. DF 14.

sh - k - k
shakk (shukūk), uncertainty. DF 12.
tashkīk, analogousness, analogous [predication], [predication by] analogy (See trans. of DF, par. 9, n. 2). DF 9.

sh - k - l
mushākalah, resemblance (See trans. of Sh, par. [10], n. 1). Sh [10].
ashkala (ishkāl), to be difficult. DF 30. Ḥ 15(3). Sh 30, [38].

sh - m - m
mashmūmāt, odors. Ḥ 11.

sh - h - d
shahida (shuhūd), to be present. DF 38.
shuhūd, presence. DF 44.
ʻilm shuhūdī, presentational knowledge. DF 44.

sh - h - d (continued)
al-shahādah, the visible world. DF 69.
'ālam al-ḥiss wa-al-shahādah, the world of sense and visibility. Sh 67.
shahādatan, in the visible world. DF 20.
al-martabah al-jāmi'ah bayn al-ghayb wa-al-shahādah, the plane linking the invisible and visible worlds. DF 68.
al-shāhid, the visible world. DF 14.
al-shāhidīyah, being present. DF 38.
al-mashhūdīyah, being the object of presence. DF 38.
shāhada, to see. DF 25. Sh 37.
mushāhadah, vision. DF 20. Ḥ 15(3).

sh - w - r
ishārah, allusion. DF 66. Sh 11.
mushār ilayh, designated. Sh 64.

sh - w - q
shawq, desire. DF 46. Sh 46.

sh - y - '
shā'a, to will, wish. DF 50, 52. Ḥ 39. Sh [38], 52.
mashī'ah, will, volition. Ḥ 39. Sh [38], 52.
mashī'at al-fi'l, the will to act. DF 50.
shay' (ashyā'), thing, anything. DF 3, 4, 5, 10, 11, 13, 14, 25, 27, 29, 32, 33, 35, 37, 39, 40, 41, 43, 44, 46, 48, 50, 51, 55, 63, 65, 66, 80, 85. Ḥ 2(3), 12, 13(3), 20, 27, 28, 31, 36, 42. Sh 1, 3, 4, 5, [2], 11, 21, 23, 25, 29, 32, 33, 34, [31], 41, 46, [42], 72, 84.
al-shay' al-'aynī, concrete thing. DF 13.
shay' bi-'aynihi, concrete thing. DF 13.

ṣ - b - gh
munṣabigh, imbued with. Sh 21.

ṣ - ḥ - ḥ
ṣaḥḥa (ṣiḥḥah), to be valid, proper, true, to apply to. DF 12, 37, 50, 51. Ḥ 2(3), 5(1), 38. Sh [38], 64, 84.
ṣiḥḥah, validity, truth. DF 61, 62. Ḥ 10, 20. Sh 5.
ṣaḥīḥ, true. Ḥ 5(1), 10.
ṣaḥḥaḥa (taṣḥīḥ), to confirm, verify. DF 12.

ṣ - ḥ - b

muta'akhkhirū al-aṣḥāb, our latter-day colleagues. Sh [43].

ṣ - d - r

ṣadara 'an (ṣudūr), to emanate from. DF 33, 37, 39, 41, 46, 48, 76, 78, 80, 83, 84, 85, 86, 89. Sh 33, 34, 46, 67.

ṣudūr, emanation. DF 2, 46, 48, 75, 77, 79, 80, 81, 84, 91. Ḥ 28, 31. Sh [31], [37], 51, 75.

ṣādir, emanation, that which emanates. DF 33, 81, 88, 89, 90, 92. Sh 34.

al-ṣādir al-awwal, the first emanation. Sh [31].

maṣdar, gerund, verbal noun. Sh 66.

al-ḥāṣil bi-al-maṣdar, state resulting from an infinitive (See trans. of Sh, par. [5], n. 1). Sh [5].

al-ma'nā al-maṣdarī, the verbal meaning. Ḥ 5(1).

ṣ - d - q

ṣadaqa 'alā, to be true of, be predicated of. DF 21. Sh 20, 28, 60.

ṣidq, truth. DF 52, 53.

ṣādiq, true. DF 50.

miṣdāq, denotation. Sh 28.

taṣādaqa, to be predicated of each other. DF 21.

ṣ - r - f

ṣirāfat waḥdatihi, His absolute unity. DF 59.

waḥdah ṣirfah, absolute unity. DF 58.

taṣurruf, control. Sh 46.

ṣ - gh - r

ṣughrā, minor premiss. DF 61, 62. Sh 61.

ṣ - l - ḥ

maṣlaḥah, benefit. DF 46, 47, 51. Sh 47, [38].

ṣ - n - '

al-Ṣāni', the Creator. DF 43. Ḥ 13(2).

maṣnū', creation. Ḥ 13(3).

ṣ - w - b

kayfīyat al-ṣawāb, the correct manner. DF 45.

ṣ - w - t

ṣawt (aṣwāt), sound. DF 62, 67. Ḥ 44. Sh 61.

ṣ - w - r

ṣūrah (ṣuwar), form. DF 20, 21, 22, 23, 24, 30, 31, 33, 35, 36, 37, 38, 39, 63, 64, 67, 69, 71, 84, 90, 91. Ḥ 13(3), 17, 25, 26, 27, 28, 31, 32. Sh 1, 20, 21, 23, 24, 26, 30, 33, 34, [31], 35, 67, 72, 84.

ṣūrah ʿaqlīyah, mental form. Ḥ 2(1).

ṣūrat al-maʿlūmīyah, the form through which something is known. DF 63, 64. Sh 63, 64.

ṣūrah mustafāḍah musta'nafah, newly effused form. DF 35.

al-ṣuwar al-maʿqulah, intelligible forms. DF 32.

ʿālam al-ṣuwar wa-al-mithāl, the world of forms and similitude. Sh 67.

ṣūrī, formal. DF 69.

al-taʿayyun al-ṣūrī, formal individuation. DF 22.

taṣawwara (taṣawwur), to conceive of, imagine. DF 20, 33, 46, 57. Ḥ 1. Sh [2], [5], 19, 41, 44b, 46.

taṣawwara bi, to assume the form of. DF 90.

mutaṣawwar, imagined. Sh [44].

ṣ - w - f

al-Ṣūfīyah, the Ṣūfīs. DF 2, 8, 11, 25, 43, 51, 52, 54, 65, 74, 79, 80, 88. Ḥ 5(2), 20, 37. Sh 25, 28, 29, [38], 65a.

al-Ṣūfīyah al-muḥaqqiqūn, the verifying Ṣūfīs. DF 49, 78, 86. Sh 37, 72.

al-Ṣūfīyah al-muwaḥḥidah, the unitarian Ṣūfīs (See trans. of DF, par. 92, n. 1). DF 92. Sh 8, 40.

ḍ - d - d

muḍādd, contrary to. Sh 21.

mutaḍādd, contrary. DF 14.

ḍ - r - r

ḍarūrata, because of, due to. DF 15.

ḍarūratan, of necessity, necessarily. DF 54. Ḥ 14, 43(2).

bi-al-ḍarūrah, of necessity. DF 56.

ḍarūrī, self-evident, necessary. DF 57. Ḥ 2(1).

ḍ - ʿ - f

ḍuʿf, weakness. Sh 9.
ḍaʿīf, weak. Ḥ 8. Sh 9.
taḍāʿafa, to double. DF 33. Sh 33.

ḍ - m - n

maḍmūn, contents. Sh [10], 72.
ḍamīr, heart; pronoun. DF 66. Sh 84.
taḍammana (taḍammun), to include. DF 40.

ḍ - y - f

aḍāfa (iḍāfah), to attribute, relate. DF 5, 6, 7, 55, 59, 66. Ḥ 2(1), 5(1), 6, 15(3). Sh 5, 67.
iḍāfah, relation, attribution. Ḥ 19, 22. Sh 5, [2].
iḍāfī, relative. DF 32. Ḥ 19.
al-wujūd al-iḍāfī, attributive existence (See trans. of DF, par. 25, n. 1). DF 25.
al-wujūd al-muḍāf, attributed existence. Sh 5.
inḍāfa, to be attributed. DF 85.

ṭ - b - ʿ

ṭabīʿah, nature. Sh 3.
kullī ṭabīʿī, natural universal (See trans. of DF, par. 12, n. 2). DF 12, 13, 17. Ḥ 14. Sh 18, 20.
al-qūwah al-ṭabīʿīyah, the physical faculty. Sh 21.
inṭabaʿa (inṭibāʿ), to be impressed. DF 24, 58. Ḥ 31, 32. Sh 33, [31].

ṭ - b - q

ṭābaqa, to correspond to, accord with, conform to. DF 30. Sh 29, 30, [42], 84.

ṭ - r - f

ṭaraf, term [of a relation]. Sh 5.

ṭ - l - b

ṭalab, desire. DF 45.
maṭlūb, thesis, conclusion. DF 17, 18. Ḥ 15(2), 30(1). Sh 18, 33, 34, 35.

ṭ - l - q

aṭlaqa ʿalā, to apply to, attribute to. DF 65. Ḥ 1, 8, 43(1).

ṭ - l - q (continued)
Sh 33.
iṭlāq, absoluteness. DF 74. Sh [16].
al-iṭlāq al-dhātī, essential absoluteness. DF 43.
muṭlaq, absolute, unrestricted. DF 4, 8, 12, 18, 20. Ḥ 12, 15(2), 20. Sh 4, [2], 9, 11, 12, 18, [16], 21.
muṭlaqan, absolutely, in an absolute sense, in any way. DF 16, 33. Ḥ 2(3), 19. Sh 37, 64.
mawjūd muṭlaq, absolute existent. Sh 25.
qābilīyah maḥḍah muṭlaqah, absolute and pure receptivity. Sh [37].
al-'uqūl al-muṭlaqah, unrestricted intellects. Ḥ 12.
al-wujūd al-muṭlaq, absolute existence. DF 6, 25. Sh 4, 5, 25.

ṭ - w - r
ṭawr (aṭwār), level. DF 11.
ṭawr al-'aql, level of the intellect. DF 11.

ẓ - l - l
ẓill, shade. DF 52.
ẓill al-takwīn, shade of creation. DF 52.
wujūd ẓillī, shadowy existence. Ḥ 2(2).

ẓ - n - n
ẓann, opinion, presumption (See trans. of Ḥ, No. 30, n. 2). Ḥ 30(1).
ẓannī, presumptive. Sh 78, 84.
muqaddimāt ẓannīyah ẓāhirīyah, ostensibly presumptive premisses. Sh 33.

ẓ - h - r
ẓahara (ẓuhūr), to appear, become manifest, apparent. DF 10, 11, 20, 21, 23, 24, 27, 37, 38, 52, 58, 59, 69, 70, 74, 89, 91. Ḥ 8, 9, 17. Sh 10, 20, 21, 24, 41, 58, 67, 69, 71, 72.
ẓāhir, apparent, obvious, external. DF 32, 64, 78. Ḥ 13(1), 13(3). Sh 37, 41, 64, 78.
ẓāhir al-'ibārah, literal meaning of the expression. Sh 28, [31].
ẓāhir al-wujūd, the outward aspect of existence. Sh 1.
al-ḥawāss al-ẓāhirah, the external senses. DF 21.

ẓ - h - r (continued)
bi-ḥasab al-ẓāhir, apparently. Sh 34.
muqaddimāt ẓannīyah ẓāhirīyah, ostensibly presumptive premisses. Sh 33.
maẓhar (maẓāhir), manifestation. DF 20, 89. Ḥ 20. Sh 67.
maẓhar al-bashar, human manifestation. Sh 67.
maẓhar al-basharīyah, human manifestation. Sh 67.
maẓharīyat al-ism al-jāmi', the manifestation of the comprehensive name [of God] (See trans. of DF, par. 21, n. 1). DF 21.
iẓhār, manifestation. Sh 72.

' - b - th
'abath, vanity. Sh [38].

' - b - d
'abd ('ibād), man, human being. DF 72, 74. Sh 72.
'ubūdīyah, adoration. Sh 37.
ma'būdīyah, being adored. Sh 37.

' - b - r
'ibārah, expression. DF 62, 63, 64, 66. Ḥ 43(1). Sh 25, [38], 64, 84.
'ibārah 'an, equivalent to. DF 63, 64. Ḥ 15(1). Sh 41.
bi-ḥasab al-'ibārah, with respect to the expression. Ḥ 39.
al-takhyīr fī al-'ibārah, to give a choice in expression (See trans. of Sh, par. 25, n. 1). Sh 25, 33.
ẓāhir al-'ibārah, literal meaning of the expression. Sh 28, [31].
'abbara (ta'bīr), to express. DF 62, 63, 71. Sh [42].
i'tabara (i'tibār), to consider. DF 21, 25, 26, 33, 38, 83. Sh 18, 26, [42], 75, 83.
i'tibār, consideration, aspect, respect, relation. DF 20, 26, 27, 33, 39, 58, 78, 80, 83, 84, 85, 86, 88, 89, 91. Ḥ 2(2), 16, 26, 30(2). Sh 1, 19, 26, 33, 40, 48, 65b.
i'tibār, point of view. Sh [31].
al-i'tibārāt al-muntashi'at al-ta'aqqul ba'ḍuhā 'an ba'ḍ, considerations whose intellections are derived one from another. DF 39.
bi-i'tibār, with respect to, in consideration of, in view of.

ʿ - b - r (continued)

DF 37, 44, 52, 59, 63, 64, 78, 80, 83, 90. Ḥ 2(3), 6, 8, 37. Sh 21, 26, 28, 47, 63, 64.

bi-iʿtibār anna, considering that, in view of. DF 38. Sh 47, 63.

bi-hādhā al-iʿtibār, in this respect. DF 27. Ḥ 14. Sh 4, 46, 51, 65b.

bi-ḥasab al-iʿtibār, as considered in the mind. DF 38.

fī iʿtibār, with respect to. Ḥ 31.

fī al-iʿtibār, in the mind. Ḥ 30(1).

fī iʿtibār al-muʿtabirīn, as conceived in the minds of those considering [this question]. DF 35.

iʿtibārī, mental, in the mind (See trans. of DF, par. 8, n. 1). DF 35. Ḥ 30(2), 42. Sh 19.

amr iʿtibārī, mental entity (See trans. of DF, par. 8, n. 2). DF 8. Ḥ 2(3), 6, 15(1). Sh 19.

kathrah iʿtibārīyah, mental multiplicity, multiplicity existing only in the mind. Ḥ 20.

mafhūm iʿtibārī, mental concept. Ḥ 4, 5(1).

nisbah ʿaqlīyah iʿtibārīyah, mental, intellectual relation. DF 88.

al-ṣifāt al-iʿtibārīyah, mental attributes [of God]. DF 77.

ʿ - j - z

aʿjaza (iʿjāz), to be inimitable, to render incapable. Sh 67.

ʿ - d - d

ʿadadī, numerical. DF 26.

taʿaddada, to be or become many, to be multiple. DF 21, 66.

taʿaddud, multiplicity, plurality. DF 10, 25, 76, 77, 89. Ḥ 2(1). Sh [2], 9, 19, 51.

mutaʿaddid, multiple, numerous. DF 3, 13, 15, 23, 24, 25, 40, 75, 76. Ḥ 34. Sh 3, 19.

istaʿadda, to be predisposed. DF 10.

istiʿdād, predisposition. DF 24, 74.

ʿ - d - m

ʿadam, nonexistence; lack. DF 25, 37, 53, 56, 57, 59. Sh 25 [38].

al-ʿadam al-dhātī, essential nonexistence. DF 37.

ʻ - d - m (continued)

ʻadam al-inqisām, indivisibility. DF 80.
ʻadamī, privative. DF 85.
maʻdūm, nonexistent. Ḥ 31. Sh 61, 63.

ʻ - r - ṣ

ʻarṣat ʻilmihi, the expanse of His knowledge. DF 51. Sh 1, 51.

ʻ r - ḍ

ʻaraḍa (ʻurūḍ), to inhere, to come to inhere in. Ḥ 5(2). Sh [5].
ʻaraḍ (aʻrāḍ), accident. DF 6. Sh 4, 37, 64.
al-aʻrāḍ al-ghayr al-qārrah, successive accidents (See trans. of DF, par. 64, n. 2). DF 64.
ʻaraḍīyah, accidentality. DF 6, 9. Sh 9.
ʻāriḍ, accident, accidental, inhering, inherent. DF 6, 9, 18. Ḥ 5(2), 7, 15(1), 15(2), 15(3). Sh 9.
maʻrūḍ, substratum, thing in which an accident inheres, inhered in. DF 6, 8. Ḥ 15(1).
mutaʻāriḍ, incompatible. DF 61, 70.

ʻ - r - f

maʻrifah, knowledge. DF 46.
ʻārif, mystic. DF 59.
ʻurfan, customarily. Sh [5].
bi-ḥasab al-ʻurf, according to custom. Sh 52.

ʻ - sh - w

ʻashā, night blindness. DF 10.

ʻ - ḍ - l

al-qūwah al-ʻaḍalīyah, muscular force. DF 46.

ʻ - ḍ - w

ʻuḍw (aʻḍāʼ), member, organ [of the body]. DF 46, 76. Sh 46.

ʻ - q - b

mutaʻāqib, consecutive, in sequence. DF 61. Ḥ 43(3).

ʻ - q- d

iʻtaqada (iʻtiqād), to believe. DF 4, 50. Sh 4, 50a.

ʻ - q - d (continued)

iʻtiqād, belief. Sh 46.
muʻtaqad, belief. Ḥ 13(2).

ʻ - q - l

ʻaqala, to apprehend. DF 31, 33, 34, 35, 36, 41. Ḥ 14. Sh 33.
lā yuʻqal, is inconceivable. DF 57. Ḥ 40.
ʻaql (ʻuqūl), intellect, mind. DF 8, 11, 12, 20, 84, 85. Ḥ 2(2), 2(3), 5(1), 11, 12, 13(2), 13(3), 14, 30(2). Sh 5, [2], 11, 28, 30, 33, 84.
ʻaqlan, in the mind; logically, rationally. DF 78. Ḥ 2(2), 15(3). Sh 3, 55.
al-ʻaql al-awwal, the first intellect. DF 84, 88, 89. Ḥ 30(2), 37. Sh [31], [37], 84.
al-ʻaql al-faʻʻāl, the active intellect. DF 76. Ḥ 23.
al-ʻuqūl al-ḍaʻīfah, weak intellects. DF 51.
al-ʻuqūl al-muṭlaqah, unrestricted intellects. Ḥ 12.
al-ʻaql al-naẓarī, the rational intellect. Sh 8.
ʻālam al-ʻuqūl, the world of intellects. Sh 41.
bi-ḥasab al-ʻaql, in the mind. Ḥ 2(1). Sh [2], [5].
fī al-ʻaql, in the mind. Ḥ 14. Sh [2].
fī khārij al-ʻaql, outside the mind. Sh [2].
ʻind al-ʻaql, rationally. Sh 34.
ṭawr al-ʻaql, the level of the intellect. DF 11.
al-wujūd fī al-ʻaql, existence in the mind. Sh [2].
ʻaqlī, intelligible, intellectual, mental. DF 20, 85. Ḥ 15(1). Sh 12.
al-jawāhir al-ʻaqlīyah, the intellectual substances. DF 36, 37. Ḥ 32. Sh 33, [31].
kullī ʻaqlī, mental universal (See trans. of DF, par. 12, n. 2). Ḥ 14.
al-muqaddimāt al-ʻaqlīyah, logical principles. Ḥ 2(3).
nisbah ʻaqlīyah iʻtibārīyah, mental, intellectual relation. DF 88.
al-qūwah al-ʻaqlīyah, the intellectual faculty. Ḥ 13(1).
ṣūrah ʻaqlīyah, mental form. Ḥ 2(1).
al-wujūd al-ʻaqlī, mental existence. Ḥ 2(2). Sh [2].

' - q - l (continued)

'āqil, rational person. DF 66. Ḥ 5(2).
'āqil, knower, apprehender. DF 32, 33, 34. Ḥ 27. Sh 33, 34.
ma'qūl, object of apprehension, known, intelligible. DF 31, 32, 87. Ḥ 14. Sh [2].
ma'qūl thānī, second intelligible, second intention (See trans. of DF, par. 19, n. 1). DF 19. Ḥ 5(1). Sh [5].
amr ma'qūl, mental entity. Sh 5.
al-ṣuwar al-ma'qūlah, intelligible forms. DF 32.
ma'qūlīyah, intelligibility. Ḥ 15(1).
ta'aqqala (ta'aqqul), to apprehend. DF 25, 31, 34. Ḥ 5(1).
ta'aqqul, apprehension, intellection. DF 31, 35, 39. Ḥ 27, 28, 30(1), 33. Sh 5, 26, 35.
fī al-ta'aqqul, in intellection. Sh 28, 35, 53.
bi-ḥasab al-ta'aqqul, with respect to intellection. DF 28, 49. Sh 28, 29.
al-i'tibārāt al-muntashi'at al-ta'aqqul ba'ḍuhā 'an ba'ḍ, considerations whose intellections are derived one from another. DF 39.

' - k - s

'aks, reflection. Sh 24.
in'akasa, to be reflected. Sh 24.

' - l - l

'illah ('ilal), cause. DF 31, 35, 40, 41. Ḥ 30(1), 30(2). Sh 5, 35.
'illah dhātīyah, essential cause. DF 40.
'illah ghā'īyah, final cause. DF 47. Sh 47.
'illah qarībah, proximate cause. DF 40.
'illah tāmmah, complete cause. DF 85. Sh 31.
'illīyah, causality, state of being a cause. DF 31. Ḥ 9.
ma'lūl, effect; caused. DF 31, 32, 35, 36, 40, 41, 55, 85. Ḥ 30(1), 30(2), 31. Sh 31, 35, 40.
al-ma'lūl al-awwal, the first effect. DF 32, 35, 40. Sh 32, 33, [31]a, 35, [31]b.
al-ma'lūl al-thānī, the second effect. DF 40. Sh 35.
ma'lūl dhātī, essential effect. DF 34.
ma'lūlīyah, state of being caused. Ḥ 9.

ʻ - l - q

taʻallaqa, to connect, be connected. Sh [38].
taʻalluq, connection. DF 30, 41, 87. Ḥ 19, 42, 45. Sh 21, 30, [38].
al-taʻallaqāt al-kawnīyah, worldly attachments. DF 11.
mutaʻalliq, connection (See trans. of Ḥ, No. 22, n. 1). DF 44, Ḥ 22, 34.
mutaʻalliq bi, connected with. DF 33, 37, 74, 83. Sh 9, [10], 33, 34.

ʻ - l - m

ʻalima, to know. DF 37, 38, 40, 41, 43, 44.Ḥ 30(1). Sh 1, 33.
min nafsihi ʻalima, to know of one's own accord. DF 37.
ʻilm (ʻulūm), knowledge, cognition. DF 27, 29, 30, 32, 37 38, 39, 40, 41, 43, 45, 46, 47, 48, 51, 53, 58, 64, 65, 66, 68, 69, 74, 84, 90. Ḥ 2(2), 2(3), 13(2), 19, 26, 30(1), 31, 32, 34, 36, 39, 44. Sh 1, [2], 26, 28, 29, 30, 31, 32, 33, [31]a, 35, 37, 40, 41, 46, [38], 51, 65b, 72, 78.
al-ʻilm al-azalī al-fiʻlī, [God's] active and eternal knowledge. DF 37.
ʻilm ghaybī, absentational knowledge. DF 44.
al-ʻilm al-ilāhī, divine knowledge. DF 91.
ʻilm shuhūdī, presentational knowledge. DF 44.
ʻilm tafṣīlī, knowledge of particulars. Sh 1.
ʻilman, cognitively. Sh 25.
ʻilman wa-ʻaynan, cognitively and concretely. DF 20.
ʻarṣat ʻilmihi, the expanse of His knowledge. DF 51. Sh 1.
fī bāṭin ʻilmihi, in His inner knowledge. DF 1. Sh 1.
majlā ʻilmī, cognitive place of manifestation. Sh 24.
al-nisbah al-ʻilmīyah, the cognitive relation. Ḥ 37. Sh [37], 48.
al-wujūd al-ʻilmī al-taʻayyunī, individuational cognitive existence (See trans. of Sh, par. 28, n. 1). Sh 28.
al-ʻAlīm, the Knowing. Sh 37.
ʻālim, knowing, knower. DF 27, 38, 41. Sh 28, 34, 41.
maʻlūm, object of knowledge, thing known, known. DF 29, 37, 38, 44, 51, 63, 64. Ḥ 2(2), 4, 41. Sh 33, 35, 37, [37], 51, [43], 63, 64.

' - l - m (continued)

ma'lūmīyah, quality of being known. DF 64. Sh 33, 35, 64.

ṣūrat al-ma'lūmīyah, the form through which something is known. DF 63, 64. Sh 63, 64.

i'lām, informing, imparting of information. Sh [44], 65b.

'ālam ('awālim, 'ālamūn), the world, universe. DF 50, 51, 52, 58, 71, 78. Ḥ 39. Sh 41, 52, 67.

'ālam al-'anāṣir, the world of elements. DF 76.

'ālam al-arwāḥ, the world of spirits. DF 71.

'ālam al-ḥiss, the world of sense. DF 71. Sh 71.

'ālam al-ḥiss wa-al-shahādah, the world of sense and visibility. Sh 67.

'ālam al-ma'ānī wa-al-ḥaqā'iq, the world of ideas and realities. Sh [37].

'ālam al-mithāl, the world of similitude. DF 69, 71. Sh 71.

al-'ālam al-mithālī, the similative world. DF 71.

'ālam al-ṣuwar wa-al-mithāl, the world of forms and similitude. Sh 67.

'ālam al-nufūs, the world of souls, Sh 41.

'ālam al-'uqūl, the world of intellects. Sh 41.

dhawāt al-'ālam, essences of the universe. DF 41.

' - l - w

al-jihāt al-'alīyah, the exalted realms. Ḥ 12.

muta'ālī, transcendent. DF 39.

muta'ālī 'an al-makān, exalted above place. DF 23.

muta'ālī 'an al-zamān, exalted above time. DF 23, Ḥ 36.

al-Dhāt al-Muta'āliyah, the Transcendent Essence. Sh [16].

' - m - m

'umūm, generality, universality. DF 90. Ḥ 14, 17.

'āmm, general. DF 8. Ḥ 2(1), 3, 15(3). Sh [2], 7.

al-wujūd al-'āmm, general existence (See trans. of DF, par. 89, n. 1). DF 89, 90. Ḥ 37.

a'amm, more general. Sh [2], 48.

' - n - ṣ - r

'unṣur ('anāṣir), element. Sh 84.

'ālam al-'anāṣir, the world of elements. DF 76.

ʿ - n - ṣ - r (continued)

abdān ʿunṣurīyah, elemental bodies (See trans. of DF, par. 87, n. 2). DF 87.

ʿ - n - y

maʿnā (maʿānī), idea, meaning, sense, concept. DF 32, 48, 50, 56, 57, 63, 64, 71. Ḥ 2(1), 4, 5(1), 5(2), 14, 28, 39, 41, 43(1), 43(2), 45. Sh 4, 5, 18, 25, 33, 44b, [38], [39], 51, 52, 55, 60, 64, 69, 72, 84.

maʿnan, in meaning. DF 4. Sh 4.

al-maʿnā al-maṣdarī, the verbal meaning. Ḥ 5(1).

al-maʿnā al-nafsī, the meaning in the mind. Ḥ 43(1).

ʿālam al-maʿānī wa-al-ḥaqāʾiq, the world of ideas and realities. Sh [37].

bi-ḥasab al-maʿnā, with respect to meaning. Sh [39].

maʿnawīyan, in meaning. Sh 4.

taqsīm maʿnawī, division in meaning, logical division (See trans. of DF, par. 4, n. 4). DF 4.

al-ʿināyah, [divine] providence. DF 37, 45. Sh 41.

ʿ - w - d

baʿdīyah ʿādīyah ittifāqīyah, coincidental customary posteriority. Sh 72.

ʿ - y - n

ʿayn, identical with, the same as. DF 4, 7, 19, 20, 26, 27, 28, 36, 37, 48, 55. Ḥ 5(1), 15(2), 15(3), 16, 31. Sh 4, [2], 12, 19, 26, 31.

ʿayn (aʿyān), individual, individual essence. DF 21, 22, 24, 89. Sh 37.

al-aʿyān al-thābitah, the fixed essences (See trans. of DF, par. 89, n. 2). DF 89, 90.

ʿayn al-baṣīrah, the eye of insight. Sh 11.

ʿaynan, concretely. Sh 25.

bi-ʿaynihi, exactly, exactly the same as. Sh 28, 41.

ʿilman wa-ʿaynan, cognitively and concretely. DF 20.

fī al-ʿayn, in the concrete world. Ḥ 20. Sh 1.

al-ījād fī al-ʿayn, to bring into concrete existence. DF 92.

shayʾ bi-ʿaynihi, concrete thing. DF 13.

ʿaynī, material, concrete, individual. DF 20, 85, 88, 90. Sh 24.

' - y - n (continued)

majlā 'aynī, concrete place of manifestation. Sh 24.
al-shay' al-'aynī, individual, concrete thing. DF 13.
umūr wujūdīyah 'aynīyah, concrete, existential entities. DF 85, 86.
al-wujūd al-'aynī, concrete existence. DF 92.
al-wujūd al-ḥaqīqī al-'aynī, concrete, real existence. Sh 28.
'aynīyah, identity. DF 4.
'ayyana (ta'yīn), to particularize, specify. Sh 35, 65b.
'alā al-ta'yīn, in specific terms. Sh 34.
'āyana, to observe. Sh 37.
'iyān, mystical insight. DF 11.
ta'ayyana, to be determined. DF 38. 65.
ta'ayyana, to become individuated. DF 1, 22. Sh 12, 19.
ta'ayyana ta'ayyunan thubūtīyan, to become individuated as fixed essences. Sh 1.
ta'ayyun, individuation. DF 10, 12, 14, 18, 19, 20, 25, 37, 89. Ḥ 15(2), 15(3), 37. Sh 12, 18, 19, [16], 20, 25, 26, 28, [37], [44].
al-ta'ayyun al-awwal, the first individuation (See trans. of Sh, par. 1, n. 1). Sh 1, [37].
al-ta'ayyun al-ṣūrī, formal individuation. DF 22.
al-ta'ayyun al-thānī, the second individuation (See trans. of Sh, par. 1, n. 1). Sh 1, [37].
al-wujūd al-'ilmī al-ta'ayyunī, individuational cognitive existence (See trans. of Sh, par. 28, n. 1). Sh 28.
muta'ayyin, individuated. DF 7, 18, 19. Ḥ 5(1), 15(2), 15(3). Sh 12, 18, 19, 25, [44].

gh - r - ḍ

gharaḍ (aghrāḍ), purpose. DF 47. Sh 63.

gh - n - y

ghanī, independent. DF 52. Sh 52.
ghinā, independence. DF 58.
mustaghnī, independent. Ḥ 44.

gh - y - y

ghāyah, goal, purpose. DF 46, 47. Ḥ 13(3). Sh 46, 47, 67.
'illah ghā'īyah, final cause. DF 47. Sh 47.

gh - y - b

al-ghayb, the invisible world. DF 69.
ghayban, in the invisible world. DF 20.
al-martabah al-jāmi'ah bayn al-ghayb wa-al-shahādah, the plane linking the invisible and visible worlds. DF 68.
ghaybī, otherworldy. DF 68.
'ilm ghaybī, absentational knowledge. DF 44.
al-ghā'ib, the invisible world. DF 14.
ghaybūbah, absence. Sh 33.

gh - y - r

ghayr (aghyār), separate entity. Sh 28, 40.
ghāyara (mughāyarah), to differ, be different from. DF 28, 29, 78, 89, 90. Ḥ 6. Sh 28, 33, 40.
mughāyarah, difference. Sh 28.
taghayyur, change. DF 24, 41. Ḥ 19. Sh 1, 24, 37.
taghāyara (taghāyur), to differ. Ḥ 2(2). Sh 28.
taghāyur, difference. DF 9, 35. Ḥ 2(1), 2(2), 30(1), 30(2). Sh 35.
mutaghāyir, different, dissimilar, distinct. DF 6, 27, 46. Ḥ 6. Sh 28, 40.

f - r - d

fard (afrād), singular, individual. DF 9, 14, 15. Ḥ 5(1), 6, 9. Sh 3, 4, [2], 7, 9, [5], 12, 20.
fard (afrād), peerless [man]. DF 87.
jam'an wa-furādā, collectively and individually. DF 39, 43.

f - r - ḍ

faraḍa (farḍ), to consider, suppose, to imagine as being. DF 20. Ḥ 2(1). Sh 25, 30.
mafrūḍ, hypothetical. DF 85. Sh [2].

f - r - '

tafrī', corollary, ramification. DF 8. Sh 50b.
tafarra'a 'alā, to follow, stem from, to depend on. Sh 35, 46, 52.

f - r - q

farīq, party, group. DF 50, 78.
firqah (firaq), group. DF 61, 70.

f - r - q (continued)

tafarraqa (tafarruq), to be divided. DF 13.
iftaraqa, to divide. DF 61.

f - s - d

fasād, error. DF 23.
fāsid, erroneous. Ḥ 43(2). Sh 41.

f - ṣ - l

faṣl (fuṣūl), [specific] difference. DF 6, 15, 16. Sh 40.
faṣṣala (tafṣīl), to particularize, detail. DF 40. Sh 41, 46.
tafṣīlan, in particular. Sh 41.
ijmālan wa-tafṣīlan, as a whole and in particular. DF 43.
tafāṣīl, particulars. DF 40.
'ilm tafṣīlī, knowledge of particulars. Sh 1.
naqḍ tafṣīlī, particular refutation (See trans. of DF, par. 9, n. 3). Sh 9.
mufaṣṣal, particularized. DF 40.
infaṣala, to be, become separate. DF 66.
munfaṣil, separate. Sh 21, 28, 41, [37].

f - ṣ - y

tafaṣṣī, escape. Ḥ 15(3).

f - ḍ - l

mufāḍalah, inequality. DF 10.

f - ṭ - r

fiṭrah, natural intelligence. Ḥ 29.

f - ' - l

fa'ala, to act. DF 50, 85. Sh [38], 52.
fi'l (af'āl), act, action. DF 39, 47, 48, 54, 56, 72, 74, 83, 85. Ḥ 38, 45. Sh 12, 37, 46, 47, [38], 51, 52, 55, 72, 75.
bi-al-fi'l, in actuality. Sh 5.
mashī'at al-fi'l, the will to act. DF 50.
al-'ilm al-azalī al-fi'lī, [God's] active and eternal knowledge. DF 37.
fā'il, agent. DF 32, 34, 46, 54, 85. Ḥ 28. Sh 4, 32, 34, 51, 84.
fā'il, subject of verb. Sh 52.
al-Fā'il al-Ḥaqīqī, the Real Agent. Sh 46.
fā'il mūjib, necessary agent. Sh 51.

f - ʻ - l (continued)

fāʻil mukhtār, free agent. DF 54, 55.
al- ʻaql al-faʻʻāl, the active intellect. DF 76.

f - k - k

infakka (infikāk), to be separated. DF 50, 53. Ḥ 16. Sh [16], [38].

f - k - r

fikr (afkār), thought, reason. DF 2. Ḥ 12, 13(2), 13(3). Sh 11.
al-qūwah al-fikrīyah, the rational faculty. Sh 11.

f - l - s - f

faylasūf (falāsifah), philosopher. DF 30, 50. Ḥ 13(2), 13(3).
ahl al-naẓar min al-falāsifah, rationalist philosophers. DF 89.

f - l - k

falak (aflāk), sphere. DF 84, 85. Ḥ 30(2). Sh 84.

f - n - y

faniya, to pass away. Sh 11.
fanā', passing away. Sh 11.
al-fanā' al-ḥaqīqī, real passing away. Sh 11.

f - h - m

mafhūm, concept; understood. DF 5, 6, 7, 8, 27, 51, 67. Ḥ 1, 2(1), 3, 15(3). Sh 5, [2], 9, [5], 21, 25, 28, 64.
mafhūm iʻtibārī, mental concept. Ḥ 4, 5(1).
mabda' al-ifhām, source of instruction. Sh 63.
istifhām, interrogation. Ḥ 42.

f - w - t

tafāwata, to differ. DF 55.
tafāwut, difference, dissimilarity, differentiation. DF 10. Ḥ 9. Sh 28, 40, 72.

f - y

wa-fīhi, in objection it may be said. Sh 5, [2].

f - y - d

fā'idah, profit. DF 51.
afāda (ifādah), to relate. DF 66, 69.

f - y - ḍ

fāḍa, to flow, effuse. Sh 46.
fayḍ, effusion. DF 50.
fayaḍān al-khayr, the effusion of good. DF 45.
al-Mabda' al-Fayyāḍ, the Effusive Principle. Sh 46.
afāḍa (ifāḍah), to pour forth, effuse. DF 66, 69, 89.
ṣūrah mustafāḍah musta'nafah, newly effused form. DF 35.

q - b - l

qabūl, receptivity, reception. DF 39, 87, 89.
qābil (qawābil), recipient. DF 10, 32, 34, 74, 76, 77, 90, 91, 92. Ḥ 28. Sh 32, 34.
qābilīyah, receptivity. DF 59.
qābilīyah maḥḍah muṭlaqah, absolute and pure receptivity. Sh [37].
qabīl, class, category. DF 64. Ḥ 2(3), 12.
qablīyah, priority. Ḥ 19.
qablīyah bi-ḥasab al-martabah, priority according to rank. Sh 37.
qablīyah dhātīyah martabīyah, priority of essence and rank. Sh 44 a.
muqābil, opposed to. Sh 26.
mustaqbil, future. DF 41. Sh 41.

q - d - ḥ

qadaḥa, to reject, refute. DF 61, 62. Sh 61.
qādiḥah (qawādiḥ), refutation. DF 78.

q - d - r

qadar, decree. Sh 41.
qudrah, power. DF 27, 29, 46, 47, 48, 50, 58, 68, 69, 72, 73, 74. Ḥ 19. Sh 72.
qādir, powerful. DF 27, 50.
maqdūr, object of power. DF 29, 46, 47, 72. Sh [44].
miqdār, measure. DF 9. Sh 9.
qaddara (taqdīr), to decree. DF 51.
al-iqtidār al-ilāhī, the divine power. Ḥ 45.

q - d - s

muqaddas, holy, sanctified. DF 24, 59.

q - d - m

qidam, eternity. DF 63. Sh 64.
qadīm, eternal. DF 27, 45, 54, 61, 63. Ḥ 41. 43(1). Sh [38], 61, 63.
athar qadīm, eternal effect. DF 54, 55. Sh 55.
al-qudamā', the early [philosophers]. DF 32.
muqaddimah, premiss. DF 12, 61. Ḥ 30(1). Sh 34, 35, 63.
al-muqaddimāt al-'aqlīyah, logical premisses. Ḥ 2(3).
muqaddimah khiṭābīyah, rhetorical premiss. Ḥ 30(1).
muqaddimāt al-wahm, premisses of the estimation. Sh 11.
muqaddimāt ẓannīyah ẓāhirīyah, ostensibly presumptive premisses. Sh 33.
muqaddimāt wāhiyah, unfounded premisses. Sh 78.
muqaddam, antecedent; prior. DF 50, 52, 53. Sh 32.
taqaddama, to be prior. DF 56.
taqaddum, priority. DF 41, 55, 56.
mutaqaddim, prior. DF 31, 55.
al-ḥukamā' al-mutaqaddimūn, the early philosophers. DF 2.

q - r - r

qārr al-dhāt, simultaneous in essence (See trans. of Ḥ, No. 9, n. 2). Ḥ 9.
ghayr qārr, successive. Sh 61.
ghayr qārr al-dhāt, successive in essence (See trans. of Ḥ, No. 9, n. 2). Ḥ 9.
amr ghayr qārr, successive entity. Sh 64.
al-a'rāḍ al-ghayr al-qārrah, successive accidents (See trans. of DF, par. 64, n. 2). DF 64.
qarrara (taqrīr), to establish. Ḥ 10.
muqarrar, established. DF 35.
taqarrur, establishment. DF 31, 32.
mutaqarrir, established. DF 31.

q - r - b

'illah qarībah, proximate cause. DF 40.

q - r - ḥ

luṭf qarīḥah, being endowed with a certain genius for. DF 81.

q - r - n

qārana (muqāranah), to be contemporaneous with, to be associated with. DF 54, 56, 72, 73. Ḥ 14. Sh 23.

iqtirān, attachment, association. DF 89. Ḥ 5(2).

q - s - m

qism (aqsām), division, part. DF 6, 60, 87.

taqsīm, division. Sh 64.

taqsīm maʻnawī, division in meaning, logical division (See trans. of DF, par. 4, n. 4). DF 4.

ʻadam al-inqisām, indivisibility. DF 80.

q - ṣ - d

qaṣada, to intend. DF 54.

qaṣd, intention. DF 45, 54, 56, 57. Ḥ 40. Sh 56.

qaṣdan, by intention. DF 55.

al-ījād al-qaṣdī, intentional bringing-into-existence. DF 55.

maqṣūd, intended, thing intended. DF 51, 55, 56.

q - ḍ - y

qaḍāʼ, decision. Sh 41.

iqtaḍā, to require, necessitate, imply. DF 10, 14, 31, 35, 43, 52, 55, 68. Ḥ 13(1). Sh 4, 5, [2], 30, 35, 51.

muqtaḍā, implication. Sh 50b.

bi-muqtaḍā, as implied by, in accordance with. Sh [31]b, 37.

ʻan muqtaḍā, as required by. Sh 67.

q - ʻ - d

qāʻidah, axiom, rule. DF 77. Sh 84.

qāʻidat al-ījāb, the rule of necessity [in bringing the world into existence]. DF 52.

q - l - l

istaqalla, to be self-sufficient. DF 3. Sh 3.

q - l - b

qalb, heart. DF 66.

q - l - m

al-Qalam al-Aʻlā, the Most Exalted Pen. DF 55, 87, 89.

q - n - ʻ

iqnāʻ, conviction. Sh 33.
iqnāʻī, convincing. Sh 78.

q - w - l

qawl (aqwāl), discourse, doctrine; saying. DF 67, 84. Sh 28, 29, 32, 60, 72.
maqūlah, category. DF 64.
muqāwalah, discourse. DF 71.
taqāwul, conversation. DF 71.

q - w - m

qāma bi (qiyām), to subsist in. DF 4, 16, 22, 27, 62, 64, 70, 71. Ḥ 5(2), 28, 43(1), 43(2). Sh 5, [2], 7, 61, 64.
al-qiyām bi-al-dhāt, self-subsistence. DF 32.
qā'im bi-dhātihi, self-subsistent. Ḥ 5(2).
al-Wāḥid al-Qā'im bi-Dhātihi, the Self-Subsistent One. DF 31.
al-qiyāmah, the resurrection. DF 67.
maqām, station. DF 68. Ḥ 9.
fī hādha al-maqām, at this point. DF 63, 65.
qawwama, to constitute. Sh 24.
muqawwim, constitutive. Ḥ 5(2).
taqawwama, to be constituted. DF 31, 65.

q - w - y

qūwah (quwā), force, strength; faculty. DF 46, 76. Ḥ 13(1). Sh 9, 21, 84.
al-qūwah al-ʻaḍalīyah, muscular force. DF 46.
al-qūwah al-ʻaqlīyah, the intellectual faculty. Ḥ 13(1).
al-qūwah al-baṣarīyah, the faculty of sight. Ḥ 13(1).
al-qūwah al-fikrīyah, the rational faculty. Sh 11.
al-qūwah al-nafsānīyah, the psychical faculty. Sh 21.
al-qūwah al-samʻīyah, the faculty of hearing. Ḥ 13(1).
al-qūwah al-ṭabīʻīyah, the physical faculty. Sh 21.
al-qūwah al-wahmīyah, the estimative faculty (See trans. of Sh, par. 11, n. 3). Sh 11.
al-quwā al-bāṭinah, the internal faculties. DF 21.
qawī, strong, substantial. Ḥ 8. Sh 9, 67.

q - y - d

qayd (quyūd), limitation, qualification. Ḥ 12. Sh 26, 41.
qayyada, to restrict, determine, limit, condition. DF 12. Ḥ 12. Sh 9.
taqayyada, to become determined. DF 74.
taqayyud, determination. DF 12, 21, 25, 37, 74.
mutaqayyid, determined. Sh 12.

q - y - s

qāsa (qiyās), to make analogous. DF 14.
'alā qiyās, by analogy with. Ḥ 15(3). Sh 67.
qiyās, syllogism. DF 61, 62, 70. Sh 61.
muqāyasah, determination by analogy. Sh 4.

k - b - r

kubrā, major premiss. DF 61. Sh 61.

k - t - b

kitābah, writing. DF 67.
maktūb, written. Sh 64.

k - th - r

kathrah, multiplicity, plurality. DF 1, 31, 75. 78, 79, 80, 81, 86, 91. Ḥ 8. Sh 1, 31, 37, [37], 75.
kathrah i'tibārīyah, mental multiplicity, multiplicity existing only in the mind. Ḥ 20.
kathrah nisbīyah, relative multiplicity. Sh 1.
kathrah wujūdīyah, existential multiplicity. DF 79.
kathīr, multiple, numerous. DF 80, 84, 85. Sh 11.
takaththara, to multiply, become multiple. DF 5, 65, 85.
takaththur, multiplicity. DF 31, 74. Ḥ 6, 34. Sh 51.
mutakaththir, multiple, many, numerous. DF 6, 24, 32, 37, 75. Ḥ 20, 34. Sh 12.

k - s - b

kasaba (kasb), to acquire. DF 72.
kasb, acquisition. Ḥ 45.
maksūb, acquired. DF 72, 74.

k - sh - f

kashf, mystical revelation. DF 11, 55. Ḥ 10, 15(3).

k - sh - f (continued)

al-kashfīyāt, mystically revealed truths. Sh 11.
nūr kāshif, revealing light. DF 11, 12.
makshūf, revealed. Sh 78.
al-makshūfūn, the unveiled. Sh 37.
mukāshafah, revelation. DF 20.
inkashafa, to be revealed, be discovered. DF 27.
mabda' al-inkishāf, the source of revelation. Sh 28, 33.
mabda'īyat al-inkishāf, being the source of revelation. Sh 28.

k - f - r

kufr, unbelief. DF 28, 29.
kāfir, unbeliever, unbelieving. DF 29.

k - f - y

kāfī, sufficient. DF 56, 57.

k - l - l

kull, whole. DF 13, 45.
kullī, universal. DF 14, 36, 37, 41, 85. Sh [2], 12, 20.
kullīyan, in a universal manner, universally. DF 37. Ḥ 2(3).
kullī 'aqlī, mental universal (See trans. of DF, par. 12, n. 2). Ḥ 14.
kullī dhātī, essential universal. Sh [2].
kullī manṭiqī, logical universal (See trans. of DF, par. 12, n. 2). Ḥ 14.
kullī ṭabī'ī, natural universal (See trans. of DF, par. 12, n. 2). DF 12, 13, 17. Ḥ 14. Sh 18, 20.
'alā wajh kullī, in a universal manner. DF 39.
'alā wajh kullī jumlī, in a universal and general manner. Sh 1.
al-ījād al-kullī, general bringing-into-existence. DF 52.
kullīyah, universality. Ḥ 17.

k - l - m

kalām, speech. DF 60, 61, 62, 63, 65, 66, 67, 69, 70, 71. Ḥ 41, 42, 43(1), 43(2), 44. Sh 60, 61, [44], 65b, 67.
al-kalām al-nafsī, the speech of the mind (See trans. of Ḥ, No. 43, n. 2). DF 64, 71. Ḥ 43(2).

k - l - m (continued)

kalāmīyah, state of being speech. Ḥ 43(2).
kalimah, word. DF 69.
kallama, to speak. DF 66.
mukālamah ḥissīyah, sensible speech. DF 71.
takallama (takallum), to speak. DF 66, 67. Sh 66.
mutakallim, speaker. DF 60, 66. Ḥ 41.
mutakallim, theologian. DF 2, 5, 12, 30, 45, 46, 49, 54, 64, 79, 80. Ḥ 2(1), 19, 30(1). Sh 32, [38], 50b, 55, 59, 63, 72, 78.
jumhūr al-mutakallimīn, the majority of the theologians. DF 5, 25.

k - m

al-kamm, quantity. DF 6.

k - m - l

kamāl, perfection, completeness. DF 2, 9, 39, 43. Ḥ 5(2), 8. Sh [38], 52.
al-kamāl al-dhātī, essential perfection. Sh 52.
al-kamāl al-tāmm, complete perfection. DF 50.
ṣifat kamāl, attribute of perfection. Sh 29, [38].
al-nafs al-nāṭiqah al-kamālīyah, the perfectional rational soul. DF 21.
al-ṣifāt al-kamālīyah, [God's] attributes of perfection. DF 50, 58.
kāmil, perfect. DF 29, 57, 58, 59. Ḥ 44. Sh 21.
kāmil (kummal), perfect [man]. DF 23, 87. Sh [37].
al-niẓām al-akmal, the most perfect order [of the universe]. DF 45, 51, 53. Ḥ 39.
kammala, to perfect. DF 29.

k - n - n

maknūnāt, mysteries. DF 66, 69.

k - w - k - b

al-kawākib al-sayyārah, the planets. DF 85.
al-kawākib al-thābitah, the fixed stars. DF 85.

k - w - n

kawn, being. Ḥ 1, 2(1), 5(1).

k - w - n (continued)

marātib al-akwān, the planes of created beings. Ḥ 8.
al-ḥaqā'iq al-kawnīyah, mundane realities. DF 91.
al-ta'alluqāt al-kawnīyah, worldly attachments. DF 11.
makān (amkinah, amākin), place, space. DF 22, 23, 41, 42. Sh 23.
muta'ālī 'an al-makān, exalted above place. DF 23.
al-mutawaghghilūn fī al-makān wa-al-zamān, those immersed in space and time. DF 23, 42.
makānī, spatial. DF 41, 42. Sh 23.
ẓill al-takwīn, shade of creation. DF 52.
al-mukawwanāt, created things. DF 52.

k - y - f

al-kayf, quality. DF 6.
kayfīyah, manner, nature. DF 77, 84, 85. Sh 34.
kayfīyat al-ṣawāb, the correct manner. DF 45.

l - ' - k

mal'ak (malā'ikah), malak (amlāk), angel. Ḥ 9.
al-malā'ikah al-muhayyamah, the ecstatic angels (See trans. of DF, par. 87, n. 1). DF 87. Sh [37].

l - b - s

talabbasa bi (talabbus), to be clothed in. DF 39. Ḥ 5(2).

l - ḥ - q

laḥiqa, to attach, adhere to. DF 38, 44, 58, 78. Ḥ 37.
lāḥiq, consequent. Ḥ 2(3), 16.

l - z - m

lazima (luzūm), to follow, be implied, to require, be necessary. DF 31, 36, 37, 40, 41, 44. Ḥ 2(1), 2(2), 2(3), 15(1), 15(2), 29, 30(1), 32, 38, 42. Sh 5, [2], 18, [38].
luzūm, concomitance. DF 50. Sh [16], [38], 51.
lāzim (lawāzim), concomitant, conclusion, thing implied. DF 6, 21, 31, 32, 37, 43, 50, 53. Ḥ 16, 37, 43(2). Sh [16], [38], 50b, 51, 52, 55.
malzūm, thing possessing a concomitant, substratum, that which implies. DF 31. Sh 52.
alzama (ilzām), to force upon. Sh 41.

l - z - m (continued)

istalzama (istilzām), to imply, require, necessitate, entail. DF 4, 40, 41, 68. Ḥ 2(2), 38. Sh 9, 31, [38], 52.

ba'dīyah dhātīyah istilzāmīyah, essential necessitating posteriority. Sh 72.

al-sababīyah al-mustalzimah, necessitating causation. Sh 72.

l - ṭ - f

luṭf qarīḥah, being endowed with a certain genius for. DF 81.

al-Laṭīf, the Kindly One. DF 43.

l - f - ẓ

lafẓan, in name only. DF 4.

lafẓah, word. Sh 21, 25.

lafẓ, utterance, word, expression. DF 67. Ḥ 1, 43(1), 43(2), 43(3). Sh [5], [10], 52.

ḥurūf al-lafẓ, spoken letters. DF 67.

malfūẓ, pronounced, thing pronounced. Ḥ 43(3). Sh 64.

talaffuẓ, pronunciation. Ḥ 43(3).

l - q - y

alqā (ilqā'), to inject. DF 71.

l - w - ḥ

al-Lawḥ, the Tablet. DF 87.

al-Lawḥ al-Maḥfūz, the Preserved Tablet. Sh 61.

l - y - q

lāqa, to be fit, be appropriate. DF 29, 67, 69. Sh 29, 46, 67, 71, 72, 84.

mā

māhīyah, quiddity. DF 4, 6, 7, 9, 24, 39, 40, 84. Ḥ 1, 2(1), 2(2), 2(3), 5(1), 5(2), 6, 37. Sh [2], 9, 40, [37].

al-māhīyāt al-ghayr al-maj'ūlah, uncreated quiddities (See trans. of DF, par. 58, n. 1). DF 58.

al-māhīyah al-naw'īyah, specific quiddity. Sh 40.

māddat al-māhīyah, the matter of the quiddity. Sh 9.

m - th - l

mithāl, analogy, similitude. DF 24, 84. Sh 67.
ʻālam al-mithāl, the world of similitude. DF 69, 71.
ʻālam al-ṣuwar wa-al-mithāl, the world of forms and similitude. Sh 67.
mithālī, similative. DF 69.
tajallī mithālī, similative manifestation. DF 71.
mithālīyah, similarity. Sh 21.
al-ʻālam al-mithālī, the similative world. DF 71.
tamthīl, analogy. DF 24. Sh 6. Sh 24.
mumāthil, similar. Sh 23.
mutamāthil, similar to each other. DF 6.

m - ḥ - ḍ

maḥd, pure, simple, exclusive. Ḥ 16, 19. Sh 85.
maḥḍummā, simple entity. DF 18. Ḥ 15(2).
qābilīyah maḥḍah muṭlaqah, absolute and pure receptivity. Sh [37].

m - d - d

māddah, matter. DF 84. Sh 84.
māddat al-māhīyah, the matter of the quiddity. Sh 9.
maddī, material. Sh 23, 37.

m - r - r

bi-al-marrah, all at once, at one time. DF 91.

m - sh - y

al-Mashshā'ūn, the Peripatetics. DF 32.

m - ḍ - y

māḍī, past. DF 41. Sh 41.
zamān māḍī, past time. Sh 41.

m - ʻ

maʻīyah, simultaneity, coextension (See trans. of DF, par. 43, n. 2). Ḥ 19.
al-maʻīyah al-dhātīyah, essential coextension (See trans. of DF, par. 43, n. 2). DF 43.

m - k - n

amkana (imkān), to be possible, contingent. DF 37, 51, 52,

m - k - n (continued)
57, 83, 92. Sh 3, [38], [39], 51, 52, 67.
imkān, contingency. DF 6, 87.
ḥaẓā'ir al-imkān, realms of contingency. Ḥ 8.
martabat al-imkān, the plane of contingency. Sh 1.
mumkin, contingent, possible; contingent being. DF 3, 6, 8, 32, 37, 72, 75, 77, 81, 87, 89. Ḥ 5(1), 12, 45. Sh 1, 3, 7, [5], 28, 31, 34, [38], 65b.
mumkinī, contingent. Sh 4.

m - l - l
millah (milal), religion. Sh 50a.
al-millīyūn, the religionists. DF 50. Ḥ 39.

m - l - k
al-Malik, the King. Ḥ 13(2).
malakūt, kingdom. Ḥ 13(2).
malak (amlāk), angel (See also under l - ' - k). Ḥ 9.

m - n - ʻ
manaʻa (manʻ), to deny, prevent. DF 76. Sh 24, 61.
mānīʻ (mawānīʻ), obstacle. DF 72, 73.
mānīʻ, denier (See trans. of Sh, par. [2], n. 1). Sh [2].
imtanaʻa (imtināʻ), to be impossible, to be unable. DF 15, 18, 20, 53. Ḥ 5(2), 20.
imtināʻ, impossibility, DF 12, 13, 14, 15, 73, 78, 79, 91. Ḥ 20. Sh [16], 64.
mumtaniʻ, impossible. DF 50. Sh 32.

m - y - z
tamayyaza (tamayyuz), to be distinguished, different, distinct. Ḥ 15(3). Sh 40.
tamayyuz, differentiation. DF 59.
mutamayyiz, distinguishing. Sh 12.
tamāyaza (tamāyuz), to be distinguished from. DF 4, 38.
imtāza (imtiyāz), to be differentiated, distinguished. DF 40. Sh 28, 40.

m - y - l
mayl, inclination. Sh 46.
mayalān, inclination. DF 46. Sh 46.

m - y - l (continued)
al-mayalān al-nafsānī, psychical inclination. DF 48.

n - b - ʾ
nabī (anbiyāʾ), prophet. DF 28, 60, 63, 67.

n - b - ʿ
manbaʿ, fountainhead, source. DF 45. Ḥ 44.

n - d - w
nidāʾ, vocation. Ḥ 42.

n - z - ʿ
intazaʿa (intizāʿ), to abstract. Sh 5, [2].

n - z - l
anzala (inzāl), to send down. DF 69. Sh 67.
tanazzala, to descend. DF 74.
tanazzul, descent. DF 74. Ḥ 8. Sh 67.

n - z - h
munazzah ʿan, exalted above. DF 75. Sh 75.

n - s - b
nasaba, to attribute. DF 65.
nisbah (nisab), relation, relationship, attribution. DF 20, 23, 38, 41, 44, 55, 58, 78, 89, 90, 92. Sh 5, [2], [10], 21, 23, 28, 40, 41, 44b, 83.
nisbah, relative adjective. Sh 21.
nisbah ʿaqlīyah iʿtibārīyah, mental, intellectual relation. DF 88.
al-nisbah al-ʿilmīyah, the cognitive relation. Ḥ 37. Sh [37], 48.
nisbah inbisāṭīyah, relation of expansion. DF 91.
al-nisab al-asmāʾīyah, the nominal relations. DF 91.
bi-al-nisbah ilā, in relation to, in the case of, with respect to. DF 44, 48. Ḥ 15(1), 19. Sh 9, [5].
mutasāwī al-nisbah, equally related. DF 41. *Ḥ 36.*
kathrah nisbīyah, relative multiplicity. Sh 1.
mutanāsib, related. DF 16.

n - s - kh
tanāsukh, metempsychosis. DF 22.

n - sh - ʼ

manshaʼ, source. DF 40. Ḥ 1. Sh 9, 37, [38], 65b.

intashaʼa, to be derived from, to arise from. DF 26, 86, 91.

al-iʻtibārāt al-muntashiʼat al-taʻaqqul baʻḍuhā ʻan baʻḍ, considerations whose intellections are derived one from another. DF 39.

n - ṣ - f

al-niṣfīyah, halfness. DF 80.

anṣafa, to be unbiased, fair-minded. DF 37. Ḥ 13(3).

n - ṭ - q

al-nafs al-nāṭiqah, the rational soul. DF 21, 76. Sh 21, 84.

al-nafs al-nāṭiqah al-kamālīyah, the perfectional rational soul. DF 21.

kullī manṭiqī, logical universal (See trans. of DF, par. 12, n. 2). Ḥ 14.

n - ẓ - r

naẓara ilā, to lead to, be conducive to. Sh [31]a.

naẓar, speculation, reason. DF 2, 11. Sh 11.

ahl al-naẓar min al-falāsifah, rationalist philosophers. DF 89.

arbāb al-naẓar, masters of reason. Ḥ 10.

al-ʻaql al-naẓarī, the rational intellect. Sh 8.

naẓīr, analogous, analogy. DF 40. Sh 40.

n - ẓ - m

niẓām, order. DF 45.

al-niẓām al-akmal, the most perfect order [of the universe]. DF 45, 51, 53. Ḥ 39.

al-niẓām al-wāqiʻ, the actual order. DF 50.

n - ʻ - t

naʻt (nuʻūt), attribute, quality. DF 26. Sh 28.

nuʻūt al-ilāhīyah, qualities of divinity. Sh 25.

nuʻūt al-rubūbīyah, the attributes of lordship. Sh 25.

n - f - s

nafs, soul. DF 84, 85. Ḥ 13(2), 30(2). Sh 84.

al-nafs al-nāṭiqah, the rational soul. DF 21, 76. Sh 21, 84.

n - f - s (continued)

al-nafs al-nāṭiqah al-kamālīyah, the perfectional rational soul. DF 21.

bi-ḥasab nafs al-amr, with respect to itself, with respect to the thing itself. Sh [38].

fī nafs al-amr, in the thing itself, in itself (See trans. of DF, par. 51, n. 1). DF 51. Sh 9, 26, [38], 58.

'ālam al-nufūs, the world of souls. Sh 41.

min nafsihi 'alima, to know of one's own accord. DF 37.

al-kalām al-nafsī, the speech of the mind (See trans. of Ḥ, No. 43, n. 2). DF 64, 71. Ḥ 43[2].

al-ma'nā al-nafsī, the meaning in the mind. Ḥ 43(1).

ḥālah nafsānīyah, psychical state. DF 46.

al-mayalān al-nafsānī, psychical inclination. DF 48.

al-qūwah al-nafsānīyah, the psychical faculty. Sh 21.

n - f - y

nafā (nafy), to deny. DF 28, 32, 41, 42, 49, 52, 54, 59. Sh [10], 25, 28, 41, 63.

nāfā (munāfāh), to be inconsistent with, incompatible with. DF 18, 20, 31, 52. Ḥ 2(3), 15(1), 38. Sh 8, 9, 11, [16], 28, 37.

intafā, to be omitted, be absent, be non-existent. DF 26, 41.

n - q - ṣ

naqṣ, imperfection, impairment. DF 2, 58, 59. Sh 1, [38].

nuqṣān, imperfection, incompleteness, decrease. DF 9, 29, 50, 58. Sh 9.

nāqiṣ, imperfect. DF 29, 57, 59.

n - q - ḍ

naqḍ ijmālī, general refutation (See trans. of DF, par. 9, n. 3). Sh 9.

naqḍ tafṣīlī, particular refutation (See trans. of DF, par. 9, n. 3). Sh 9.

manqūḍ bi, refuted by, contradicted by (See trans. of DF, par. 9, n. 3). DF 9.

n - k - r

ankara (inkār), to deny. DF 50. Ḥ 20. Sh 11, 72.

n - k - r (continued)

mustankar, objectionable. DF 51.

n - h - y

nahā, to prohibit. DF 60, 62, 63.
nahy, prohibition. Ḥ 42. Sh 60.
lā nihāyata, infinite. DF 83.
bilā nihāyah, infinite. DF 83.
ilā mā lā yatanāhā, to an infinite degree, to infinity. DF 43. Ḥ 37.
'adam al-tanāhī, infinity. Sh 83.
ghayr mutanāhī, infinite, DF 20. Sh 83.

n - w - r

nūr kāshif, revealing light. DF 11, 12.
nūr al-wujūd, the light of existence. Sh 24.
al-nūr al-wujūdī, existential light. DF 58.
al-nūrīyah, luminosity. DF 38. Ḥ 8.
tanawwara, to be illumined. Sh 72.

n - w - '

naw'(anwā'), species; type. DF 15, 16. Ḥ 2(2), 13(1), 42. Sh 3, 40, [42], 84.
al-māhīyah al-naw'īyah, specific quiddity. Sh 40.

h - w

min ḥayth huwa huwa, as he is in himself. DF 26. Sh 26.
huwīyah, ipseity (See trans. of DF, par. 22, n. 2). DF 22, 39, 65.

h - y - l

Hayūlā al-Hayūlayāt, the Substance of Substances. Sh 72.

h - y - m

al-malā'ikah al-muhayyamah, the ecstatic angels (See trans. of DF, par. 87, n. 1). DF 87. Sh [37].

w - t - r

tawātara (tawātur), See trans. of DF, par. 60, n. 2. DF 60.

w - j - b

wajaba, to be necessary. Sh 3, 35, [38].

w - j - b (continued)

wujūb, necessity, being necessary, necessary existence. DF 18, 72. Ḥ 2(3), 5(2), 15(1). Sh 28.

wājib, necessary existent; necessary, necessarily existent. DF 3, 50, 51, 55. Ḥ 2(2), 5(1), 12, 20. Sh 3, 4, 28.

al-Wājib, the Necessary Existent. DF 3, 4, 7, 18, 25, 29, 77. Ḥ 2(2), 4, 5(1), 5(2), 15(1), 15(2). Sh 5, 7, [5], 18.

al-Wājib li-Dhātihi, the Necessary Existent in Himself. DF 2, 55.

Wājib al-Wujūd, the Necessary Existent. DF 31.

al-Awwal al-Wājib, the Necessarily Existent First. DF 36.

al-Wujūd al-Wājib, Necessary Existence. DF 8.

wājibī, necessary. Sh 4.

al-Wujūd al-Wājibī, Necessary Existence. DF 8.

al-wujūd al-khāṣṣ al-wājibī, the proper existence of the Necessary Existent. Ḥ 5(1).

awjaba (ījāb), to necessitate, require, to imply. DF 9, 41, 57. Ḥ 40. Sh 4, 5.

ījāb, necessitation, creation or causation by necessity (See trans. of DF, par. 50, n. 2). DF 50. Ḥ 40.

ījāb, affirmation. Sh 44b.

ījāban, by necessity. DF 55.

qā'idat al-ījāb, the rule of necessity [in bringing the world into existence]. DF 52.

al-ījād al-ījābī, necessary bringing-into-existence. DF 55.

mūjib, necessary agent, necessary cause. Ḥ 38. Sh [38].

fā'il mūjib, necessary agent. Sh 51.

w - j - d

wujida, to exist. DF 3, 15, 90. Ḥ 42. Sh 3, 46, [42].

wujūd (wujūdāt), existence. DF 2, 3, 4, 5, 6, 7, 11, 12, 13, 16, 17, 18, 28, 31, 35, 36, 37, 38, 44, 45, 54, 55, 56, 61, 64, 72, 84, 85, 87, 89, 91. Ḥ 1, 2(1), 2(2), 4, 5(1), 5(2), 6, 8, 9, 15(1), 15(2), 15(3), 16, 19, 20, 31. Sh 1, 3, 4, 5, [2], 8, [5], 24, 25, 29, 32, [31]a, 35, 37, 40, [38], 52, 72, 84.

al-wujūd al-'āmm, general existence (See trans. of DF, par. 89, n. 1). DF 89, 90. Ḥ 37.

al-wujūd al-'aqlī, mental existence. Ḥ 2(2). Sh [2].

w - j - d (continued)

wujūd aṣīl, basic existence. Ḥ 2(2).

al-wujūd al-'aynī, concrete existence. DF 92.

al-wujūd al-baḥt, pure existence. Sh 1.

al-wujūd al-basharī al-jismānī, bodily human existence. Sh 11.

al-wujūd al-basharī al-rūḥānī, spiritual human existence. Sh 11.

al-wujūd al-basīṭ al-ḥaqīqī, real and simple existence. Sh 25.

al-wujūd al-dhihnī, mental existence. Sh 4, 40.

al-wujūd fī al-'aql, existence in the mind. Sh [2].

al-wujūd al-ḥaqīqī, real existence. Sh 29, 58.

al-wujūd al-ḥaqīqī al-'aynī, concrete real existence. Sh 28.

al-Wujūd al-Ḥaqq, the True Existence. DF 26, 74, 87, 89, 90.

al-wujūd al-iḍāfī, attributive existence (See trans. of DF, par. 25, n. 1), DF 25.

al-wujūd al-'ilmī al-ta'ayyunī, individuational cognitive existence (See trans. of Sh, par. 28, n. 1). Sh 28.

al-wujūd al-khārijī, external existence. Ḥ 2(2), 2(3). Sh 4, [2].

al-wujūd al-khāṣṣ, proper existence (See trans. of DF, par. 4, n. 3). DF 4, 7, 8, 25. Sh 4, 5.

al-wujūd al-khāṣṣ al-wājibī, the proper existence of the Necessary Existent. Ḥ 5(1).

al-wujūd al-khayālī, imaginary existence. Sh 58.

al-wujūd al-muḍāf, attributed existence. Sh 5.

al-wujūd al-muṭlaq, absolute existence. DF 6, 25. Sh 4, 5, 25.

al-Wujūd al-Wājib, Necessary Existence. DF 8.

al-Wujūd al-Wājibī, Necessary Existence. DF 8.

wujūd ẓillī, shadowy existence. Ḥ 2(2).

bāṭin al-wujūd, the inner aspect of existence. Sh 1.

bi-ḥasab al-wujūd, with respect to existence [outside the mind]. DF 28.

mustaḥīl al-wujūd, impossible of existence. DF 51.

nūr al-wujūd, the light of existence. Sh 24.

w - j - d (continued)
waḥdat al-wujūd, the unity of existence. DF 8, 25, 74. Ḥ 5(2). Sh 37.
Wājib al-Wujūd, the Necessary Existent. DF 31.
ẓāhir al-wujūd, the outward aspect of existence. Sh 1.
wujūdī, existential. DF 78, 79, 85, 87.
umūr wujūdīyah, existential entities. DF 87.
umūr wujūdīyah ʻaynīyah, concrete, existential entities. DF 85, 86.
al-kathrah al-wujūdīyah, existential multiplicity. DF 79.
al-nūr al-wujūdī, existential light. DF 58.
wājid, giver of existence. DF 38.
al-wājidīyah, giving existence. DF 38.
mawjūd (mawjūdāt), existent, existing; that which exists. DF 3, 8, 12, 15, 16, 18, 20, 25, 27, 36, 40, 41, 43, 44, 55, 56, 83, 85, 87, 88, 89, 90. Ḥ 2(2), 4, 5(1), 5(2), 6, 9, 11, 14, 15(1), 17, 31. Sh 3, 5, [2], 18, 20, 24, 25, 33, [31]a, 35, 37, 40, 41, [37], 44b, [42], 63.
mawjūd bi-dhātihi, self-existent, Sh 4.
mawjūd bi-nafsihi, self-existent. Sh [5].
mawjūd dhihnī, mental existent. Sh 4, 25.
al-mawjūdāt al-ḥālīyah, presently existing things. DF 44.
mawjūd khārijī, external existent. Sh 4.
mawjūd muṭlaq, absolute existent. Sh 25.
mawjūd zamānī, temporal existent. Sh 41, 44b.
Mabdaʼ al-Mawjūdāt, the Source of Existents. DF 18. Ḥ 15(1). Sh 18.
al-mawjūdīyah, receiving existence, being in existence. DF 38. Sh [2].
wijdān, inner sense. DF 56, 57, 59.
awjada (ījād), to bring into existence, to create. DF 3, 32, 37, 54, 55, 72, 92. Ḥ 39, 45. Sh 32, 46, 84.
ījād, creation, bringing-into-existence. DF 47, 48, 50, 51, 52, 54, 56. Ḥ 39. Sh 56.
al-ījād fī al-ʻayn, to bring into concrete existence. DF 92.
al-ījād al-ījābī, necessary bringing-into-existence. DF 55.
al-ījād al-kullī, general bringing-into-existence. DF 52.
al-ījād al-qaṣdī, intentional bringing-into-existence. DF 55.

w - j - d (continued)
martabat al-ījād, the stage of bringing-into-existence. DF 3, 87.
mūjid, creator. DF 87. Ḥ 2(3).

w - j - h
al-jihāt al-'alīyah, the exalted realms. Ḥ 12.
'alā wajh kullī, in a universal manner. DF 39.
'alā wajh kullī jumlī, in a universal and general manner. Sh 1.
tawjīh, justification. Sh 52.
ghayr muwajjah, unjustified. Sh 61.

w - ḥ - d
waḥdah, unity. DF 1, 24, 25, 26, 31, 65, 74, 75. Ḥ 7. Sh 1, 9, 24, 26, 37, [37].
waḥdah shakhṣīyah, individual unity. Ḥ 20.
waḥdah dhātīyah, essential unity. DF 78. Ḥ 20. Sh 40.
waḥdah ṣirfah, absolute unity. DF 58.
waḥdat al-wujūd, the unity of existence. DF 8, 25, 74. Ḥ 5(2). Sh 37.
martabat waḥdatihi al-dhātīyah, the plane of His essential unity. Sh 51.
ṣirāfat waḥdatihi, His absolute unity. DF 59.
waḥdānīyah, unicity. DF 25.
wāḥid, one, single. DF 5, 6, 8, 14, 16, 22, 23, 24, 29, 31, 32, 35, 37, 41, 51, 75, 76, 77, 78, 80, 81, 84, 85, 87, 89, 92. Ḥ 6, 7, 20, 36, 42. Sh [2], 9, 12, 21, 28, 35, 37, 40, 41, [42], 72.
wāḥid (āḥād), unit. DF 13.
al-Wāḥid, the One [God]. DF 26.
al-Wāḥid al-Awwal, the One First Being. DF 81.
al-Wāḥid al-Ḥaqq, the True One. DF 24.
al-wāḥid al-ḥaqīqī, what is really one. DF 78, 79, 80, 91.
al-Wāḥid al-Qā'im bi-Dhātihi, the Self-Subsistent One. DF 31.
al-Mabda' al-Wāḥid, the One Principle. DF 84.
wāḥidī al-ṣifāt, single in attributes. DF 51.
wāḥidīyah, singleness (See trans. of DF, par. 26, n. 1). DF 26. Sh 26.

w - ḥ - d (continued)

aḥadī al-dhāt, one in essence. DF 51.

dhātuhu al-aḥadīyah, [God's] unitary essence. DF 52. Sh 72.

aḥadīyah, oneness (See trans. of DF, par. 26, n. 1). DF 26, 44.

al-aḥadīyah al-dhātīyah, essential oneness. DF 26. Sh 26.

aḥadīyat jamʿ jamīʿ ṣifātihi wa-asmāʾihi, the oneness of the aggregate of all His attributes and names. DF 74.

waḥḥada (tawḥīd), to assert the unity [of God]. DF 25. Ḥ 20.

tawḥīd, unification. Sh 67.

al-Ṣūfīyah al-muwaḥḥidah, the unitarian Ṣūfīs (See trans. of DF, par. 92, n. 1). DF 92. Sh 8, 40.

ittiḥād, unity, union. DF 21, 32, 48. Ḥ 2(1), 20.

muttaḥid, united. DF 27. Ḥ 30(1), 30(2).

w - r - d

warada ʿalā, to be raised against, brought against [in objection]. DF 17.

mawrid (mawārid), source. DF 66.

awrada ʿalā, to raise an objection against. DF 37. Ḥ 5(2), 42.

w - s - ṭ

wāsiṭah (wasāʾiṭ), intermediary. DF 40, 55. Ḥ 8. Sh 34, 35.

bi-wāsiṭah, through the mediacy of, by means of. DF 44, 78. Ḥ 32.

bilā wāsiṭah, immediately. DF 75.

tawassuṭ, mediacy. DF 32, 69, 81, 85, 86. Ḥ 31. Sh 32.

w - ṣ - f

waṣf (awṣāf), quality, attribute, attribution. DF 14. SH 9, 28, 33, 35.

ṣifah (ṣifāt), attribute. DF 2, 18, 27, 28, 29, 30, 32, 37, 39, 45, 48, 49, 61, 62, 63, 64, 65, 66, 67, 68, 69, 70, 74, 78. Ḥ 8, 13(3), 15(2), 19, 20, 22, 40, 44. Sh [2], 12, 19, 21, 26, 28, 31, 41, [37], [38], 63, 75.

al-ṣifāt al-iʿtibārīyah, mental attributes [of God]. DF 77.

al-ṣifāt al-ḥaqīqīyah, real attributes [of God]. DF 41, 45, 77. Ḥ 19. Sh 1.

w - ṣ - f (continued)
al-ṣifāt al-mu'aththirah, effective attributes. Sh 28.
ṣifāt al-rubūbīyah, attributes of lordship. DF 65. Sh 25.
ṣifat kamāl, attribute of perfection. Sh 29, [38].
al-ṣifāt al-kamālīyah, [God's] attributes of perfection. DF 50, 58.
al-ṣifāt al-salbīyah, the negative attributes. Ḥ 19.
wāḥidī al-ṣifāt, single in attributes. DF 51.
aḥadīyat jam' jamī' ṣifātihi wa-asma'ihi, the oneness of the aggregate of all His attributes and names. DF 74.
mawṣūf bi, qualified by. DF 32.
ittaṣafa bi (ittiṣāf), to be described, be qualified by. DF 14, 87. Ḥ 2(2), 2(3). Sh 4, 5, [2], 9, 21, 35.
muttaṣif bi, qualified by. DF 14. Ḥ 42. Sh 12.

w - ḍ - '
fī mawḍi'ihi, in its place [in works dealing with this subject]. DF 4. Ḥ 2(2), 15(1). Sh 4, 6, 18, 32.
mawḍū', subject [of a proposition]. Ḥ 2(1). Sh [2].

w - ṭ - '
muwāṭa'atan, univocally. Ḥ 5(1). Sh [5].

w - ṭ - n
mawṭin, place. DF 68.

w - gh - l
al-mutawaghghilūn fī al-makān wa-al-zamān, those immersed in space and time. DF 23, 42. Sh 41.

w - f - q
wāfaqa (muwāfaqah), to agree with. Sh [43], 84.
ittafaqa ma' (ittifāq), to agree with. DF 53, 54. Sh [39].
ittifāqan, unanimously. Sh 47.
ba'dīyah 'ādīyah ittifāqīyah, coincidental customary posteriority. Sh 72.
muttafiq al-ḥaqīqah, with the same reality. DF 6.
muttafaq 'alā, agreed upon. DF 50. Sh 11, 25, 78.

w - q - '
waqa'a 'alā, to subsist in, inhere in. DF 13.

w - q - ʿ (continued)

waqaʿa (wuqūʿ), to occur. DF 46, 52, 68, 70, 71, 72, 73, 74. Ḥ 12. Sh 37, 46, [38], 51.
wāqiʿ, actual. Sh 37, 67.
al-wāqiʿ, actual fact, what actually occurs. DF 51. Sh [43].
fī al-wāqiʿ, in actual fact. Sh 1.
kamā huwa al-wāqiʿ, as is the actual case. Sh [16].
bi-ḥasab al-wāqiʿ, with respect to actual fact, in actuality. Sh 29, [38], 78.
khilāf al-wāqiʿ, contrary to actual fact. Sh 3.
al-niẓam al-wāqiʿ, the actual order. DF 50.
awqaʿa (īqāʿ), to bring about, cause the occurrence of. Sh 46, 47.

w - q - f

mawqūf ʿalā, dependent on. Sh 5.
tawaqqafa ʿala (tawaqquf), to depend on. DF 56, 87. Ḥ 2(3). Sh 5, [2], 41.

w - l - d

al-mawālīd al-thalāthah, the three generations (See trans. of Sh, par. 84, n. 2). Sh 84.
wallada, to generate. Sh 33.
tawlīd, generation. Sh 72.

w - l - y

walī (awliyāʾ), saint. DF 28.
awlā, superior, more appropriate. DF 10. Ḥ 8.
awlawīyah, superiority (See trans. of DF, par. 9, n. 2). DF 9, 51.

w - h - b

al-Wahhāb, the Bestower. Ḥ 13(1).

w - h - m

wahm (awhām), estimation, estimative sense (See trans. of DF, par. 12, n. 1). DF 12, 23, 42. Sh 11.
muqaddimāt al-wahm, premisses of the estimation. Sh 11.
al-qūwah al-wahmīyah, the estimative faculty (See trans. of Sh, par. 11, n. 3). Sh 11.
wahhama, to give the illusion of. Sh 33.

w - h - m (continued)

tawahhama (tawahhum), to imagine. DF 25, 51, 52. Ḥ 42. Sh 4, 9, 28, 41, 48, 51, 52.

w - h - y

muqaddimāt wāhiyah, unfounded premisses. Sh 78.

y - q - n

yaqīn, certainty. Ḥ 13(3). Sh 84.
'alā al-yaqīn, to the point of certainty. DF 17.
yaqīnī, certain. Ḥ 13(2). Sh 78.

PERSIAN WORDS

būdagī, being in existence. Sh [5].
būdan, to exist. Sh [5].
chīz, thing. Ḥ 41.
dill, heart. Ḥ 44.
Khudā, God. Ḥ 44.
Khudāvand, God. Ḥ 41.